"*Where There's a Will* aim... social reluctance to talk ab... guiding us gently through som... it encompasses... Kerrigan's tone is carefully balanced and the writing is compelling... he urges us to seize the day before it seizes us."
DYING MATTERS COALITION

"An invaluable asset... informative and fascinating in equal measure... sensible and forthright. I would recommend it as a practical and helpful guide."
JAFFAREADSTOO, BOOK BLOGGER

"A repository of incredibly useful information... interesting and enlightening... it even has a sense of humour. I would recommend *Where There's a Will* as a key addition to anyone's reference library."
READER REVIEW, GOODREADS

WHERE THERE'S A WILL

A PRACTICAL GUIDE TO TAKING CHARGE OF YOUR AFFAIRS

MICHAEL KERRIGAN

Saraband

Published by Saraband
Suite 202, 98 Woodlands Road
Glasgow, G3 6HB, Scotland
www.saraband.net

Copyright © 2012 Saraband (Scotland) Ltd.

All rights reserved. No part of this publication may be reproduced,
stored in a retrieval system, or transmitted, in any form or by any
means, electronic, mechanical, photocopying, recording, or otherwise,
without first obtaining the written permission of the copyright owner.

Project editor: **Sara Hunt**

Project consultant and contributor: **Ronnie Scott**

Contributing editors:
Clare Haworth-Maden, Craig Hillsley

Interviews in 'Reflections' section: **Jennie Renton**

ISBN: 978-1-887354-93-6

Printed in the EU
on paper sourced from sustainably managed forests.

3   5   7   9   10   8   6   4   2

Cover illustration: © 2012 **Lesley Barnes**

"Short days ago
We lived, felt dawn, saw sunset glow,
Loved, and were loved, and now we lie
In Flanders fields."

John McCrae

CONTENTS

PREFACE   7

INTRODUCTION   9

CHAPTER ONE
   Last Orders:
   What Instructions Do You Want to Leave Behind?   23

CHAPTER TWO
   Shuffling Off This Mortal Coil:
   How Do You Want to Go?   59

CHAPTER THREE
   Pomp and Circumstance:
   What Kind of Send-off Do You Want?   91

CHAPTER FOUR
   Your Last Resting Place:
   Where Do You Want to End Up?   131

CHAPTER FIVE
   In Memoriam:
   How Do You Want to be Remembered?   165

CHAPTER SIX
   A Happy Ending?   192

REFLECTIONS   209

RECOMMENDED RESOURCES   244

INDEX   254

ACKNOWLEDGEMENTS   260

✳ PREFACE ✳

'There are eight million stories in the Naked City...,' the old TV voiceover intoned. Whatever your state of undress, that's a lot of beginnings, middles and, consequently, ends. No book could conceivably deal with death in all its guises or explore its implications for an endless succession of individual lives – so *Where There's a Will* doesn't even try. It seeks only to acknowledge the myriad possibilities of mortality whilst at the same time trying to point out the common ground. And, it's hoped, to offer a little of the sort of support that all of us are liable to find we can do with at one time or another.

That support itself must come in many different forms, however: we all have our own individual challenges to confront as we approach our ends. Which is worse, the terror of death or the fear of filling in forms, the dread of decision-making? That isn't the facetious question it may at first seem. For some of us, the thought of dying in itself is less alarming than that of losing our sense of control, our dignity as death approaches; for others, it's our anxiety at leaving emotional loose ends that will now have to remain untied.

If our own deaths come to us in all sorts of ways, so do our experiences of others'. Any bereavement brings with it a whole host of challenges, from the most metaphysical (How can this make sense?) to the most mundane (Just where did she leave that spare front-door key?) In between comes a whole gamut of emotional, legal, financial and practical matters: it's hard to think of anything much that isn't at least touched on here. The great thing about this book, we like to think, is that it's open to the enormous diversity of demands death makes on us, whether it's our own mortality or someone else's that's involved.

In keeping with this, its writing has been very much a collective effort. While its author takes the lead, tackling key questions and developing ideas in a more or less conventional way, it is to Ronnie Scott that credit is due for the early stages of this book's development and for being the major contributor to Chapter Three, Pomp and Circumstance. There's a chorus of other voices (often unexpected ones) here besides, bringing special expertise on everything from life-expectancy statistics to storytelling and shiatsu, as well as personal experiences that all of us would hope never to encounter. Some of these contributions are to be found interspersed in the main body of the text, whilst others are presented in a special 'Reflections' section towards the end. This way the hope is that the book will entertain as wide as possible a range of perspectives without suffering any significant loss of focus along the way.

Last, but by absolutely no means least: some readers will find the last section to be the most useful bit of the book; and that's fine by us. The Recommended Resources section offers suggestions as to where you might go to find further information and, if necessary, help.

Michael Kerrigan

INTRODUCTION

Few of us really want to die. In fact, in an ideal world, we'd live forever, if we had any say in the matter. If you are religious, however strong your belief in salvation, it's still scary to think of the awesome, and irreversible, step into the unknown that you'll be taking as you make your final exit from this mortal world. And it's just as frightening for the godless, even though we may rationally ask ourselves why oblivion – why simply ceasing to be – should be such an unnerving prospect. Some branches of self-help psychology would have us look on the bright side of everything, to see our glass as being half full, and consequently somehow to celebrate death, or, at least, its positive aspects (if any). Yet death is a bitter cup that we have to drain to the very bottom, and many of us have found another, simpler way of dealing with our fear of death: denial. The trouble is, though, that too determined an avoidance of the subject only stores up trouble for later on, and not just for ourselves, but also for those we love.

This book sets out to find a sensible middle way. We know that we're never going to defeat death, for even the most miraculous works of modern medicine can only hope to hold it at bay for a few months or years. What we can do, however, is rob it of a great deal of its destructive force by preparing ourselves for it thoughtfully, by facing it calmly and by carefully taking charge of our affairs.

You may be reading this book because you, or someone you're close to, are facing imminent death. If so, this book should help to guide you through some of the issues that you need to think about yourself, or else will help you to consider how best to approach the subject openly with the person who may now be in real need of your help or support. Helping our friends and loved ones is a basic human instinct. And when those we care for are going through difficult times, such as one of life's challenging transitions, it's gratifying to know that we have the power to make their situation a little easier for them. Remember that it can often be the small kindnesses, rather than the grand statements, that help the most. 'Being there' for someone might be as simple as listening to him or her, or it may involve giving advice, sharing knowledge or offering practical support.

Every life is framed by birth and death, which are sometimes said to be the only certainties (apart, maybe, from taxes). When a healthy baby is born, there is no difficulty in sharing the consequent happiness. People are relaxed about exchanging anecdotes, and there can almost be an overload of shared wisdom as the new parents are inundated with well-meaning advice. Yet when it comes to death and bereavement, we often feel lost for words, perhaps because there is still a real taboo surrounding the subject. We may consequently feel panicky and unprepared or ill-equipped to deal with death's emotional or practical aspects. Yet giving comfort to someone who is dying can be as easy as gently stroking his or her arm, thereby maintaining a profoundly supportive human connection through touch, with no words being required.

Down the centuries, successive civilisations have developed their own ways of handling the transition from life to death. Many of us belong to cultural and religious groups in which such inherited beliefs and traditions still run strong, and this book will refer to them where appropriate, while also bringing in alternative viewpoints for you to consider. This is just one of the illuminating ways in which *Where There's a Will* throws light on dying, death and bereavement, areas of life that all too often remain in the shadows, but where ignorance does not equal bliss.

DYING IS FORBIDDEN

In ancient times, the Athenian tyrant Pisistratus forbade dying on the Greek island of Delos.

The island was deemed a sacred centre, and the prohibition was intended to purify the place and thus make it fit for the gods to be worshipped in (births were forbidden, too).

There are some modern towns – in France and Spain, Brazil and Norway, for example – that also have laws prohibiting death. In France and Spain, these laws are political manoeuvres designed to pressurise governments into authorising more land for cemeteries. In the Brazilian city of Biritiba-Mirim, however, the mayor's intention was for the law to put pressure on citizens to take better care of their health so that they did not take up space in an already full cemetery before their time. (And it seems that relatives of the deceased in Biritiba-Mirim may face punitive fines and even jail sentences.)

In the Arctic town of Longyearbyen, there is room for the dead, but no burials take place there because the underlying permafrost prevents bodies from decomposing. All of Longyearbyen's dead are therefore buried on the Norwegian mainland instead, to which seriously ill people are flown as a precaution in case they die.

Nor are commoners, members of parliament included, allowed to die in the Palace of Westminster – theoretically, at least – on account of it being a royal palace. Deaths are instead recorded as having taken place at St Thomas' Hospital, the nearest hospital.

A MIGHTY LEVELLER

Death comes to us all. That is not the most original of observations, it has to be said, but sometimes the obvious point needs to be made. However diverse we may be in terms of our ethnic background, culture, class or wealth; however different the details of our lives; and whether we 'go gentle into that good night' or 'rage, rage against the dying of the light' – the simple fact remains that we're all, without exception, going to die. We may be able to postpone it, that is, if we're lucky and up to a point; we may be fortunate enough to have good health for longer than the average; and we may ultimately be blessed with a long life, as well as with loving family and friends to help us through our declining years. One way or another, though, death awaits us, whether we're ambushed by accident, carried off unexpectedly early by illness or pass peacefully away, having reached a ripe old age.

Given that death is unavoidable, we might as well be as ready for it as we can. In earlier, more religious times, that might have meant being spiritually prepared for the Last Judgement of Judaeo–Christian belief and for the world to come, and for many of us that remains of the utmost importance. This book doesn't pretend to resolve any big spiritual questions, though (there's already a huge theological and spiritual body of literature out there dealing with those). In any case, there are other ways in which it makes sense to ready ourselves for death, notably by preparing ourselves mentally for what lies ahead and by taking the practical steps that will help us to smooth the way for ourselves and for those who love us. Death is daunting, whatever we do, or don't, believe about our final destiny, but at least it is comforting to know that there are things that we can do to arm ourselves against being overcome by fear.

A Sparrow's Flight

Life is short: this is yet another hackneyed thought that nevertheless bears restating. So what's a lifetime – any lifetime – in the eternal scheme of things? This point was memorably recorded during the eighth century by St Bede, when the Christian chronicler described how a Northumbrian courtier explained to his pagan lord why he felt drawn to Christianity, which seemed a strange and alien religion at that time.

The present life of man, O King, seems to be, in comparison with that time which is unknown to us, like the swift flight of a sparrow through the room wherein You sit at supper in

*winter, with your commanders and ministers, and a good fire
in the midst, whilst the storms of rain and snow prevail abroad;
the sparrow, I say, flying in at one door, and immediately out
at another, whilst he is within, is safe from the wintry storm;
but after a short space of fair weather, he immediately vanishes
out of your sight, into the dark winter from which he had
emerged. So this life of man appears for a short space, but of
what went before, or what is to follow, we are entirely ignorant.*

Not everyone will agree that Christianity has the answers, but
we can still relate, with a shiver, to the thought of that dark and
dismal eternity outside. We can bandy statistics around, maybe
pointing out that people live longer in London than in Glasgow's
East End, or that the poorest in Britain fare far better than the
majority in sub-Saharan Africa. The truth, however, is that the
longest human life lasts for less than the blink of an eye in cosmic
terms. But then what does that matter when our life is everything
to us as individuals?

What Really Matters?

The real significance of life-expectancy figures is not what
they say about the speed with which death rushes up on this
or that social group. Far more important is what they imply
about quality of life. Economic factors play a major part in this,
but, rich or poor, we're all individuals and therefore in any case
have different lives.

A memorable account of the Industrial Revolution and its
impact on a northern town, Charles Dickens' novel *Hard Times*
(1853) is among his most obviously socially conscious in its
outlook. Yet at a time when new technologies, economic development and political conflict were transforming life completely,
what really mattered, Dickens insisted, was the personal experience of every individual man, woman or child. When Louisa
Gradgrind balks at the prospect of marriage to the much older

man favoured by her father, she makes the age-old point that life is short. Her father, who had made a study of what was then called 'political economy', is ready with his reply, however:

'It is short, no doubt, my dear. Still, the average duration of human life is proved to have increased of late years. The calculations of various life assurance and annuity offices, among other figures, which cannot go wrong, have established the fact.'

'I speak of my own life, father.'

'O indeed? Still,' said Mr Gradgrind, 'I need not point out to you, Louisa, that it is governed by the laws which govern lives in the aggregate.'

'While it lasts, I would wish to do the little I can, and the little I am fit for. What does it matter?'

Mr Gradgrind seemed rather at a loss to understand the last four words; replying, 'How, matter? What matter, my dear?'

Most of us like to think that we matter, even if we know that we don't really count in the calculations of society as a whole, and still less in the overarching eternal scheme of things. Yet however insignificant we know we are, we still have to feel that our existence has meaning of some sort, and that we don't end up having lived our lives in vain.

KNOW YOUR PLACE

You can stoke up your anxiety (or anticipation) by considering the influence of where you live on how long you've got left. There are massive differences between places in terms of how long the average person lives. So if you're looking for a quicker exit, a move to Glasgow would put you in the city with the UK's lowest average life expectancy. Want to stick around longer? London's Kensington and Chelsea is the place to be, with its residents enjoying the UK's highest average life expectancy.

OK, OK, so it's not actually that easy . . . Differences in life expectancy from place to place reflect a complex mixture of things. A large part of it is that wealthier folk tend to be healthier, by virtue of having easier lives and being better behaved (smoking fewer ciggies, for example). Kensington has great average life expectancy because it's full of wealthier people.

How you look after yourself (or not) is a bigger factor than where you live in determining when you go, but it's not the whole story. Lots of pollution, cold weather and streets that suit traffic more than pedestrians, for example, may be features of your area that can curtail your life. Cleaner air, greener streets and supportive neighbours can help you last a bit longer. About 10 to 15 per cent of the difference in average life expectancy from place to place is down to characteristics of the area. In all, it might be time to think about moving house.

Contributed by **Richard Mitchell,** Professor of Health & Environment at the University of Glasgow, he specialises in the influences of physical environment on health and mortality.

A Foregone Conclusion?

More, perhaps, than the generalised fear of the unknown, or more specific anxieties about an afterlife, the dread of death is that of a life left unfulfilled. Death is the defining moment that not only concludes, but completes, our life: the point at which our narrative finds its final 'closure'. Only when we die does the overall trajectory of our existence become apparent. As Aeschylus (525–456 BC), the Greek tragedian, wrote: 'No man's life may be considered happy until he has ended his days in prosperity'. Only when we die does it become clear what our lives added up to: only then does what we achieved – or didn't achieve – in our lives at last stand revealed.

But it is not revealed to us: being dead, we don't get to read our story. And a narrative only has a shape from the outside, anyway. Neither do we have script approval on the stories that others tell about us, so it won't be up to us how well we emerge from them. Whatever we may believe, or don't believe, about any life that is to come, historically, we have tended to regard death as a sort of judgement day for our mortal lives: the moment when we're weighed in the balance. How did we do, when all was – literally – said and done? Where the medieval mind envisaged impish demons dousing the souls of sinners in pools of fire, today we may be more inclined to imagine those who knew us lined up like the judges at a figure-skating competition, holding up their marks.

The Story of My Life

For all our concerns that they may judge our lives and find us wanting, our loved ones are typically slower than we may think to find fault with us. Indeed, they may well 'read' our life stories more charitably than we would ourselves, so that their judgements are less harsh than we fear. If our youthful fantasies of world domination went unrealised, that's partly because, as time went by, we found ourselves prioritising other things, they might say. Or if we didn't make our family's fortune as we always dreamt we would, we may instead have enriched them more than we knew in other ways. Maybe we met our setbacks with a cheerful courage that gave them hope; perhaps we showed a determination that inspired them. Maybe we helped them to fulfil ambitions that we didn't manage to achieve ourselves, or maybe we enabled them to cope with challenges of their own. Indeed, how we handled failures may have been as important as being a success.

So in the end, it seems that our 'story' – if we want to see it that way – is for others' benefit, rather than our own, and that we can only hope they'll see us the way we'd want them to. Is this a vain and pointless hope? Perhaps, but then it's only human to want to present yourself to the best advantage – anyone who ever put on make-up, or dressed to impress, knows how that feels. As in life, so in death (or, at any rate, in its anticipation): we want to leave a good impression, to be liked and respected, even when we're gone.

'And so it is for each man the praise of the living, of those who speak afterwards, that is the best epitaph', says the Seafarer in the Anglo-Saxon poem of that name. He is talking, one imagines, about exploits on the wild ocean or on the field of war, but much the same could be said for our own, more humdrum, heroics. To be remembered fondly by our friends and relations, or to be recalled at our former place of work as having been a reliable colleague: these things mean a lot to us as we approach our end.

STILL TALKING . . .

When we face the final curtain, talking is good, and the conversation can now continue after death (up to a point, at any rate). Ever since the introduction of the camcorder, the practice of leaving a last, spoken testament, a message to loved ones from beyond the grave, has been catching on. Such recordings range from brief and simple declarations of love and words of reassurance to lengthy life stories or defiant speeches of self-justification ('I did it my way . . .'). Many serving soldiers record bedtime stories for their children before they go off to war; these will also be there as mementoes should they never make it home again.

In the age of VHS recordings, taped testaments like these were very much for private usage, but the advent of digital recording has changed all that. The Facebook generation sees privacy differently from its predecessors, and if our drunken exploits are to be posted for all to see, why shouldn't our thoughts on death and life be, too?

Neat and Tidy

Ultimately, while it's gratifying to be liked and respected, what sort of story our life makes isn't really the main issue. We may want our narrative to reach the 'right' conclusion so that everything is neatly rounded off, but that's perhaps mainly because we don't want to leave any difficulties for those we love to have to deal with. In life, we generally hope to treat those around us with respect and care, and to acknowledge and accommodate their needs as far as possible, and the same goes for us in death. We want the best for our loved ones, and following on from how we feel about them from day to day is the desire that our passing should not cause them too much pain or trouble.

In truth, once we've thought about it and unravelled it a bit, much of what we think of as being a simple fear of death tends to come down to our anxieties over the confusions, quarrels, responsibilities and burdens that we're going to leave behind us. Be they unpaid bills, unresolved quarrels or unexpressed sentiments – the things that we always meant to say, but never quite got around to – if we stay in denial for too long, we're liable to leave unfinished, unpleasant business of all sorts when we die.

DEATHLESS PROSE

Perhaps it is because death is such a taboo subject that we often can't bring ourselves even to utter the words 'die', 'died' or 'dead', for example, when talking of those who have died, and instead seek refuge in euphemisms. Here are just a few:

- to pass on/over/away;
- pushing up daisies;
- with God;
- gone to meet his/her maker;
- to give up the ghost;
- to bite the dust;
- the deceased;
- to shuffle off this mortal coil;

- moved on;
- bought it;
- bought the farm;
- joined the choir invisible;
- the dear departed;
- kick the bucket;
- no longer with us.

Ourselves and Others

While this book sets out to help readers to think about ways of mentally preparing themselves for the fact of death, or of helping someone else to prepare for it, it does so mainly by considering the things that could ease our passage for other people. Most of us live our lives through our relationships, which means that we can't be at peace if we feel that we're stacking up problems in life for those we leave behind us when we're dead.

As ever, however, it's important to face up to your limitations, to appreciate how far your actions are circumscribed, and then to come to terms with that. You can't set everything to rights in death any more than you could in life, so there's no point in torturing yourself (or others) with thoughts of what you can't do. You can't leave your children a Georgian townhouse if your only home is a council flat, for example, any more than you can end feuds when the antagonists are determined to fight on. When you're dead, your now grown-up son who is lacking in life skills is going to have to find a way to cope without you, while a loving spouse or partner will inevitably grieve and miss you – these are situations that simply cannot be helped.

Feel the Fear, and Prepare Anyway

There may be things that you can't change or put right before you die, but there are useful actions that you can take, whoever you are and whatever your life is like. In particular, there are ways that you can make things easier for those who'll have to mourn you, thus making sure that your loss is no more painful than it has to be. And doing that will help you to face the prospect of death, if not with eagerness, then at least with the quiet confidence that you're leaving your affairs – and your relationships – in order, as far as is feasible. A challenge engaged with can be a challenge substantially met, and a little thought, a little effort can go a long way in this respect. If you take control of what can be controlled, then the rest won't feel half as frightening.

Taking control is what this book will try to help you to do. Organise yourself, and you will find yourself banishing the paralysing, rabbit-caught-in-the-headlights type of terror that may take hold whenever you even start to think about death. This book can't banish that fear completely, but the advice that it offers may enable you to replace it with a purposefulness that is as effective as courage, from which real feelings of strength and fortitude may come. It will also arm you with ideas and insights that may enable you to help another person tackle some of their worries when it is they who are facing death, not you – yet, at least.

FAMOUS LAST WORDS

Be they profound or banal, significant or inconsequential, tragic or amusing – certain famous people's last words have proved somehow memorable.

"DON'T DISTURB MY CIRCLES!"

Greek mathematician Archimedes, who was doing a bit of geometry during the Roman sacking of his city and didn't want a soldier to disturb his drawings. The soldier ran him through with his sword..

"VIVO!" (I LIVE!)

Roman emperor Caligula, delusional to the end, before he was assassinated by his own soldiers.

"I'M BORED WITH IT ALL."

British politician Sir Winston Churchill.

"ALL MY POSSESSIONS FOR A MOMENT OF TIME."

Queen Elizabeth I of England.

"I CAN'T BELIEVE, AFTER ALL THIS TIME, IT WAS A BLOODY BANANA THAT KILLED ME."

Seventy-three-year-old Slovenian Ivanka Perko, who had survived living under Nazi and Communist regimes, but died after a scratch from the pointed end of a banana skin didn't heal properly.

"FREEDOM!"

Scottish patriot William Wallace.

Chapter One
LAST ORDERS:

WHAT INSTRUCTIONS DO YOU WANT TO LEAVE BEHIND?

Death, where is thy sting? For most of us, that sting won't be physical, fortunately, for modern medicine has much reduced the pain of dying. It can't free us from the fear of death, however. Maybe nothing can, if truth be told: what sterner test could there be of secular stoicism or spiritual faith?

For many, death's cruellest torments are those arising from the helpless realisation that their personal and financial affairs are in disarray. That they're departing life too late to take meaningful action, leaving their loved ones to deal not just with heartbreak, but with a major headache. Bank accounts; internet passwords; wills and insurance policies; possessions ... in the eternal scheme, such things may sound banal. But those who outlive us are going to have to handle them on our behalf. We can make that task easy for them, or we can leave them with a tangled confusion to try to unravel, with all the distress (and perhaps the tension and bitterness) that this may entail. Take a little time and trouble now, and we can ensure that our deaths, however painful they may be for them, don't have a sting in the tail for those who love us most.

On the other hand, perhaps your worries are not so much about your own affairs, but someone else's. Is your elderly parent losing the sharpness that he or she once displayed, and might the life-insurance certificate now be filed under the sofa cushions, or the passport in the laundry basket? How will you find them when they are needed? It would be reassuring for both parties to know that you've anticipated some of these practical questions before it's too late.

It isn't morbid or gloomy to acknowledge the inevitability of death, just common sense. As in other areas of life, a challenge addressed may not be a challenge done away with, but it's certainly a challenge cut down to size. If we organise our affairs well – and well in advance – we'll be able to face death with the confidence of knowing that we've done everything we can to smooth the way for those we leave behind. Denial simply stores up suffering for ourselves, and for others. We may 'know not the day nor the hour', as St Matthew's Gospel has it, but the odds of us knowing when we will die are certainly shortening year by year. For most of us, there *will* be plenty of time to make preparations. How we decide to use that time is up to us, but it makes sense to start getting these things sorted out now by ordering our estates and writing a will. Opinions differ widely on the existence and the nature of the afterlife, but no great world religion believes that you can do your filing from the beyond.

ORDER OR CHAOS?

While it's crucial to be clear in your own mind that you've or-dered your affairs to your satisfaction, it's also important to try to put yourself in your loved ones' shoes, to imagine what they'll be faced with after your death and to try to make dealing with this as easy as possible for them. Writing down your wishes, along with as much practical information as you can, will give you peace of mind and will also help your next of kin.

Spelling It Out

Many of the tasks that we have to do to order our affairs before we die are obvious, so much so that they may end up being over-looked. Remember that you really can't be too clear and explicit because things that may seem to you to go without saying often don't. If they've known you by a nickname for years or decades, for example, it may be that your neighbours (and even your close friends) don't know your real name. The most devoted children may also be hazy about your date of birth. Too much is too easily taken as read, especially things that we're liable to regard as done and dusted, but that may not be readily available to those we leave behind. It's no use having made a will, for instance, if no one can find it when you're gone: there have to be clear instructions to help your next of kin locate it. Moreover, even when they have found it, how will they know that what they've got is really your 'last will and testament' – your final word – unless you've been completely clear as to its date?

Far-sightedness is good, but it's important to stay on the ball as well, and not to lose track of the things you so prudently took care of way back when. Any life-insurance policy that you may have will typically have been taken out years – or even decades – before you finally round the turn into life's final straight. So is the documentation readily to hand in the here and now? Are there any other insurance policies, stocks or shares or other assets that your next of kin should know about? Or, for that matter, any liabilities, such as loans or hire-purchase plans? Perhaps you've gone to the lengths of contributing to a prepaid funeral plan; that foresight may well be wasted if you haven't told your next of kin about it. And who else might need to know about it? A local tax inspector? Your accountant?

The same goes for any instructions that you may want to leave for your funeral: if you haven't made them clear already – and even if you have, it can't hurt to spell it all out again – then now's the time. Are you hoping (or have you arranged) for a particular person to take charge of the arrangements for your funeral? Do you want a certain individual to officiate? Have you chosen specific readings, hymns or poems? Do you have a cemetery in mind for your burial, or a special spot in which you'd like your ashes to be scattered? Our nearest and dearest they may be, but our relations can't be expected to read our minds, so the more clearly you can make your feelings known in advance, the better. And do it in writing, if at all possible, because the scope for misunderstanding is considerable, and those attempting to make these arrangements may well anyway be in a state of shock. It's a kindness to them, and will give you a sense of security, if you set out what you want as explicitly as possible so that they will know that they're doing things the way you'd like them to be done when the time comes.

Given the clear advantages of setting out your wishes for your funeral explicitly and in writing, the obvious answer may seem to be to include them in your will. Bear in mind, though, that in the shock of bereavement and in the frantic administrative rush that follows, the will is often seen as being something that can safely be left for another day. It may not be read – or even found – until after the funeral. If you're going to add instructions for your funeral to your will, make absolutely sure your loved ones are aware of this; you might be just as well preparing a separate document in any case.

So important is the paperwork – and, for many of us, so forbidding – that we may easily forget more everyday arrangements. Try to think about those, too. Are your house or car keys easy to find, for example? Are there spares 'out there' with neighbours that shouldn't be lost track of? Are there friends or relations who should immediately be told of your death? And what should be done when you die if you spend much of your life online?

KEEPING IT CLEAR

It makes sense to write down specific instructions for your next of kin or your executors listing the immediate actions required in the days after your death. Here are a few key issues that you may want to bear in mind as you do so.

- your full name, address and any other contact details that you think will be useful;
- your date and place of birth;
- the name of your husband or wife or partner;
- the names of your children, and, if appropriate, their telephone numbers;
- your NHS number and your doctor's name and contact details;
- whether you are an organ donor and, if so, where your donor card can be found;

- whether you are leaving your body to medical science and, if so, where the consent form is lodged (see also page 134);
- whether you have a funeral plan and, if so, where it is held and who should be contacted;
- any instructions for your funeral and the disposal of your body (see also Chapters 3 and 4);
- the date when you made your will; where you've lodged it; and, if you've lodged it with a solicitor, his or her name and contact details;
- where any financial paperwork can be found, along with lists of the types of accounts, direct debits, investments, policies, mortgages, loans, hire-purchase agreements, credit cards, store cards and so on that you hold and the name in which they are held (but not any PIN or account numbers, for reasons of security);
- details relating to any insurance policies that you may hold; your television licence details and those of your cable- or satellite-television provider; details of your internet service provider (ISP) and of your mobile-phone supplier;
- where any important documents can be found (e.g., birth and marriage or civil-partnership certificates; your passport, driving licence and any identity cards; the deeds to your house or any lease or rental documents);
- the names and contact details of anyone you would like to be informed of your death (e.g., family members and friends, as well as your employer, bank and/or building society, doctor, accountant and/or tax advisor, solicitor, and the local register office where your death should be registered);
- the names and contact details of any local service providers whose services should be cancelled (e.g., the newsagent or a window cleaner);
- the names and contact details of anyone who holds spare sets of house or car keys that should be retrieved for safe-keeping;

- instructions regarding any pets or animals for which you are responsible;
- any other instructions or information that you think your next of kin or executors will need to be aware of on your death.

When you are satisfied with your instructions, seal them in an envelope, label it 'instructions upon my death', date it and address it to your next of kin or executors. Finally, remember to tell your next of kin or executors that you have written down your wishes and instructions, and where they can be found.

Virtual Life Ends, Too

In the digital age, more and more aspects of our lives are being conducted online. Instead of keeping physical diaries and photo albums, we are increasingly using blogs and photo-sharing websites, for example. Rather than writing letters, we are sending e-mails or texts or are communicating via social-networking sites like Facebook and Twitter. But what happens when you die? Will your family or friends be able to access your online accounts if they have to? What happens if you've used online banking to deal with your finances, for instance? And who will shut down your PayPal account (if you have one)?

The situation varies, and is constantly evolving, but it seems safe to say that while internet service providers (ISPs), e-mail and website hosts and social-networking sites will provide information or limited access to the friends or family of someone who was registered with them before they died, this, crucially, does not include passwords. Some companies are increasingly offering a service by which you can store passwords – and even a video – online, which will then be sent to a list of your chosen contacts on confirmation of your death. But then how will they know that you've died, and can you really trust these companies to do all that they promise anyway? If you decide that you want a trusted someone to have complete access to your digital life after your death, it's probably best to give them your passwords yourself.

LOGGING OFF

These days, lots of us spend so much of our lives online that we have cyberselves. These online dimensions of who we are bring real responsibilities that we probably haven't thought through, and about which our loved ones very likely don't have a clue.

The security issues are the most obvious: whilst it's important that our partners or executors should have access to our financial data, it's just as important that other people shouldn't. This means that some careful thought has to be given to how user-IDs and passwords are communicated to those who need them.

There are questions of privacy to be considered as well, and it isn't just our own privacy that's at stake. We have responsibilities towards those with whom we're in touch online and those that we work for. Who's going to read our e-mails when we no longer can? Do our computers provide direct access to confidential databases or other items belonging to our employers?

And then there's online etiquette, itself still very much a work in progress. Should news of our deaths be posted on Facebook, for instance, or do we want our details or accounts to be deleted? Do we have avatars that should be activated to take their leave of longstanding forum-friends?

Here's a list of some of the things you have to consider if you want to ensure that the people you leave behind can access and sort out your virtual remains:

- Your computer password: you may have documents on your computer that friends and family need to access after your death.
- Secret documents: if you have documents or files that you don't want anybody to see, you can protect them with a special password that you take with you to the grave.
- Online banking: ensure your passwords are safe (or not written down) to prevent identity theft. Bank policies do differ but often, once the bank is informed of your death, the executor of your estate will automatically gain access to manage your accounts and won't need your passwords. It is worth making

a list of all your bank accounts so that none is forgotten.

- Social networking: at the time of writing, sites like Facebook will allow a deceased person's profile to remain as a tribute site, but will remove it at the request of close family, though legal challenges may change this.

- Address books: many people now keep their address books in electronic formats. Consider tidying up your address book, getting rid of contacts for 'expired' relationships and leaving instructions on who should be contacted at your death. You may also need to ensure that the necessary passwords to online address books, e.g. in email accounts, are left behind for your executor to find.

- Emails: if leaving behind your email account password, consider whether there is correspondence that you feel somebody may want to keep (nowadays love letters and other correspondence are rarely in paper format) or that you don't want anybody to see.

- Professional virtual networks: if you are a regular participant in professional or special interest networks or forums where you have become known in a group, consider leaving instructions for a message to be posted to inform such contacts. In some cases, you may be a specialist in a field to an extent that only such a group can appreciate.

- Work-related documents or connections: should be terminated or protected for confidentiality (could be documents saved when working from home or special access to databases or virtual information on work computers or in cloud spaces). Remember that many passwords are often saved in the cookies on your computer so if you give an executor your general computer password, they may automatically gain access to confidential work accounts, email accounts and other types of accounts if your cookies are not cleared.

- Libraries: if you have virtual libraries you feel should be saved for the future, be they of pictures on Flickr, videos on You-

Tube, music play lists on Spotify (before, a record collection could be a very personal and valuable thing to leave behind; it might still be in its virtual form), or document collections on Scribd, ensure your executor knows about them and have the necessary passwords.

- If you have your own website(s), consider whether you want them closed down or if you want to appoint a new administrator to ensure their continued existence. You may have to discuss such arrangements in advance if you want to ensure the appointed person is capable and willing to take on the task and has access to the necessary software and/or passwords.
- Online or virtual calendars: does your executor need to know any plans in your diary to be able to cancel appointments? There's another password you may want to pass on.

YOUR ESTATE AND YOUR HEIRS

'Estate' sounds such a grand word – far too grand, perhaps, to be applied to the assets that we'll be leaving behind us when we die. Yet however modest they may seem, our assets have value to those who survive us, particularly if they feel that they've missed out on an inheritance.

A Family Affair

Time was when we 'passed away' at home in bed, in the bosom of our family, attended by a weeping wife or a gravely stoic husband. And as we commended our soul to God, it was wafted gently heavenward on our children's prayers. So affecting a scene must almost have seemed worth dying for.

So much for the idealised version. The reality was rather different, however. They had accidents and heart attacks in the past as well, of course. And because they also had far fewer effective ways of managing pain, comparatively few people can have departed life in anything like such serenity.

This sort of Dickensian deathbed scene seems more fictional than ever now that the stereotypical Victorian family is very much a distant memory and our society is both multifaith and much more secular. Such a tableau would often be too big and too complicated today, when even the happiest of families are now likely to include a bewildering web of civil partners, stepchildren, half-siblings, former wives and husbands and such hitherto unheard-of categories as ex-in-laws. In addition, friendship groups are as important as families for some, with many of us feeling a closer bond with former schoolfriends, college classmates or service comrades than we do with distant parents or with siblings from whom we've grown apart.

Another mainstay of death as described in the nineteenth-century novel is alive and well, however: that of 'great expectations' – and of unseemly wrangling when these are disappointed. Granted, the stakes aren't usually quite so high as they were then: in the costume dramas, the inheritable estates in question are often quite literally that, i.e., stately homes set in rolling acres, with the rights to grandiose titles being at stake, too. Nowadays, although class distinctions are by no means in the past, they have certainly been much diminished in recent years. Even the upper classes tend to be in paid employment, so inheritance isn't a case of all or nothing the way that it once was. The system of primogeniture prevailed in England until as late as 1925, by which it was assumed that a first-born son would inherit his father's fortune by default. Anything that a woman was given in her father's will went straight to her husband the moment that she got married. Women have since won a far greater degree of financial autonomy, of course, whilst the state provides a safety net of sorts for those who need it. Few of us, then, depend entirely on inherited wealth and status for our livelihood and, beyond that, for our sense of who we are. Even so, few of us are so unworldly that we do not care at all about what we may, or may not, inherit.

Beneficiaries

What happens to our property or money when we are gone may make a significant difference to important individuals in our lives, and perhaps to more people than we may at first assume. That holds whether you're the owner of a Scottish castle, a country pile in Hampshire or a two-up, two-down in Salford, or whether you're a south London housing-association tenant who's just managed to put a few hundred quid aside. That is why it's so important to prepare a will, and to do so now, not when it's all become critical. Remember that it's in everybody's interests that your intentions should be clear.

There's no use denying that any property or capital that we leave may make a considerable difference to those whom we also leave behind. Modesty forbids many of us from recognising that we're wealthier than we think, but these days, if we own our homes, we may be sitting on a fortune. That fortune may have no more than a 'paper' value should you be thinking in terms of your position on the property ladder (for if your home has doubled in value since you bought it, so has any other property that you'd like to buy), but would be real enough to anyone who received it as a windfall.

Even if what we have to leave isn't enough to change our heirs' financial or social destiny, it may still help to shape their immediate future: quite a small sum can jump-start saving for a holiday or car, for example. Conversely, those who feel that they haven't been favoured by a bequest are likely to resent what they may perceive as an injustice. And because the 'family circle' has been growing, both in extent and in complexity, the scope for misunderstanding has increased. Hence the importance of making a will. Whilst it's asking too much of a piece of paper for it to heal all wounds, at least it can spell out your intentions. After all, the least we can do is leave what clarity we can.

MAKING A WILL

Die without having made a will, and it's quite possible that any assets that you leave won't go to those who you'd dearly like to benefit from them, maybe because no one knew your intentions, for example, or perhaps because someone else has a better legal claim to them. Making a will that clearly lists your property and states your wishes should ensure that your assets are distributed according to your instructions, and should spare your loved ones the additional grief of apparently having been 'disinherited'.

Death-Deniers

The Law Society estimates that only about 40 per cent of us ever get around to drawing up a will. Although we know that we should, most of us are rather reluctant to do so. The reasons for this are many and varied, and add up to procrastination on a major scale. First, there's our tendency to shrink from *any* administrative task; then there's the fact that this one is so easily postponed (until suddenly it can't be). There's the assumption, too, that it 'goes without saying' that whatever we have will automatically go to our spouse or partner, or to our children (which is true only up to a point, if it's true at all). And then there's the unspoken – and often unconscious – fear that by making arrangements for our death, we'll somehow help to bring about that moment.

Throughout this book, we keep coming back to nineteenth-century examples, and it's true that the Victorian age was big on death and mourning, with its five-star funerals and its elaborate mourning rules. There's also something about the thought of all of those 'testators' and 'legatees', and those 'whereuntos' and 'hereinafters', that smacks of another age. And then there's the new culture of denial: if sexual intercourse began in 1963, as the poet says, dying came to an end around the same time. Or so it seems from the way that it generally goes undiscussed.

It's often said that baby boomers grew up to become 'kidults' – eternal adolescents – with their rock music, their partying and their all-round sense of entitlement. Regardless of whether that's really true or not, it does appear to be the case that they often haven't been in too much of a rush to think about their futures, or those of their families. Wills don't just make us think of death: worse still, for many of us would-be BoBos ('bourgeois-bohemians'), they suggest financial planning, which in turn conjures up images of carpet slippers, secateurs and the *Daily Telegraph*. So wills have come to seem 'uncool', and even somehow anachronistic, at a time when they're arguably needed more than ever before.

WHO GETS THE HOUSE?

Living longer, reduced pensions and a generally shaky economy – all of these factors have contributed to creating less financially stable senior citizens. A survey quoted by the *Daily Telegraph*'s personal finance editor in April 2010 found that over half of the UK's pensioners are in debt, with the average amount for those in debt standing at £36,000 per person, rising to £40,000 for those aged seventy and above. Faced with reduced incomes and high interest rates (interest from debt consumes about one-third of pensioners' incomes), many are turning to their homes as a source of income, not by renting out rooms, but instead by entering into equity-release schemes for cash.

The schemes work like this. An owner-occupier aged between fifty-five and seventy, with a home worth at least £30,000, can apply for a loan equal to the value of their home, in the form of either a lump sum or monthly payments. No interest or capital is repaid during the individual's lifetime, but the house must be sold and the lender paid on their death. The owner-occupier will usually be guaranteed the right to remain in the home for the rest of his or her life, and most schemes will not lend more than the house is worth. These schemes may prove helpful for some, but they are of course weighted towards the lender in terms of financial reward, and Age UK recommends seeking independent legal and financial advice before entering into any such plan (indeed, assuming that there is an advisor that you consider trustworthy). Its rising popularity suggests that many pensioners are finding this a tempting way of boosting their income, but is it wise, and will it really benefit you? As ever: there is no free lunch, so caution is essential.

One group of people may not be happy about senior citizens handing over their homes in this way: those who anticipate inheriting the properties in question. Any adult children who view their parents' home as a source of future income to offset their children's university debts, for instance, may be upset to learn that rather than receiving a fat inheritance, they are legally bound to sell their parents' home and repay the lender before seeing a penny of the proceeds themselves. So if you are considering such a scheme and don't mention it to your heirs, be warned that it could come as a nasty shock to them if you went ahead and they only found out when the money-lender came knocking. (Then again, it's your money, and you're entitled to spend it in whatever way you choose, and that may be treating yourself by taking a world cruise!)

Where There's a Will . . .

Essentially straightforward, a will is a typed or written statement saying what you want to happen to your property and assets after your death. You have to be eighteen or over to make one – old enough to make a mature decision – and, in the traditional formulation, you also have to be 'of sound mind' so that everyone can be sure that this really is your considered will and that you haven't been subject to manipulation in making it. Your signature has to be witnessed, too, so that it's clear that it really is your will and that you made it freely, and there have to be two witnesses to reduce the risk of a will being signed under coercion or through undue influence. (Under Scotland's more trusting system, one witness will do.) The will also has to be dated so that any chronology is clear: many people make more than one will over the years as their circumstances and feelings change, and it's important that there should be no ambiguity over which will represents their final thoughts. Once signed and witnessed, the will is either kept in a safe place at home or at the office of a solicitor. It is typically accompanied by an inventory identifying exactly what the property and assets mentioned in the will are, making administering the will much easier when the time comes.

The formalities of making a will are relaxed if you are a soldier or seaman in active military service. In these cases, the law allows an unwritten will, known as a 'privileged will', to be made. This covers situations such as that of a soldier who has been wounded in combat saying who should inherit his or her estate upon his or her death. It is valid even if the soldier is under the age of eighteen.

It's customary to appoint one or two trusted friends or relatives to act as executors to oversee any breaking-up and distribution of property or other assets from your estate. This probate process, as it is called, can be time-consuming, and executors are responsible for making sure that it all goes as it should. It's a big responsibility, and you will have to ensure that a chosen executor is willing to take it on; you can't just nominate someone without their advance agreement. Or, rather, you can, but they'll be entirely within their rights if they choose to refuse the role – or if they allow the other executor(s) to go ahead and administer the estate as they see fit, whilst keeping the 'power reserved' to step in at a later date if they so wish. An executor can be a lawyer, and if your estate is big and complicated, opting for one may make sense, but in many cases a competent layperson will cope just fine (perhaps with a little help from your solicitor in a background role). So it's important to discuss your plans as fully as possible with your chosen executor(s) so that they know what they're getting themselves into and can then make a realistic judgement as to whether they're up to it and what advice or assistance they feel they're likely to need.

Whilst a professional can clearly bring invaluable experience and expertise to the role of executor, they can also play a crucial role simply by virtue of not being too involved. Where your beneficiaries are likely to disagree – perhaps because their interests are conflicting (those of your present partner and of your children from a previous relationship, for example), there's obvious scope for difficulties, and for rancour. Your executors need to agree to all decisions made regarding the administration of your estate, so it is better to appoint somebody independent than two people who are likely to disagree.

When deciding upon possible executors, you'll also have to bear in mind the fact that you won't be calling on their services for quite some time (touch wood!) This is one area in which it may not make so much sense to trust in experience and age. Are your favoured candidates likely to be around when you die yourself? It doesn't matter how reliable your executors are if they've been dead a decade by the time they're needed. Not to beat about the bush, this is another reason for having more than one executor: it improves the odds that there's actually someone around when they are required!

Self or Solicitor?

This book is all about taking charge of your own affairs, but do-it-yourself is not necessarily always the right way. Straightforward as it is, in principle, to write a will, a fair few pitfalls lie in wait for the unwary and inexperienced, and mistakes tend not to emerge till it's too late. Problems typically arise from simple errors, such as forgetting to include certain assets, or not getting the document properly signed and witnessed. If you don't have much money or property to leave, you may feel that the expense and hassle of hiring a solicitor isn't warranted, but then there's a case for saying that the more modest your estate, the less you can afford to get things wrong. (Bear in mind that you may be able to get legal aid to help you with this.)

Most independent experts believe that it makes sense for most of us to call in a solicitor for help in drawing up a will, if only to give it a once-over before it's signed and witnessed. This is especially the case if what you have in mind for your estate is anything other than straightforward. If you want anyone other than your spouse, civil partner or children to inherit it, for instance; or if you want things distributed in specific ways: to leave more to X than to Y, for whatever reason; or if you want stepchildren or other relatives or friends to be beneficiaries. However simple your situation may be on the face of it, if you also have property or investments abroad, it makes sense to have the help of a professional with the appropriate experience (again, *ask* about this before appointing them), and likewise if you run your own business or are self-employed.

MAKING IT LEGAL

The following requirements are necessary in order to create a valid will:

- the maker of the will must be eighteen years old or older;
- the will must be made voluntarily, with no outside pressure ('undue pressure", that is: gentle prompting that it might be a good idea to get things sorted out is obviously fine. That said, this is clearly a grey area: whatever the pressure, a will is assumed to be valid unless the contesting party can persuade a court that unreasonable pressure was brought to bear.);
- the person making the will must be of sound mind (that is, aware of what he or she is doing);
- the will must be made in writing;
- the will must be signed by its writer in the presence of two witnesses;
- the will must be signed by the two witnesses after the person making the will has signed it;

- the witnesses should not be beneficiaries of the will (a will signed by beneficiaries is still valid, but the beneficiaries cannot then inherit anything).

Although it is not legally required, it is advisable to date any wills that you may make. Also, bear in mind that a will may need to be updated following major changes in your circumstances, such as a marriage, the birth of children, a divorce and so on. The will can be kept at home, or else it can be lodged with a solicitor or at a bank.

THE PROBATE (OR CONFIRMATION) PROCESS

Probate (or, in Scotland, confirmation) is the process of officially proving that a will is both authentic and valid so that a deceased person's estate can accordingly be dealt with by a personal representative. Before this can be done, a 'grant of representation' authorising him or her to do so must be issued by the Probate Service (in England and Wales; the process differs in Scotland and Northern Ireland). Broadly speaking, it is necessary if the deceased has left at least £5,000, stocks or shares, certain insurance policies, or property or land, and without it control of such assets will not be granted to an executor or administrator (i.e., the personal representative). After a person has died, the executor(s) named in his or her will therefore applies to the Probate Registry for a 'grant of probate', as it is called in England and Wales (or, in Scotland, a 'grant of confirmation'), which will give them the right to administer the deceased's assets. (If the deceased did not leave a valid will, however, a relative can apply for a 'grant of letters of administration', or, if a valid will was left, but there is no executor, a 'grant of letters of administration with will'.)

Once a properly completed application for a grant of probate has been sent to the probate registry, it will generally be processed within two to three weeks. If all of the information about the estate is to hand and the papers are completed straight away, therefore, the entire process may be completed in as little as a month. But it generally takes six to nine weeks and could easily take several months, depending on the nature of the assets and how well organised the deceased person's affairs are. If there is a house to be valued, for example, it may take several weeks for the valuer to send the formal valuation report. And if there are a number of share holdings, it may be necessary to instruct a stockbroker to value the shares. Sometimes it will take executors a long time to sort through the paperwork to ascertain what assets form part of the estate.

This is just a brief outline of the probate process; further information is given on the www.direct.gov.uk and www.hmcourts-service.gov.uk and www.hmrc.gov.uk websites, and elsewhere.

Death and Taxes

Death and taxes, the two great certainties of life, often go together, but not always. In the UK, inheritance tax kicks in at £325,000 (the figure for 2012/13); above that threshold, it takes 40 per cent of anything you leave − with certain exemptions: for example, assets passing to a spouse or civil partner; assets passing to charity; or assets that qualify for inheritance tax relief, such as Agricultural Relief or Business Property Relief.

Inheritance tax was introduced by a Labour government during the 1970s as a way of clobbering the rich. The housing boom of later years transformed many people's fortunes for the better, yet by the end of a credit-crunched 2011, the average UK house price had fallen to £160,780 (the Land Registry figure for England and Wales) − well within the nil tax zone, in other words. This means that inheritance tax isn't really an issue for most of 'Middle Britain', with only 5 per cent of the population being believed to be affected. On the other hand, that's still a fair few people, while houses worth £300,000 or more hardly have to be stately homes these days. Throw in some savings and a life-insurance policy, and many men and women who see themselves as belonging to perfectly ordinary middle-class families will find themselves facing the prospect of a significant demand from HM

Revenue & Customs. And whilst a widowed spouse or civil partner won't have to pay out on his or her inheritance, how matters are handled can still have important consequences later on.

If you have significant savings that you think you may be bequeathing to someone, you'd be sensible to take professional advice about inheritance tax: there are so many ways that you can be stung, but also so many ways around them. It may be that, rather than waiting until after you have died, it makes more sense to give the sums that you have earmarked as gifts to your chosen recipients well in advance of your death, or to set up trusts whose funds are protected for specific purposes. A solicitor's services start to cross over into those of a tax advisor here, and because good solicitors (ask around for recommendations) are unlikely to come cheap, the bigger and more complicated your estate, the more expensive their services are likely to be. But it's almost always a price worth paying for peace of mind, and for the confidence of knowing that you have your affairs sorted out how you want them, and that what you're intending to leave your dependants won't go straight to the taxman.

DIGITAL WILLS

A digital will can take two forms: It can be a conventional will and testament in digital format, or it can comprise instructions for dealing with the deceased's digital possessions.

Although the second option is typically for online accounts, more and more people are looking into the first. Apps are now available to help you make your will (digital or conventional), or you may record a video in which detailed instructions are provided.

You could post a digital will on a website, although you may not want your final bequests to be publicly accessible, or, indeed, to be viewable on a website like YouTube (www.youtube.com), where they can be given approval ratings. Note, too that a video will cannot stand alone as a legal document in the UK, but must be supported by a written will.

Changing and Complex Times

Most of our ancestors didn't have too much to leave behind them when they died – maybe some clothing and tools, or a few sticks of furniture, perhaps. The nearest they got to investment was paying a penny-in-the-pound of all their earnings into a funeral fund so that they could spare themselves the disgrace of a pauper's burial. Even among the middle classes, things were relatively simple, with the possessions typically bequeathed being a house, some jewellery and some (smarter) furniture. There might have been savings in the bank, but few had elaborate investment portfolios.

Whilst it's true that crazes for playing the stock market briefly swept North America and Europe from time to time during the nineteenth century, they never outlasted the bear markets that inevitably came. And the effects of the 1929 Crash on financial traders have been much exaggerated, for they didn't really pitch themselves off Wall Street window ledges in their droves. The main impact of the catastrophe was on the little guy (and gal): the shopkeepers, schoolteachers and secretaries of the Midwest, who lost everything as their savings shrivelled and their homes were repossessed. If the Great Depression dominated life in the 1930s, it also cast its shadow over the decades that followed, with a whole generation growing up with a profound suspicion of anything that smacked of speculation; the bank deposit account or building-society savings account was about the limit. In Britain, that changed with the advent of Mrs Thatcher's 'shareholding democracy' of the 1980s. 'Maggie's' Conservative government had already created a new population of homeowners – in other words, 2 million more people with something to bequeath. Now, with the privatisation of the big utilities, Joe Public – or rather, 'Sid' – was encouraged to invest in stocks and shares. Many became shareholders without even trying: financial naïfs who'd opened savings accounts as a simple step up from hiding their money under the mattress metamorphosed into minicapitalists when the building societies suddenly demutualised during the 1990s. By this time, the effects of the Big Bang of 1986 had spread out from the City to make themselves felt at high-street level. Financiers, freed by deregulation, were offering a widening variety of ever more ingenious investment and savings packages, many of them specifically aimed at (and energetically marketed to) 'ordinary people'.

The inevitable result of postwar economic history has been that when it comes to financial matters, what constitutes an 'ordinary person' has completely changed. From internet accounts to ISAs, from multiple mortgages to bonds and unit trusts, our financial arrangements are of a complexity that would have amazed and bewildered our grandparents (indeed, they often amaze and bewilder us!) And while hype has exerted a strong influence on those with money to invest, they've also been pushed into doing so by a growing sense that the state pension provision won't be enough. The recent near-collapse of the international banking system may have curbed enthusiasm for the more extravagantly imaginative plans, but there's no way we're going to put the clock back now.

You can deplore these trends or rejoice in them. You can argue that they've promoted the freedom of the individual and have rewarded hard work and enterprise, or you may feel that they've made society more selfish and uncaring, enriching the already affluent at the expense of the already poor. One thing is for sure: whether or not the financial reforms of the past decades produced the trickle-down in wealth that their proponents promised, they certainly caused a trickle-down in financial complexity. Men and women of quite modest incomes now have investment and savings arrangements so intricately ordered that they would have shocked a captain of industry a few decades ago. Whilst it's true that an excluded 'underclass' at the bottom of the heap can't get any access to banking at all, it's all different even only a rung or so up the social ladder.

If we struggle to keep track of our various financial activities ourselves, what are our executors supposed to do? Our financial affairs will typically have evolved in semichaotic fashion over years, and unless we're organised and efficient by nature, it's very easy to lose control. So it actually makes sense to stop and take stock, and to examine and overhaul our existing arrangements, closing down accounts that have become redundant or once attractive savings plans that have now passed their shelf life. Generally speaking, the simpler, the better. In any case, it's crucial that some overall system is in place so that we (or our executors) can clearly see what we have, and the position with each account or investment. It will certainly make life easier for those who come after us.

Dying in Debt

For many of us, our complex financial situations mean that we have some debts, and it's important to remember that our estate includes liabilities, as well as assets, and that these include everything from outstanding water rates and income tax to credit-card bills. It's not that your appointed heirs will inherit your debts as such, but rather that your creditors will get first dibs on anything that you leave. Your executors are required by law to see that these debts are paid, and there's a pecking order. There may be complicating factors, but the usual priority order of creditors is: 'reasonable' funeral and administration expenses; debts due to the government (such as income tax or overpayment of benefits); secured creditors (for example, for a mortgage over property); preferential debts, in relatively rare cases (such as wages due to employees); ordinary debts such as utility bills; interest on unsecured debts; and 'deferred debts', such as informal loans between family members).

It's worth checking what protection, if any, you have against these liabilities. For instance, in more conservative times, mortgage providers typically insisted that you took out a life-insurance policy as part of the package. This would mean that if you died before the term of the mortgage had ended, it was paid off automatically. The more creative schemes of the 1980s and 1990s didn't necessarily do this, however. Nor, frequently, did those second mortgages that became so popular during the housing boom of more recent years. So it may well be worth taking out insurance to cover this eventuality even at a comparatively late stage. You can also take out payment-protection cover for credit-card debts.

Whilst it may be the case that our heirs don't inherit our debts, if they've shared our homes with us, they may be liable for outstanding domestic bills. More seriously, perhaps, a jointly owned property may have to be sold after your death so that your (or, rather, your creditors') debt can be recovered. This means that your spouse or civil partner will get their share, but at the same time, they'll lose their home.

A Settling of Accounts

It isn't just money that we need to set to rights, of course. With death comes the final auditing of our emotional accounts, and our last chance to show our loved ones how we feel. The hope, in the first instance, is that we will leave our partners, immediate families or other existing dependants financially secure – something that we've probably always striven to do during our lives. After that, though, we may perhaps want to acknowledge any other bonds or obligations that we may feel. How we allocate any legacies we leave sends a clear message to those left behind. In many cases, even cash bequests are likely to be received in an emotional spirit, valued not just in monetary terms, but as signs that the receivers are remembered. And if we know that a friend or relation will particularly prize our old Biggles books or ballet programmes, our Alan Shearer autograph or our antique asparagus tongs, this is our big chance to make their day.

By the same token, if you'd rather your money went to the Battersea Dogs' Home or Cancer Research, this is the time to make those intentions clear. The only way to ensure that a charity benefits on your death is to leave a legacy in your will. (Assets passing to charity under your will are exempt from inheritance tax.) Likewise, if you want to divide things up in a way that you know members of your family won't all understand, you will have to make it absolutely clear that this is what you want, whatever they may think. Don't expect to be understood unless (or even if!) you explain yourself. You can outline the reason for your bequest in the will itself – for example, 'I give to X the sum of £500 in recognition of his years of loyal service'. To this day, though, scholars squabble over whether Shakespeare left his wife his 'second-best bed' as a slight or as a tender token of remembered intimacies (the 'best bed' would have been for guests, it's argued). You can't expect to please everyone in death any more than you can in life. In the end, you're not responsible for others' unrealistic expectations. Neither are you being realistic if you expect that long-simmering disputes or rankling rivalries will miraculously be resolved when you pass on.

Yet again, clarity is crucial: the more explicitly everything can be spelled out in your will, the easier it's likely to be all round. If I *know* that I've been passed over, I may not like it much, but at least I have a hope of putting the hurt behind me and moving on. If I remain convinced that I've been badly served, but have no way of establishing it, resentment may eat away at me for years.

The Clutter Question

Most of the stuff you leave behind is not going to be the subject of emotional arguments between your friends or relations, however. The trip to the charity shop with clothing and clutter that is no longer needed is one of the grimmer rituals of modern-day bereavement (even if it plays a part in the important process of 'letting go'). Although you can usefully anticipate and deal with this problem only to a limited extent, if you can see that you have heaps of junk that you're never going to use and that is only going to be a headache for those you leave behind, then why not get rid of it? Anyway, a bit of streamlining seldom hurts at any time of life.

It's also worth thinking about whether anything you have might be more than mere clutter. Do you have things that you're sure would actually be useful to any people or organisations that you know? Do you own any old items that a local museum might appreciate? You'll have to be realistic here because there's clearly scope for embarrassment on all sides. Your leather-bound Complete Jane Austen may look lovingly well thumbed to you, but to your old school library, the covers may just seem old and the pages simply tatty. But this shouldn't be a reason not to think positively about more constructive ways in which the clutter that squats on your life like a dead weight might be of help to others. Feeling that things that you can no longer use may be of benefit to someone else can be very cheering, and also to your loved ones at what is inevitably an upsetting time (however well you manage your death).

Think, as well, about whether any of your possessions may have sentimental value to someone – not just the obvious heirlooms (like jewellery and antiques), but maybe items like childhood toys or trophies, once-prized LPs or birdwatching binoculars. You can't necessarily expect the person clearing out your things to know what the important mementoes are, or who will value something that, to others, will be just junk. So as far as is feasible, identify what's likely to be of interest, and to whom.

Also consider whether you have any letters or journals that you'd like your partner or children to see when you are gone, or, for that matter, that you'd very much not like them to see. Either way, you'll need to make provisions for them before you die.

Of course, some of the most important things we would like to pass on are difficult to include in a will. Saying that we love or appreciate someone before it's too late is a common desire that is nevertheless often put off for too long. Family trees, stories and other morsels of information also need to be communicated to the next generation if we don't want them to be lost forever. So if you want to let others know about the family's distant relationship to a famous historical figure, or to remember Uncle Bert's heroic wartime feats, or even if you just want to preserve Grandma's fabulous chutney recipe, you need to consider the best way of passing on this knowledge.

TAKING IT TO THE GRAVE

Although the pyramids are the most famous mortuary symbol in the world, no one is sure exactly how the ancient Egyptians built such impressive structures. But that is only one of the many secrets that have gone to the grave with people. Buried treasure, for example, is a common plot device in novels and movies, but only one pirate, William Kidd, is known to have buried some of his ill-gotten gains. After Kidd was hanged in 1701, the search for his buried treasure began – and has continued ever since.

The most beautiful violin music is made, it is said, by Stradivarius violins, but no one knows how the master made his famous instruments. And whilst Lee Harvey Oswald is widely reviled as the man who shot US president John F Kennedy in 1963, Oswald's own assassination in the same year prevented a trial, and there consequently remains a question mark over the true identity of Kennedy's assassin. In the case of the Mongol ruler Genghis Khan, the location of his burial place remains a mystery to this day, because everyone who knew it was killed.

Will Power

The importance of making a will is most powerfully illustrated by a look at what happens when a person doesn't leave one when he or she dies.

Strict rules govern what happens when a person dies 'intestate', or without having made a will. Then, the Crown takes charge and appoints an administrator of its own to play the part that would otherwise have been performed by the executor. He or she has to do it without fear, favour – or, it may seem – much compassion. And even if it works out well for everyone, the process is often slow.

After first making sure that any liabilities are settled in the customary order (see page 46), any remaining assets are distributed. Again, a set order is followed.

If a person with a surviving spouse or civil partner, and with children, dies intestate, the spouse or civil partner will inherit everything up to a value of £250,000, as well as the personal possessions. From any remaining assets, one half is divided equally amongst the children. The spouse has the right to receive the income from the other half for the rest of his or her lifetime, and thereafter this also passes to the children.

If a person with a surviving spouse or civil partner, but without children, dies intestate, the spouse or civil partner inherits everything up to a value of £450.000, and the personal possessions. From the remainder, the spouse or civil partner inherits one half, and the other half will be inherited by other relatives. Of these, parents come first, and if there are no surviving parents, siblings. If there are neither surviving parents nor siblings, more distant relatives, such as nieces and nephews, will benefit.

It's important to bear in mind that partners inherit only if their relationship with the deceased has been officially sanctioned: 'common law' doesn't recognise the common-law wife or husband, in other words. Nor does it recognise a partner, be it gay or straight, however intensely loved or longstanding in devotion. If there is no legal attachment, there is no right to inherit under intestacy law.

Children are in a stronger position. It makes no difference whether they're born of the first, second or subsequent marriages, or, for that matter, of no marriage at all. If they're the children of the deceased, they're entitled to their equal share.

Although every family is different, the law cannot easily take account of that. Individuals who feel that they're not being justly treated can challenge intestacy arrangements, but it's typically a long-drawn-out and difficult affair. If you have reason to want your estate to be distributed along any other than these rigidly straightforward lines, then it really is important that you make a will, and that you take good care of it. Because you're also deemed intestate if your will cannot be found. So don't go to the trouble of making a will if it's only going to end up being lost.

Common-Law Misconceptions

The importance of clarity really can't be overstated when making a will, not least because the law can't cope with anything that isn't set down in black and white. This is particularly problematic for those free (or simply lackadaisical) spirits among us who've more or less muddled through life, leaving important things not just unwritten, but unstated. If that's a problem when X gets the rosewood table that we 'always meant' Y to have (yet never said so), it can be a tragedy when the whole status of a family is at stake.

Consider this: 'My partner and I are married in all but name; we've been together for twenty-two years; we have children; and everyone who knows us thinks of us as man and wife.' That doesn't mean that the legal system does. It's the easiest thing in the world to assume that the law will naturally recognise the things that everyone else does. But the law is intolerant of vague assumptions by its very nature. It has to be, for everyone's protection. This literal-mindedness can be irksome when the law is resolutely refusing to acknowledge the blindingly obvious, but then what's obvious to me may not be anything like as obvious to someone else.

So it's no use being outraged that the state regards our partnership as an overgrown one-night-stand. We will have to tell it if we see our relationship as something more. The 'common-law marriage' isn't quite a myth, in legal terms, but it's really rather an airy-fairy philosophical concept that cuts very little ice when it comes to the big concerns of life like the rules of inheritance, which simply don't come into play here. In the law's eyes, your partner is neither your 'natural' heir nor your next of kin. That doesn't mean that you can't leave him or her your home and your belongings, but that you'll actually have to take steps to *do* that – it won't just happen automatically. So if you want your partner to inherit your possessions automatically, you will either have to marry him or her or form a civil partnership. Otherwise, you will have to set down your wishes officially in a will.

Guardian Angels

If you have a child or children, this is also the time to appoint a guardian or guardians to look after them in case you should die or become incapacitated before they're able to take care of themselves. The guardian(s) would then be formally named in your will.

It's an honour to be asked, but taking charge of someone else's children is potentially both an enormous commitment and an immense responsibility, so whoever you nominate must give their full agreement first. And it's in everybody's interest that they should be given the opportunity to think it through for a while at leisure – and without pressure – so that they don't sign up to something that they don't really want to do.

First, though, you and your spouse or partner need to talk it through together yourselves, to think around the decision and to look at it carefully from every angle. The person you're thinking of asking may be a fantastic friend, or a doting aunt or uncle, but would he or she make a good replacement parent? Would they be able to offer not just the love, but the patience, the tolerance, and, at times, the strictness that your offspring will need? Are their lives also likely to be stable enough to give your child(ren) their full support?

If you've grown away from your family – not necessarily in terms of affection, but maybe in terms of lifestyle and attitudes – you may be more likely to see the qualities you're looking for in a friend rather than a family member. Your family may find this hard to understand, however, which is all the more reason for spelling out your intentions in your will – again, the more explicit and unambiguous you are, the better.

A DOG'S LIFE

Animals have a special place in many people's hearts and many of us would often be extremely upset to think of our pet being uncared for, or even made homeless, in the event of our death. Under UK law, pets are treated as property and so it is possible to insert a clause in a will ensuring that care of the animal will be transferred to a new owner. Naturally it is vital to discuss such an arrangement fully with that person before making provision in a will.

The RSPCA provides a free Home for Life service, which means that after an owner's death, care of the pet is handed over to the charity. As well as looking after the animal, the RSPCA endeavours to find it a new home. For more information, see www.homeforlife.org.uk.

A BIRTHDAY BEQUEST

Scottish writer Robert Louis Stevenson left his friend Annie H Ide his birthday. Apparently, she had often complained about having a birthday that fell on Christmas Day, so when he died in 1894, Stevenson left her his birthday of 13 November.

Full Disclosure

When it comes to clarity, what goes for the law also goes further than you may think for families, which means that you'll have to be prepared to come out and say exactly what you want to be done after your death. Think about it:

- Does 'everyone' really see things the way you do?

- Does Dad believe that he knows better than your 'deadbeat' partner what's good for his 'little girl' and grandchildren?

- Does your partner's mum think that you were never good enough for him?

- Have you always been (in the nicest possible way) bullied by a big brother or sister who invariably knows best?

Even if such common familial tensions don't exist, you can't necessarily expect even those who know you well to read your mind, while even the most well-meaning relation may go too far in interfering – or, alternatively, may hang back out of diffidence.

So whilst financial details should be set down in your will, you should also be aiming to prepare the important people in your life for how you want things to be when you are gone. The more you can get things out into the open, the better (short of boring everyone to tears or getting everybody down). Without coming on like the angel of death, you should be trying to have conversations in which you establish the idea that you have a view on how you'd like your affairs to be arranged after your death, and you should do this sooner rather than later. You should also – as gently as possibly – be nudging your partner into thinking things through himself, and then into having the same sorts of conversations with his or her family. You can't make family members behave well when the time comes, but by making your wishes clear, you can at least give them the chance to do the right thing. They certainly can't do it if they don't know what it is.

And what goes for us goes for those we love as well. If we feel that a friend is sleepwalking towards intestacy, with all of the chaos and heartache that it can bring for loved ones, then it's only right that we should raise our concerns. Not that this friendly duty is a license to nag or bully: in the end, if they don't take action, then it's their denial, and it has to be respected. If it's our partner who's being so passive, then that's a bit different. It's harder to see where the boundary should be between undue interference and responsible prompting, but giving up and sleepwalking in the same direction ourselves is hardly the answer.

Altogether, talking is the key to dealing with just about all of our various fears of death, whether we're talking about the animal fear of dying, the philosophical fear of oblivion, or the sheer administrative funk that we may get into when faced with putting our financial and legal affairs in order. There's a danger that you may bang on too much about it all and end up being a bore – just as you may when talking about coarse fishing or your holiday in Turkey – but if you're reasonably tactful and sensitive, there's no need for talk of death to be a dampener on life. We can do away with denial using honesty and frankness, so allowing the idea of death to be normalised as just another subject for discussion. That way we, our partners, our children and our friends will be able look forward to our deaths – not, perhaps, with enthusiasm (at least, we hope not!) – but with a degree of acceptance, with courage, and also with calmness.

A GOOD CAUSE?

Among the medieval mortal remains moved to Ilford's Clark Road Cemetery in 1874, when the church of St Martin Outwich, in the City of London, was dug up for construction work, were those of a certain Mrs Abigail Vaughan. In her will, she left four shillings a year (quite a sum in those days) towards the cost of buying firewood for burning heretics.

DON'T GET MAD . . .

Many people fantasise about using their wills to settle old scores, although rather fewer can hold on to a grievance for quite that long. Yet there are those in every generation for whom the prospect of eternal darkness is as nothing when compared to the opportunity to have their posthumous revenge. Men like US attorney T M Zink, for example, who died in 1930 leaving his daughter a fortune of $5. That was still $5 more than his widow got. Instead,

$50,000 was left in trust to be used for building a 'womanless library'. Not only were no women to be admitted to this place of learning, but it was to contain no work by a female author.

Samuel Bratt, who died in 1960, left his widow £330,000 – on the strict condition that she smoked five cigars each day for the rest of her life. She'd made his own life miserable, he felt, by refusing to let him smoke the cigars that he so loved in either his house or garden, so he devised this special purgatory just for her.

Misogyny is a recurrent feature in 'revenge-will' stories. So maybe it's no surprise that so many women decided that man wasn't a girl's best friend. When she died in 2007, American hotelier Leona Helmsley, 'Queen of Mean', left her white Maltese dog, Trouble, $12 million. (Her indignant family managed to get this figure reduced to $2 million.) But Trouble was a pauper-pooch by comparison with Gunther III, the dog who belonged to Germany's late Countess Carlotta Liebenstein. She died in 1991, leaving her pet a cool £43 million.

BONA BONANZA

If you are not yet persuaded how crucial it is to make a will, perhaps this final nugget of information might just bring you round: HM Treasury's own figures for the amount it helps itself to in the form of *bona vacantia* (literally 'vacant goods'). This is money and property on which no will has been left, and where no kin can make a claim. By law, accordingly, it goes straight to the state. And it seems there are an awful lot of people who die unmourned by any near or dear. In the year ending March 2011, there were 26,481 new cases, involving some £55 million. It's hard to imagine that a fair proportion of those who left this money didn't have better uses for it than as a gift for the government – however public-spirited that may seem.

Chapter Two
SHUFFLING OFF
THIS MORTAL COIL:

HOW DO YOU
WANT TO GO?

Will you get to choose how you'll die? Quite possibly not. Traffic accidents claim in the region of 3,000 lives a year in the UK; house fires account for a good 300 more. Some people have dangerous jobs: soldiers and police officers (obviously), and also seafarers, scaffolders, roofers, miners, forestry and quarry workers. You may have the misfortune to meet a mad axe-murderer (they do exist, even if the odds of you winning the lottery are better than you encountering one), or you may find yourself caught up in a drive-by shooting. But when it comes to unexpected deaths, the real mayhem is medical. Flu and pneumonia can strike almost as suddenly as any violent attacker, and 13,000 people in England and Wales die of them each year. You could also keel over at a moment's notice – and many thousands do – carried off by a heart attack or stroke.

Yet the chances are that you will succeed in escaping all of these fates. And if you do, you may well find that you have more control over your destiny than you expect. Not that you will have the option of dodging death altogether, of course, but you may find yourself with a degree of choice over how you approach it, and how your doctors do, too. Advances in medical science, technology and practice have not only allowed many thousands of us to live much longer than our predecessors, but have also enabled our final illnesses to be better managed. The pain and indignity that, historically, were such inseparable parts of death have today been considerably allayed, although not, unfortunately, eliminated.

A 'long life' can be a curse as well as a blessing, as it also means a long old age. For too many it has come to mean an endless round of frustration, humiliation and loneliness. Whilst some of us fear the onset of old age, the fact remains that there's never been a better time to grow old. Great news? Well, yes and no. We've all lived long enough to see that progress is problematic, and have seen quite clearly that the cutting edge is also double-edged. Every time technology answers a question, it raises a new – and perhaps more intractable – one: today's industrial revolution is tomorrow's global warming, for instance. The fact that so many millions of men and women have been able to enjoy a better quality of life for longer has to be a good thing, despite the sneers about doddery driving and Saga holidays. But what of those who feel that they've outstayed their time; that they're trapped in an existence they can't enjoy; that they're the prisoners of well-meaning medics and families?

Along with the long life, moreover, has come the 'long death': what was once the matter of a moment may now be a protracted process, with weeks, or even months, perhaps being spent on life-support. And we've given ourselves new and terrifying powers: if we haven't made a formal resolution about it in advance ourselves, we may leave our families with the terrifying responsibility of debating the precise instant at which we should be switched off at the mains. (In fact, it is doctors who have the ultimate authority in these circumstances, in consultation with the next of kin. They must act in the best interests of the patient, and if this brings them into conflict with family members, there will be considerable distress added to an already agonising situation.)

The science and organisation that characterises even the post-mortem procedures nowadays does mean that you can plan ahead to an extent that people would never have considered in the past. In many cases you even have the opportunity of designing your final moment, though the time leading up to it may be equally challenging. Death used to be a simple matter – not an *easy* one, but certainly straightforward. All you could do was tuck the patient in and be as sympathetic and supportive as you could. And if *you* were the patient, all you could do was face death as bravely as you could. Now mortality has become a moral minefield all of its own, while old age is hardly unproblematic.

DECLINING YEARS

Thanks to medical advances and a better standard of living, we are now living longer than ever before. Yet this brings its own problems in an age when changing familial and social structures and support networks can no longer be relied upon to respect or take care of those who are elderly, frail and increasingly impoverished. It's a problem for society, and, at the more personal level, it's also a problem for those of us who are contemplating what lies ahead in old age.

The Prime of Life?

They've 'never had it so good', said Harold Macmillan, notoriously, in 1957, but the British people were to have it even better when they retired. Not all of them, of course: many were poor in 1957, and were destined to remain so, yet even then, they received some protection from the welfare state. For many, though, there were advantages aplenty. With a shot in the arm from the NHS and a leg-up from the Education Act of 1944, they entered the world of work as Britain moved towards full employment. Experience and continuity were valued then (the age of mergers and buy-outs had not yet arrived), and they remained in place, paying into gilt-edged pension schemes year after year. They could often take early retirement on favourable terms. Yet even if they stayed on at work until their sixties, they still felt physically young and fit by comparison with earlier generations, and the golf course, the cruise and the Spanish timeshare beckoned. And when their liberation from salary-slavery coincided with a new era of cheap airfares, the world really did appear to be retired people's oyster.

So much for the pensioner stereotype, though. For even the most fortunate had their ups and downs: marriages were less stable and families were more fragmentary than they'd been before. By no means everyone was anything like as affluent when they reached retirement, and not everyone had the blessing of good health. The headline figures might have indicated that the NHS had transformed the well-being of the nation, but that didn't mean that every individual felt fine. In its own, unspectacular way, a chronic illness can slowly drain the joy out of living, making each new day an ever-more unrewarding struggle.

Nor was longevity evenly distributed across the population: as ever, the rich outlived the poor. Women, meanwhile, frequently lasted longer than their husbands. Men who bucked this trend found themselves ill-equipped to take care of themselves domestically, or even to do the sort of basic social networking they'd tended to leave to ''er indoors'. Meanwhile, for every widow who had a new lease of life when freed from a man who'd beaten or bullied her, or had simply got under her feet at home, another felt lost and lonely, adrift in a society that was losing sight of the elderly in its midst.

SEQUESTERING SICKNESS

Historically, we didn't lead such sheltered lives as we do today. Even young children would have known full well what sickness could be like. Many would have helped to tend a dying parent or grandparent at home. The modern hospital has done great things, and no one in their right mind would want to put the clock back, but it has had the effect of sequestering the sick, taking suffering out of the everyday world. The hospital is a place apart, as surely as any prison: it isn't meant to be that way, but that's the way it often seems. One of the most positive aspects of hospice care, by contrast, is the welcoming environment in which family members and friends are encouraged to visit and spend time with their relative or loved one, keeping everyone connected.

Liberated, or Marooned on the Margins?

The reasons for the decline of the extended family are complex, but they include the simple fact that, for all its virtues, many people didn't like living in it: they didn't like its feuds, its power struggles and its sense of overwhelming and inescapable surveillance. But there's no doubt that the rise of the nuclear family left the older generation increasingly marginalised. Weekend visits to gran and granddad could easily become a chore. Help, when given, could be begrudged, and even when it wasn't, could subtly stigmatise elderly relatives as recipients of charity. Everyone could have a state pension or receive social security; many could fall back on quite generous private pensions; the elderly could be independent, society seemed to reason, and the tendency was to feel that they therefore *should* be.

In truth, many older men and women have been only too happy to oblige, having enjoyed their independence – or having enjoyed it while their health and financial means permitted. Many found it liberating to keep their families at arm's length: the freedom to see their grandchildren, offer help with their care as and when it might be needed and yet be free to lead their own lives, suited a great many grandparents down to the ground. But this new role has not been without its tensions: a grandparent's status suddenly became negotiable in a way that it hadn't been before: a grandparent's contributions could be taken for granted on the one hand or resented on the other, while sage counsel might now be rejected as interference.

In former times, the elderly paterfamilias was the head of the household, with the matriarch its ruling heart: their years and their experience commanded unquestioning respect. They weren't necessarily obeyed, but their authority was acknowledged, and their hard-won wisdom was recognised by society as a whole. Those who grew old in the final decades of the twentieth century found a very different status awaiting them, however, along with very different attitudes. Times had not only changed, but seemed to have entered fast-forward mode. And in such times, what application does the 'wisdom' of old age now have? Conservative commentators may berate the young for their illiteracy and innumeracy, their textspeak and their obsession with celebrity, but it is their elders who are conspicuously at sea, if we pay heed to the media. The times seemed to be conspiring to cast ridicule on a generation born and educated before the computer age. Physically fit they may be, but as they struggle to work a cash-point machine or find themselves baffled and bamboozled by a call-centre queuing system, the elderly are often portrayed as having become more helpless than they've ever been.

An Onerous Responsibility, or a Boon for Society?

Despite families spending less and less time with their elderly relations, one result of this situation has been the feeling, which has slowly and stealthily been gaining ground, that elderly people may be a burden. A burden on the state because all they do (supposedly) is draw pensions and soak up health treatment, home-help assistance and, in many cases, residential care. And a burden on the nuclear families that have grown increasingly inward-looking and exclusive over time.

The postwar consensus was that the welfare state could, and should, be expected to provide care and support 'from the cradle to the grave'. This has given way in recent decades to the idea that taxation is an imposition upon hardworking families, and that taking 'hand-outs' is somehow not strictly honourable. The elderly are generally net 'takers' in such a scheme (however much they may have given during the course of their working lives), and the result has been that they (or their supportive families) have often had to fight for whatever help they receive from health or council services, while such help as they get may be viewed with resentment by those around them.

Within the family itself, communication has inevitably suffered as elderly mothers, fathers and parents-in-law have been recast as outsiders. Misunderstandings have underlined the differences between the generations. Media stories of elder abuse are thankfully an extreme exception, but we should be aware that the underlying norms have gradually been changing. Giving support to the elderly once seemed like part of the ordinary familial give-and-take, but now feels like providing special care, a duty of the sort that, over time, is only too liable to become irksome.

Most insidiously of all, the idea of being a burden has taken root in the minds of many elderly people, who have come to sense that they've outlasted any useful function. And although few families would explicitly endorse such a view, more may encourage it (if only subconsciously), whilst the most devoted don't necessarily do enough to banish such anxieties. Once more, communication is at issue: many people simply don't see where a gulf of misunderstanding has opened up between themselves and their elders.

The reality, however, is that plenty of older people do still contribute to society and are anything but helpless. Public figures such as Tony Benn, Maggie Smith and David Attenborough have continued educating and entertaining until well into their seventies and eighties, attaining 'national treasure' status in the process. And it is not only these famous characters that make a positive difference to our world. Think of the thousands of grandparents providing free, daily childcare for young working couples, or the retirees dedicated to charity work and local churches. Often it is not until after they have gone that we realise both our gratitude for their constant support and the valuable connection to our own pasts that they embody. And that, certainly for most, is a boon that outweighs the burden.

GROWING OLD DISGRACEFULLY

Today's media may put a great deal of emphasis on youth culture, but many retired people feel that at last they're free to enjoy the time of their lives. For retirees in good health, with a thriving social life and financial security, this may be the first time they've been able to celebrate a carefree existence, free from family responsibilities, work pressures and the insecurities that characterised their youth and middle age. And with a mature self-knowledge and a sense of being glad to be alive, as well as the time to express themselves, travel or just relax – what's not to like?

"Life should not be a journey to the grave with the intention of arriving safely in an attractive and well-preserved body, but rather to skid in sideways – Chardonnay in one hand – strawberries in the other – body thoroughly used up, totally worn out, and screaming – WooHoo! What a Ride!"

www.hellsgeriatrics.co.uk

Taking Stock

Many retirees do continue to live life to its fullest, but it is also the case that from now on, a proportion of our elderly people are likely to find themselves increasingly hit by a double-whammy of age-old old-age problems and of a new poverty many of us felt we'd put behind us. As time has gone on and fiscal difficulties have grown, the state pension has greatly decreased in value, whilst many companies have closed their final-salary pension schemes. Indeed, the last twenty years or so have seen a large-scale casualisation of labour across a wide range of industries and businesses that once offered long-term employment, with all the benefits that it brought. Typists, TV repairmen, teachers, telesales staff . . . a huge variety of workers are now officially classed as self-employed. The short-term contracts under which they typically work don't tend to be particularly generous in terms of pay, but such workers are still supposed to fund their own pension plans.

In addition, councils, badly strapped for cash themselves, are making what cuts they can, which inevitably has an impact on the elderly. It is, after all, the local authorities that assess an individual's care needs and different councils inevitably interpret the rules in different ways, meaning that the provision of long-term care for the elderly can vary greatly across the UK. Moreover, the system is complex and it can be difficult to understand exactly what care provision an elderly person is entitled to. And all the indications are that things are going to get worse before they get better. Many people are therefore going to find themselves facing difficulties at a time of life when they're least equipped to deal with them. It's something that we have to address as a society, and it's also something that we may have to think about in terms of ourselves.

DECIDING ON DEATH

It may be the last thing that we want to think about, but it's far better to face and resolve the question of how we'd like to die (given the choice, of course) while we can still communicate, or act on, our wishes rather than leaving it until it's too late and we're powerless to help ourselves. The issues involved are complex, and often painful, but thinking about them, and preparing yourself – and maybe also your loved ones – will make taking life-or-death decisions easier for you all when the time comes.

Decisions, Decisions

Many of us are already likely to be in a vulnerable state when serious illness eventually catches up with us. How we respond, how we cope and how far we feel that we can call on those around us for help and support – this is likely to depend in part on how much self-confidence we have, and on how secure we feel.

All of the previously outlined context should be borne in mind when treatments of terminal illness are considered, and also the idea of assisted suicide. This question has become increasingly contentious in recent years because living longer has also meant dying longer. For as preventative medicine and improvements in surgery have been bearing down on deaths from other causes, cancer has become increasingly pre-eminent as a killer. Typically, that means long and difficult periods of outpatient treatment followed, if we're unlucky, by a protracted terminal illness. But death from cancer doesn't tend to come as a bolt from the blue:

we generally have time to think, to take decisions and to make plans. These may simply be about whether we want to die at home or in a hospice, or about how far we want our carers to go in order to try to extend our life.

How we want our life to end is ultimately a personal decision, whatever ethical considerations come into play. Usually, we'll take into account how we feel about it ourselves, and also how we imagine our families and other loved ones will feel, and how we can make the situation as easy as we can for them. At the same time, this is one of those cases in which we must stand up for ourselves, and for what we want, rather than passively accepting the course that we believe to be the most obliging. Even if we do decide that we don't want our carers to fight to keep us alive to the bitter end, and at any cost, it's important – for them, as well as for us – that it is our own choice, made without pressure from others.

This is where the question of coercion can come in, and where, correspondingly, family and friends may have a responsibility to help. The fear is not so much that wicked relatives are going to press unwilling patients to 'do the decent thing' so that they can inherit their property (although it's amazing what people will do in certain circumstances). It's more that many men and women – particularly in older generations – have been schooled in self-sacrifice. Fathers who've got up at the crack of dawn and have worked long hours all their lives in order to feed their families, women accustomed to taking the smallest piece of cake and giving up the comfy chair – they're not about to start thinking about putting their own needs first.

Thinking Ahead

We can't know how we'll feel when the moment comes to face death, and yet by then it may be too late to make a sensible decision. So we'll have to make the best guess we can as to what our choices would be. Whilst we don't have any experience of what dying's like, we at least know how we feel about things in general, and we also know the kind of person we are. Fear of death, humiliation or helplessness, the possibility of pain (however well we're tended), and any ethical convictions – we'll have to factor in all of these issues as far as we feel able.

This is an impossible ask, but then if it's impossible for us, it's going to be even worse for anybody else. So there's no real alternative, then: we'll have to be the ones to do the thinking. And it makes sense to start thinking well in advance of the critical moment, and to involve your family as much as you can. If you're the prospective patient's child, parent or partner, your dilemma is different; remember that although you can't usefully push him or her, you can invite discussion and be as supportive as you can. You can also encourage your loved one to try to think about what lies ahead, and not about what you, or others, will want, but about what is likely to feel right for him or her. Make it clear that you're not afraid of listening whenever he or she wants to air these feelings.

Of course, you may think all of this through and discuss it with loved ones, and still reach the conclusion that you'd rather let nature, doctors or a deity take the lead whenever the time comes. But you'll benefit from the confidence of having considered the issue and made a positive decision, whatever that may be.

Polar Opposites

However personal decisions about dying may be, we cannot help but be aware that we have to take them in the context of a debate about assisted death that seems to rage more fiercely by the year. The stakes also seem to have risen in direct relation to the increasing degree of control that our doctors have gained – and, through our doctors, also we ourselves – over our lives.

The problems with any debate are, firstly, that it's abstract; and, secondly, that it's a conflict that, by its very nature, is a back-and-forth tussle between opposing points of view, when most of us want a point of application to our own lives. Conducted as it is by people who feel strongly, the debate tends to express itself in absolute terms: it's our inalienable right to decide when we die, on the one hand; or it's completely wrong, on the other. Those religious or adamantly secularist commentators who take up such uncompromising positions on either side of the question are entitled to their views, of course. But many of us are likely to feel that, whatever the black and white may be, the broadest of grey areas lies between them.

Conviction and Creep

'I am the master of my fate ... the captain of my soul.' If agnostics could have a patron saint, it would be William Ernest Henley (1849–1903), whose scorn for the fear of death – and of any judgement that might await him – was eloquently expressed in his most famous poem. 'Invictus' (the Latin for 'unconquered'), a declaration of defiance, romantic and heroic, was written in 1875. Whilst agnosticism (which literally means 'not knowing') is not, in theory, a belief system, but rather the absence of one, Henley's assertion, as quoted above, is very clearly a statement of faith. Those who believe that they have the right to decide the moment of their deaths are arguably making a comparable claim, as dogmatic in its way as anything that Henley wrote.

Those with strong religious convictions are more upfront about the theological basis of their views, which does not mean that we should necessarily regard them as being right (indeed, we may well consider their position misguided). Devout Catholics see this debate as ultimately overlapping with that over birth control and abortion: are we going to snuff out any life that we deem to be 'not worth living'? Who are we to judge the quality of someone else's existence? Who are we even to judge the quality of our own? Our duty is not to assert our 'rights', but to endure any suffering that existence sends our way. What right do we have to second-guess our creator? And where's it all going to end? What if a sufferer was unable to express a view? Or if they asked to live, but their family felt strongly, and sincerely, that they were wrong?

Slippery-slope arguments are notoriously ungovernable, and no one's suggesting compulsory euthanasia for the over-65s, or the over-95s, yet the dangers of 'ethics creep' cannot be dismissed.

Modern Modes

We may well believe that we have the right to decide how we are going to die, and if we do, we should stick to our guns. But it's surely true, too, that in the case of assisted death, we shouldn't simply acquiesce because so many people seem to see it as the 'modern' way. Faced with what we may fear is likely to be a long-drawn-out, painful and humiliating end, it's also natural that we would hanker for something less messy and more streamlined – for 'dying with dignity'. And that may indeed be much the best way for us; we just shouldn't jump to that conclusion because everyone else seems to be doing so.

The question of what's 'modern' is actually a problematic one. For a start, there's nothing really so cutting-edge about 'mercy killing'. It's true that this is very much a modern problem, and not only because, until recently, we simply died before these dilemmas could present themselves. There's also a real danger of being blinded by science and technology. The situation of the individual patient can be lost sight of when doctors and hospital care systems take over. (And the patient can almost literally be lost sight of: when he or she is linked up to drips and monitors, with every pulse being measured – and, in some cases, every breath being made mechanically – the patient on life-support may appear to have been incorporated into a larger medical machine that is working away to rhythms of its own.)

This may seem a frightening, Frankensteinian vision, yet we shouldn't be too quick to let it spook us. Few of us are really going to want to experience death *au naturel*, so it would be silly to disregard the immeasurable advantages that all of this high-tech hardware has given to terminal patients, not least in terms of pain management. The key thing is to remember that it's the patient who really matters: that what they want, and what they need, has to remain the central focus.

GOD'S WILL?

Newspaper stories reporting how Jehovah's witnesses opted for a certain, 'natural' death rather than a life-saving medical treatment have fed the belief that the members of this Christian Church refuse medical intervention as a matter of course. In fact, the only such prohibition is concerned with blood transfusions, the justification for which is cited as being Biblical (Acts 15:29, for example: 'That ye abstain from meats offered to idols, and from blood . . .') Other religious groups whose members may refuse certain types of medical intervention include Christian Scientists (who may prefer to leave their fate in the hands of God and advocate prayer as a healing tool).

Time may be of the essence in an emergency, life-or-death situation, so if it is of vital importance to you, be it for religious reasons or otherwise, that you are not subjected to an invasive form of medical intervention, writing a note to this effect and keeping it on your person is probably a sensible precaution.

Dying with Dignitas

Attitudes to assisted suicide vary considerably in Britain, and, more problematically, so, too, does the judicial response. Some parents and partners of those who have died have been charged with murder and, in a few cases, have been convicted, while the charges against others have ended up being dismissed. Faced with something of a judicial lottery then, those contemplating getting help to bring their suffering to an end have tended to look abroad, to countries where this course of action is allowed (or ignored) by law.

The last few years have seen the British government locked in an undignified struggle with Dignitas, the Swiss-based support group for assisted suicide. At the time of writing, up to a hundred Britons have made the journey to Zürich, where the group has its headquarters. Here, those who wish to die are helped to do so comfortably. Since the British authorities are unable to take any meaningful action against a group of people who are not breaking any law of Switzerland, they have been reduced to acting against their British clients – or, rather, against the relatives who helped them to travel to Switzerland.

There was little sign that Britain was ready for anything so macabre as 'suicide tourism', but the prosecution, or threatened prosecution, of parents and partners who were clearly deeply grieving, and had patently acted with the most compassionate of intentions, caused a backlash that surprised many social commentators. These people were viewed with a great deal of sympathy – even support. Although the law against assisting suicide (which carries a jail term of fourteen years) currently remains unchanged, the government has let it be known that it doesn't expect to enforce it against those who are believed to be acting in good faith.

In early 2012 a report commissioned by the campaign group Dignity in Dying suggested that this state of affairs was unacceptable, and even went so far as to propose that assisted dying for terminally ill people could be allowed, providing that proper safeguards were put in place. The report, by the Commission on Assisted Dying, attracted accusations of bias, but the media coverage it provoked illustrates the huge public interest in the issue and that the debate is likely to continue for some time yet.

There are clear signs, therefore, that assisted suicide is well on the way to becoming much more widely accepted, if not actually normalised. Yet Dignitas' role remains contentious, and attracts vehement criticism. Even those who believe that assisted suicide may represent a merciful release may draw the line at the ultra-libertarian view that our lives are ours to end as we please. Hence the controversy when, in 2009, the English conductor and composer Sir Edward Downes and his wife had their lives brought to an end with the help of Dignitas, for whilst Lady Joan was suffering from terminal cancer, Sir Edward was not. Ludwig Minelli, the founder of Dignitas, defended his decision to allow this assisted suicide to go ahead, as have over a thousand others since the centre was established in 1998.

Those applying to end their days at the Dignitas clinic must, in fact, go through an extensive selection process: medical records are examined and second opinions sought. Many don't go through with it: indeed, 80 per cent of those who get the green light from the clinic's staff end up deciding not to exercise their option to go ahead. (See also pages 231–33.)

Preparation is Power

From a practical point of view, it makes sense to inform ourselves as far as we can about what we might be facing towards the end of our lives. Informing ourselves in general can't hurt, and certainly not in particular either, if the case arises. If we've been diagnosed as having an illness (or a loved one has), what can we find out about its likely course? This is one overwhelmingly positive way in which we can take a degree of control – not just by grilling our doctor, but by reading around the subject. What palliative treatments are available? What sort of dilemmas can we expect to face? And not just the immediately medical dilemmas, but the indirect ones: will we need to change our living arrangements, reallocate rooms or even move house? Can we carry on working for now, or, realistically, do we need to resign? If we're going to be a partner-carer, do we need to talk to our employers?

And then, of course, we can start taking steps to prepare ourselves for our big confrontation with death itself. What can we do now that may make things easier later on? This is the time to think about what is commonly known as a living will, if we haven't already: what do we want our doctors to do – or not to do? We can either spell it all out explicitly and specifically (which makes most sense if we've already been diagnosed and have a good idea of what's coming) or we can grant power of attorney to somebody whom we trust.

While the popular term 'living will' is commonly used to mean a statement of your wishes on how you would like to be treated, or not treated, if you become incapacitated, in the eyes of the law a living will may mean one of two things: an 'advance statement' or an 'advance decision' (for those in England and Wales, for whom the law was clarified by the Mental Capacity Act of 2005. Check the guidelines on Directgov, or from a local Age UK, see page 248, for Scotland and Northern Ireland.)

The first of these, the advance statement, is not legally binding, but is an expression of your views that may include not only your wishes concerning medical treatment should you become incapacitated, but also more general preferences that might, for example, reflect your religious views if they could affect aspects of your treatment. If you appoint someone as your attorney, you can choose to record your advance statement in your Lasting Power of Attorney for personal welfare (LPA) document. Whether or not your advance statement is part of an LPA, your attorney will be required to take the wishes expressed in your advance statement into consideration when making decisions on your behalf when, or if, the time comes.

The second possibility, the advance decision, is a legally binding, written, witnessed decision to refuse treatment, even if that refusal will result in death. It should specify what sort of treatment you are refusing and the circumstances in which you want it to apply – for example, resuscitation after cardiac arrest – and you must be legally competent when making it. If you want to make an advance decision, consult your solicitor and/or doctor for advice, because there are risks in making the details either too loosely defined or too specific. If you have already made any form of advance decision, you should also check periodically that it is still valid, in case the law or your circumstances have changed since you made it. You may cancel an advance decision at any time, and appointing an LPA will nullify your advance decision and make your LPA responsible for your healthcare choices.

By appointing someone as your attorney, you are effectively handing over to him or her your decision-making power; this will presumably be someone you feel knows you very well. Even so, it's best not to assume that he or she knows your views on these matters, but instead to be as clear as you can in stating your specific requirements (as far as you can say what they are), and then allowing for your proxy to make whatever other decisions may be needed once you are no longer in a position to make them for yourself. Above all, it makes sense to talk things through with your proxy as thoroughly as you can.

Ultimately, it's the doctor's decision as to whether an advance decision is valid, and whether, for example, to issue a Do Not Resuscitate (DNR) order or discontinue life-saving treatment if there is any doubt about the validity of an expression of wishes. A doctor *cannot* do anything to hasten a patient's death, and it is his or her responsibility to keep him or her as comfortable as possible even if life-preserving treatment is considered inappropriate.

There are two types of LPA: one of these deals with your health and welfare, as described above. The other type deals with your property and financial affairs, and it is advisable for most people to prepare one of these. This type of power of attorney can be used if you become either physically or mentally unable to look after your own finances. You can give your attorney the power to, for example, pay bills on your behalf or, if necessary, sell your home to pay for the costs of any care you may need.

You can only make an LPA while you have the mental capacity to understand the nature and effect of the document and to give your instructions. It is not wise, therefore, to leave this unattended to, in case you miss your window of opportunity altogether. If you become mentally incapable of looking after your own affairs but don't have an LPA in place naming a representative to look after your financial affairs on your behalf, an application must be made to the Court of Protection for someone to be appointed to do this for you. This is a time-consuming and costly process.

SUCH AN UNCONSCIONABLE TIME A-DYING?

Devised by medical and nursing staff at the Royal Liverpool Hospital in cooperation with the local Marie Curie hospice, the Liverpool Care Pathway (LCP) set new standards in end-of-life care for the NHS. Constantly reviewed since its introduction in the 1990s, the scheme offered guidelines for the administration of palliative care, whilst also establishing criteria by which it could be decided when specific treatments were to be maintained and when they should be discontinued. The LCP approach puts the 'whole patient' at its centre, including psychological and spiritual support in the context of the patient's family and/or carers, rather than focusing narrowly on the medical issues alone. It has been hailed as a major success, for the most part. Medical opinion has been overwhelming in its support; patients – as far as can readily be judged – have mostly found it helpful too; whilst relatives of the sick and bereaved have queued up to record their gratitude.

But controversy is never far from our deathbeds, and this hasn't been the whole story. Concern has been expressed by some that the LCP can be, on occasion, a little too eager to speed up the dying process. Some families fear that a loved one's death may have been hastened by the decision to stop giving them fluids. Some experts, moreover, worry that the LCP could mask signs of a health condition improving. Withdrawal of fluids and food from a patient, the frequent use of powerful painkillers, stopping basic treatment and tests (such as the measurement of blood pressure) – after a few days of this under the LCP, it would be all too easy for someone who, although frail and vulnerable, hadn't actually been at death's door, to cross its threshold.

Such differences in approach often boil down to the question of whether life is worth preserving at any cost, or whether the focus should be quality of life. It was King Charles II, in 1685, who apologised to his doctors for being 'such an unconscionable time a-dying': but dying just takes as long as it takes.

Home or Away?

When someone with a terminal illness reaches the point at which treatment is either no longer desirable or unlikely to be effective in combating the disease, it's time to shift the focus from medical intervention to quality of life; in other words, to embark on a programme of palliative care. Each person will have his or her own priorities in this situation, but most people need practical and emotional support, effective relief from pain and invasive procedures, an emphasis on dignity, and to have his or her voice heard and respected.

After prolonged treatment, which most terminally ill patients will have endured, there is often a strong desire to stay at home if appropriate support is available. Some opt for hospice care – but these are not mutually exclusive choices. In most parts of the UK, people can attend a hospice as an outpatient for daytime support or receive care at home from visiting hospice staff.

Hospices have their roots in monastic institutions that provided refuge for the dying, especially during the Middle Ages, but these refuges all but disappeared with the subsequent decline of the monasteries. The modern hospice movement began in the 1960s, when Dame Cicely Saunders, a British nurse, defined the concept of 'total pain' as consisting of not only physical affliction but also spiritual, practical and emotional pain and the social isolation that resulted from the cultural taboo surrounding the dying. She founded St Christopher's Hospice in London in 1967 and pioneered the development of compassionate care, taking her message around the world in an outreach campaign that would revolutionise end-of-life practice.

For the uninitiated, a hospice may appear to be a place to die, but the ethos of hospice care is entirely the reverse: instead, it is a place to live. A hospice is set up to celebrate life, to nurture hope and to meet the needs of the whole person, concentrating on comfort in the spiritual, emotional and physical senses.

Degrees of Death

Whether we spend our final days in a hospice or a hospital, the Do Not Resuscitate order has its place because patients' lives can often be extended by today's medical technology for lengthy periods: for weeks, or even months, after the normal functions of 'living' have shut down. Yet many patients feel that they don't want to be kept alive in these circumstances: it's not the sort of life they want to be prolonged.

No one objects to a miracle cure. The cardiac patient who has been plucked from the brink of death, nursed back to health and sent home safely, for example, may often be able to resume life as before, albeit with a bit more exercise and less cholesterol, perhaps. The accident victim whose heart has stopped in the trauma of a fall or car crash may otherwise similarly be a picture of good health. The trouble is that in a terminal patient, what remains after resuscitation may be a 'life' in only the most limited of senses. The patient may have been saved from death only to slump into a coma of deep unconsciousness: unwaking, unsleeping, unaware of light and darkness, sounds, smells or even pain. Or they may live on at a slightly shallower level of unconsciousness, responding to the most basic stimuli, but showing no signs of awareness, in a condition referred to as a 'vegetative state'. After four weeks without change, such a condition is categorised as a 'continuous vegetative state'; after a year (or three months in the case of anoxic – oxygen-deprivation – brain injury), it is deemed 'permanent'. Clearly, it can't be known with absolute certainty that this state is permanent, but by this time, it seems that there is very little chance of meaningful recovery.

In extreme cases, the heart and lungs can be kept functioning long after all indications of neurological activity have gone, hence the idea of 'brain death', when the brain-dead patient is alive, yet not alive. Officially, in fact, the view is that he or she is dead, but many people feel that it isn't quite so clear-cut. What if there is activity in the brain, but we just haven't identified it? The science of neurology is still at quite an early stage. If this question can be asked about the brain-dead, how much more pertinently can it be asked about those in lengthy vegetative states or comas, from which we know patients have occasionally (and quite unexpectedly) come round – albeit usually with profound disabilities?

For centuries, the boundary between life and death was fixed. Indeed, it could hardly have been more definite (even if we did die in the 'sure and certain hope of the Resurrection to eternal life', as the Anglican prayer book has it). In the last few decades, though, that boundary has been blurred: there are degrees of death, and dying is in many cases not a moment, but an artificially managed phasing-out of life. This existential no-man's-land may cause prolonged anguish for loved ones (see pages 227–31).

A Life Worth Living?

Being in a permanent vegetative state can't be much of a life. 'As far as we know', comes the rejoinder from the anti-euthanasia lobby. It may not, perhaps, be as profoundly philosophical as the question 'What is life?' but the question 'What makes life worth living?' is, in many ways, more pressing.

Who are we to say what makes life worth living? And how are we to know when a life is worth living when we know so little of ourselves, let alone of others? Is the life of an individual with severe disabilities, maybe a quadriplegic person, not worth living? 'I don't want to live . . .' says the jilted lover – before picking him- or herself up off the floor a few weeks later and carrying on as usual. 'I wish I was dead', says the person in a depression that's deep, but perhaps not enduring.

On the other hand, the 'Who are we to say?' question cuts both ways. If a sick person truly, deeply and consistently believes that their life is insupportable, do we have the right to tell them that they don't know their own mind? Perhaps they don't – we don't know our own much of the time, it often seems, and prolonged suffering and humiliation is all too likely to distort perceptions. Maybe we have to 'protect' them from making what might be a huge mistake. And yet, if anyone's going to be able to weigh things up and come to any sort of informed decision, there surely can't be anybody better placed than they are themselves.

There's certainly no harm in thinking such things through as far as possible, and in talking them through with those around us: not just with medical professionals, but with our loved ones. After all, as individuals, we are heading into uncharted existential territory (and despite some extraordinary advances, it's still something of a wilderness for science, too). Once established, communication should be assiduously maintained, and if you're a relation, friend or lover of the person at the centre of these issues, this may well be where you come in. We may change our minds (more than once), we may falter, and we may feel the need for bracing counsel or reassurance, but we'll always want to feel that we're being listened to.

DEATH IN DISCWORLD

Sir Terry Pratchett's extravagantly quirky, comic Discworld novels have always had their darker side, with Death appearing as a character throughout. After 2008, however, when the then-fifty-nine-year-old author revealed that he'd been saddled with the 'embuggerance' of early-onset Alzheimer's, he became an outspoken and eloquent advocate for assisted suicide: 'I don't want to be there for the endgame', he said.

Pratchett was at the forefront of a campaign to have assisted suicide legalised in Britain, for full immunity to be granted to those who helped their loved ones make their final exit. In guidelines issued late in 2009, however, the government refused to take so radical a step: relatives would still be in line for murder charges under the law – at least in theory – although there were clear hints that their cases would be viewed sympathetically.

The author was unimpressed by what he saw as a craven compromise. In February 2010, he called for 'euthanasia tribunals'. Experts in both medicine and family law would sit on these, he envisaged, and would consider applications for assisted suicide case by case. Everything would be above board. Those who won the support of a tribunal would then have the legal right to take their own lives, and their partners and families would have the legal right to help them.

Pratchett even visited the Dignitas clinic himself as part of a controversial BBC documentary, which showed Peter Smedley, an English hotelier, taking a lethal dose of barbiturates at the Swiss clinic. The 2011 broadcast attracted criticism from the likes of Michael Nazir Ali, the former Bishop of Rochester, who said the programme 'glorified suicide'. However, Pratchett defended the programme, saying he believed that the right to an assisted suicide should extend to anyone over the age of consent.

His continued commitment to a campaign for a change in the law was confirmed when the writer partially funded the controversial Commission on Assisted Dying, which recommended in 2012 that the terminally ill could be offered the choice of assisted dying if they met certain eligibility criteria (see page 74).

THE HOUBEN HOAX?

In 1986, a young Belgian man was all but killed in a car crash. Rom Houben didn't die, but was left in a lasting coma. Or so, at least, it seemed, until, in 2009, it turned out that he hadn't been unconscious at all: rather, he had been 'locked in' – so badly paralysed that he was unable to respond to stimuli of any sort. Now, however, it was discovered that he could communicate, with a speech therapist acting as 'communication facilitator' enabling him to point to the letters on a keyboard. In eloquent terms, he described his nightmare: twenty-three years imprisoned within his paralysed body: 'I dreamed myself away . . . I screamed, but there was nothing to hear'.

Houben's case was a human-interest story like very few others, but it was also important in its implications for medical ethics. How many other patients were in what appeared to be vegetative or comatose states, but were actually still 'all there', albeit imprisoned by paralysis?

In the end, Houben's story disappeared as abruptly as it had arrived. In 2010, investigators tried to repeat the earlier findings experimentally. Once again, they attempted to 'unlock' Rom from captivity within his own, helpless body to enable him to talk to the outside world again. They were unsuccessful, however, and as further efforts failed, Rom's doctor admitted defeat. It became clear that only when therapist Linda Wouters was with Rom as his facilitator did any 'communication' take place. It seemed that it had all been a hoax, or, at best, wishful thinking.

ASCERTAINING
AND CERTIFYING DEATH

Not many of us come face to face with death on a daily basis, and so may wonder what sort of checks are performed to make sure that someone really has died when it seems as though they have breathed their last. And what happens next?

Time of Death

It's telling that the UK has, as yet, no official legal definition of death. The law is struggling to catch up with science, which is itself unsure. However, in 2008, the Academy of Medical Royal Colleges issued a code of practice that included specific guidance on how a decision as to whether death has taken place or not should be reached.

Some of the academy's advice was obvious: if death has taken place some time before, there may be rigor mortis – the telltale stiffening of the body and limbs that takes place after death. Hypostasis may also be evident, when the unpumped blood in a dead body is drawn naturally downwards by gravitational force to whichever part of the corpse is lying the lowest, causing a visible reddening beneath the skin. In terms of more immediate signs, some again seem self-evident to most of us. A dead person doesn't breathe, for example, so apnoea – stopping breathing – is one clear sign. It isn't necessarily a conclusive sign, though: it may only just have happened. The medical practitioner therefore has a moral duty to make 'full and extensive attempts' to restart respiration and revive the patient by whatever means appear possible. The same goes for the heart, when that's stopped beating.

If all of these attempts fail and the absence of a pulse – or, in the hospital context, the flat-lining of an electrocardiogram (ECG) monitor – shows that cardiorespiratory arrest has truly taken place, the patient must be kept under observation for five minutes. If any momentary sign of cardiorespiratory activity takes place, even if attempts at full revival then fail, a further five minutes must elapse before a final check is made by lifting the eyelids and shining a bright light into the person's eyes to test for corneal reflex, or blinking. If the reflex is absent, the patient is pronounced dead, and the time of death is officially recorded. In the kinds of cases we've looked at above, in which patients may have spent some time in an ambiguous situation – in a coma or vegetative state, for instance – a specialist neurologist may be brought in to confirm that death really has taken place.

It's all a little less formal when a GP is called out on a home visit. None of the high-tech equipment of the hospital is available here. Instead, having looked for signs of movement, the doctor has to spend a minute checking for respiratory effort and trying to find a pulse. Then, again, he or she checks the eyes for any corneal response.

TO DEATH AND BACK

There has been considerable debate about near-death experiences (NDEs) ever since the establishment of the spiritualist movement during the nineteenth century. In a typical NDE, someone who has apparently been on the point of death, like the victim of a car crash or a patient on an operating table, comes around to recall an utterly vivid vision in which they've hurtled down a dark tunnel towards a blinding light.

A poll conducted during the early 1990s recorded that 8 million Americans firmly believed that they had undergone a NDE. It's probably not difficult to find 8 million people who'll believe just about anything, you may say, and there's no doubt that – along with alien abductions – NDEs are both 'out there' and in fashion. Yet it seems possible that these claims may be true.

That such experiences happen has, indeed, become generally accepted, with examples being reported in the renowned medical journal the *Lancet*. Now, scientists are debating exactly what may be responsible for some NDEs, particularly in the case of people who 'wake up' from comas. For if an NDE is a product of the conscious mind, how are we to explain the many NDEs reported by patients who were then in a coma, when no electrical activity was detected in their brain?

There's no question that modern medicine has saved many thousands of patients who were 'dead' – at least in the traditional sense, in that their hearts were no longer beating. These patients were genuinely hovering for a time in the no-man's-land between death and life, from which no one would have returned in earlier centuries. So it's hardly surprising that they may have strange stories to tell, or that they should attach a mystic significance to what they 'saw'.

One possible explanation for this phenomenon is chemical imbalances in the brain, such as raised levels of carbon dioxide, as a Slovenian research team suggested in 2010. Leading authority Peter Fenwick, a Fellow of the Royal College of Psychiatrists, is amongst those who reject this conclusion, however, because there remain too many unexplained cases.

EXISTENTIAL LEGALITIES

In the USA, death is followed by the removal of 'personhood' (the legal state of being a person), as brain activity, or the ability to resume brain activity, is required for legal personhood. (This is why 'pulling the plug' on a 'brain-dead' person isn't a crime: legally, the patient is no longer a person.)

Post-Mortem Paperwork

When they are certain that the patient is dead, an attending GP will typically issue a death certificate – assuming that they feel that the cause of death is clear. (In the hospital context, it could be any of the attending team who would do so.) To avoid any unnecessary mistakes, the doctor who signs the certificate has to have attended the patient at some point during their final illness and (if that's been protracted) to have seen him or her within the past fortnight. Only if the GP feels confident about the cause of death should they go on to sign the certificate. If not, the case will have to go to the coroner.

In the first instance, though, the certificate is given to the next of kin, or, in their absence, to any relative who lives nearby or is visiting at the time. Failing that, it may be given to a landlord or co-tenant, or to an undertaker, if one has been appointed by the family. The certificate now has to be taken or sent to the office of the registrar of births and deaths, which will then decide whether a coroner needs to be informed.

A coroner is automatically informed when the cause of death has apparently been an accident or crime, or when the attending doctor has felt unsure about it. But the coroner's office will also interest itself should death seem to have been caused by an industrial disease (like asbestosis or chemical poisoning) because agencies of state will want to investigate such cases. Likewise, deaths caused by drug abuse may be of relevance to law-enforcement and social-services agencies; so, too, will cases of self-neglect. In any of these instances, a post-mortem examination may be ordered; this may in turn lead to a full-blown inquest.

In the majority of cases, there are no complicating factors, so the coroner's office issues a (green) certificate for burial or cremation. Basically, this confirms that all legal procedures involving the death have now been completed and that the next of kin are free to hold the funeral. Along with the burial certificate, the coroner's office provides a certificate of registration of death (BD8), which is required if the deceased was receiving a state pension or other benefits before they died. For a fee, the office will also issue copies of the death certificate: these are likely to be needed later, during probate, as proof of death for banks or insurance providers.

One other bureaucratic burden – that of informing various government departments (such as the Pension Service, the Passport Office or the DVLA) about a death – will soon be eased. The government is now rolling out the 'Tell Us Once' service across England, Scotland and Wales, so that you only have to inform your local authority, which will then contact other government departments for you. For more details, see page 249.

TO EXAMINE OR NOT TO EXAMINE?

A post-mortem, or autopsy, is the full physical examination of the deceased by experts. It involves dissection, is time-consuming and expensive, does violence to the body and, in perhaps 90 per cent of cases, is unnecessary. Families must wait for the process to be completed before they can reclaim the body of their loved one and proceed to a funeral.

A post-mortem is appropriate either as part of an ongoing criminal investigation or when there is real doubt as to the medical cause of death. But a leading pathologist has argued that the state presently intervenes in far too many cases – 22 per cent of deaths in England and Wales – leaving families distressed and frustrated by excessive intrusion into their private grief. Professor of forensic and legal medical issues Derrick Pounder made the case in January 2011 (in the *Journal of the Royal Society of Medicine*) for a move toward the system in Scotland, where only 6 per cent of deaths are investigated in this way, with simpler external examinations being more widely used instead. The large increase in post-mortem rates in England and Wales resulted from the 2005 recommendations of the Shipman Inquiry that doctors be subject to greater supervision by coroners, to prevent any repeat of the serial-killing Dr Harold Shipman and his murders of hundreds of patients.

The inquest is a legal hearing, to which witnesses are summoned to give evidence so that the coroner can piece together a narrative of how death came about and establish its cause that way.

There are therefore two distinct aspects to the coroner's work: one medical, and one legal. Coroners may be recruited from either field.

IMAGINING YOUR DEATH BED

You may just want to slip away with as little fuss as possible, or you may wish to see the faces of those you love ranged around you when you die. If you have any strong wishes about how you'd like to experience your final hours, it's a good idea to express them before it's too late.

The Hour of Our Death

So much for the clinical procedures and the bureaucratic kerfuffle that kicks off when the moment of death finally comes – but what about you? You're actually going to be dying here! Vital as it is to your peace of mind to know that you've done all you can to put your affairs in order, what feelings do you have about the experience of dying itself? It can be helpful, up to a point, to make practical plans as a displacement activity, a distraction from what may be more sombre thoughts. But musing on the moment to come can be positive and helpful, too.

Who do you want to be with you when you die, for example? Just your partner, or other family members or friends? Depending on who you are, and how you may be feeling (you're going to be ill and may not feel yourself), you may either want to fade away quietly or make a more public exit, saying goodbye to everyone you can during your final hours. What's going to be more important to you: privacy or people? You may begin by feeling that it'll be a case of the more, the better, but may then find that you can't face a crowd when the moment arrives.

Obviously, it's up to those we love to try to use a bit of sensitivity when the time comes, but even so, the more we've talked things through with them, the easier they'll find it to respond appropriately. And if you're caring for someone who's terminally ill, try to create the opportunity for your patient to express his or her wishes in this regard. It will make the moment of death easier for the patient, and for you as it becomes imminent. See pages 214 to 216 for an experienced perspective on this time, and ask a GP, hospice or other care worker for advice.

Many of us may want to pass away without an all-singing, all-dancing party raging around us, but we wouldn't want to have forgotten people who've been important to us. So if there are friends or family members who you've been meaning to see, but haven't yet managed to, or things you've meant to say, but haven't yet found a way of saying, it's really worth making the effort to see or say them now.

Chapter Three
POMP AND
CIRCUMSTANCE:

WHAT KIND OF SEND-OFF
DO YOU WANT?

Ceremonies mark our passage from one phase of life to another, often providing comfort and a sense of belonging. Christenings, baptisms and naming ceremonies welcome us into the extended family, biological or metaphorical; graduations often mark our entrance into the adult world; weddings and civil-partnership ceremonies confirm our commitment to our other halves, creating a single unit in the eyes of society. And at the end of an earthly existence, a funeral both celebrates the life of the person who has died and provides comfort for those left behind.

A death leaves a hole: in the family, the workplace, the school – whatever community the dead person was part of. By reminding those left behind that the deceased lived a worthwhile life and was loved and respected by many people, funerals are a way of helping to close that gap. They also affirm that all of us are part of an extended family, and of a number of social networks, and that these groups will help to provide affection and support to those left behind. In short, funerals are an important part of the grieving process.

LARGER THAN LIFE EVENTS

Different cultures cope with death in different ways, and there have been some pretty extreme funerals through history. The ancient Egyptians were famously interred in their pyramids, for example. And the word 'mausoleum' comes from the towering monument that was built for Mausolus of Caria (modern-day Turkey) by his sister-wife Artemisia (who reportedly spent two years mixing his ashes into her wine). Important Vikings would be placed in ships that were then set on fire. Slaves were often sacrificed so that they could continue serving their masters in the afterlife. Another extreme example was the ancient Indian custom of *sati*, or *suttee*, in which a dead man's widow threw herself (or was thrown) on to her husband's funeral pyre to be burned alive with his corpse.

In modern times, such extravagant ceremonies have mostly disappeared. But not entirely: after the death of Princess Diana on 31 August 1997, for instance, over 1 million bouquets of flowers were laid outside her Kensington Palace home. In addition, more than 3 million mourners crowded into London for the princess's funeral at Westminster Abbey, with the ceremony itself being watched by 2.5 billion people worldwide.

IT'S YOUR FUNERAL

Until recently, the majority of funerals were religious affairs, conducted according to long-established rituals; however, a growing number of people are finding that these religious traditions have little relevance to them today. There has therefore been a gradual shift towards families and friends taking control of funerals and planning events that both reflect the personality of the deceased and meet the emotional needs of the people attending.

Still, planning a funeral in the days immediately following a death is very distressing for those who have been bereaved. So why not make the process easier for your loved ones by taking control and making your own decisions and funeral preparations well in advance of the actual event? Just as most brides and grooms have taken control of planning their marriage ceremony (a task traditionally undertaken by the bride's parents), so people can now determine, in advance, what kind of ceremonial exit they would like to make. The point of this is not usually to ensure that you'll have one final 'designer' party or chance to show off in front of your peers as much as to relieve those who survive you of as much uncertainty as you can about your funeral preferences.

Funeral Plans

The growth of funeral plans has made it easier for anyone, of any age, to design their own funeral in advance, and even to pay for it. For example, the Cooperative Funeralcare company offers both fixed-price options and a tailor-made one that allows for detailed forward-planning. The Golden Charter funeral plan, which is offered by independent funeral directors, also offers an *à la carte* approach. Both of these schemes allow customers to pay for the funeral of their choice at today's prices, and guarantee that there will be no further charges. In January 2011, prepaid funerals accounted for 10 per cent of the Cooperative Funeralcare's business, but, said spokesman David Collingwood in a BBC interview, the prepaid, preplanned trend is increasing. If you want to set up this sort of arrangement, make sure that you choose a reputable company, and that you read all of the small print.

It's worth pointing out that purchasing one of these funeral plans does not guarantee that your wishes will be carried out to the letter, however. Relatives can add or change details, if they are willing to pay any price difference, and could, in extreme cases, ignore your arrangements altogether and instead insist on a completely different funeral that reflects their beliefs and wishes rather than yours. (Note that unlike in the USA, there is no set legal definition of next of kin in the UK. In general, the order of next of kin is: married spouse/civil partner; adult children; parents; siblings. So if you do not leave clear instructions, these are the people who will get to decide on your funeral arrangements.)

For most of us, the primary reason for setting out our wishes in advance is to ease the task of our nearest and dearest when the time comes for them to make decisions about our funeral – a time when they're least prepared to cope with the stress, and sometimes the family conflict, that a death in the family may involve. Knowing that you took the time to think through your requests would certainly eliminate much of the heartache that planning your funeral could involve for your loved ones. Some people, however, want to make sure that their funeral stipulations are carried out come what may, and if you are one of them, the only way to guarantee that they are is to specify them in your will. Appointing an executor will ensure that this happens, so if you need to, see a lawyer about setting this up (see pages 38 to 39). The will is not generally read until after the funeral, so it is vital that you let the appropriate people know in advance that you have included instructions for your funeral in your will. You can even specify penalties in case of your wishes being ignored.

SPLASHING OUT: FUNERALS IN JAPAN

Funerals are typically expensive affairs in Japan, with the average Tokyo funeral costing 3.5 million yen, or about £26,000 in 2010. One might imagine that this could be explained in part in practical terms: Japan doesn't have much space. But with more than 99 per cent of the population being cremated, this is scarcely a factor. Although Japanese traditions, including Buddhism, emphasise simplicity, it's simply a cultural fact that funerals tend to be elaborate by comparison with those in other cultures.

Thinking Outside the Box

A coffin is central to the funeral ceremony. In the past, the only question was how much you wanted to spend on this typically wooden box and its furnishings. The choices available to us today are very much wider, however, ranging from biodegradable cardboard and wicker containers to the elaborate products available from specialist suppliers.

For most of us, the choice generally comes down to a wooden, cardboard or wicker container. The traditional pine or oak coffin is typically offered with a selection of 'furnishings' (embellishments) – from handles to nameplate – made of metal (for burials) or plastic (for cremations). The interior may be plain, or may be lined with padded silk or another luxurious material, an option that may be desirable should the open coffin be displayed at some point before the funeral ceremony.

The coffins created by some manufacturers are sometimes surreal. Vic Fearn & Company Ltd, for example, started out during the 1860s making oak and pine boxes of traditional shape and design. Recently, though, its craftspeople have been turning their hands to more individual designs, with the company's workshops in Nottingham and the Isle of Wight producing coffins in such shapes as cricket bats, bowling pins, Guinness cans, red telephone boxes, wine bottles, running shoes, books, carrots and clouds. Another British company, Colourful Coffins, can print any photograph or graphic on to its wooden or cardboard coffins. Among the designs chosen by its customers are tramcars, religious scenes, montages of personal photographs, scenic sunsets, flowers and even brick walls.

It may seem like tempting fate, but a practical possibility is to buy your coffin now, and to make use of it around the house before you die. Some coffins intended for this dual purpose are available as benches with padded lids, while others can be cunningly assembled to create a temporary bookcase, and some people have even been known to sleep in their coffins. If you are a sports or gaming fan, you may also be interested in the products of companies like Casket Furniture of British Columbia, in Canada, which offers poker tables, cribbage boards, pool tables (which have a somewhat telltale shape) and blackjack tables.

Your choice of ideal coffin may also be dictated by how environmentally friendly you want to be, and whether you would like to be buried in a churchyard, cemetery or woodland burial site, or, alternatively, whether you would prefer to be cremated (see Chapter 4). Cost may be a concern that influences your choice of coffin, too. Cardboard containers are available at prices below £100, or roughly a quarter of the average cost of a standard coffin. (See pages 122–25 for information on budgeting for a funeral.)

GA COFFINS

In the UK, unusual coffins are just that – unusual. But for the Ga tribe of Ghana, highly individual coffins are the norm. A Ga funeral is a celebration of the deceased, with the coffin being personalised to reflect his or her life. It is considered bad form to start making a coffin ahead of time, which means that a coffin often won't be finished until a month or so after its future occupant's death. Examples of the shapes into which Ga coffins are fashioned include cigars, Coke bottles, cars, shoes, fish and pineapples.

You *Can* Take It With You

People have been buried since the earliest times with their favourite possessions, or else with grave goods that they believed would prove useful in the afterlife. In ancient Greece, for instance, coins were laid over the deceased's eyes so that he or she could pay Charon to ferry them over the river Styx, which was considered the boundary between the earth and the underworld. The British Museum's 2011 exhibition 'Journey through the afterlife' included examples of goods placed in ancient Egyptian graves (see the feature overleaf). Ceramic and glass bowls, perfume bottles, spurs and other equestrian equipment were just some of the items that went to the grave with the ancient Romans. In more recent times, Pre-Raphaelite poet and painter Dante Gabriel Rossetti sentimentally placed a folio of his unpublished poems in the coffin of his beloved, Elizabeth Siddal, after her suicide in 1862; seven years later, however, he was persuaded to exhume the poems in order to publish them.

These days, we are more likely to place the mobile phone from which someone was inseparable in life in his or her coffin, or maybe a symbol of a hobby, such as a football season ticket or scarf. (A passion for golf or fishing may similarly be commemorated with a scorecard or well-used flies.) Toys are sometimes tucked into children's coffins, along with greetings cards or photographs. People who were born in another country may be buried with the flag or another emblem of their homeland. Along with diaries, love letters and service medals, among the more unusual items put in coffins are bingo daubers, sunglasses, bars of chocolate, bottles of whisky, pieces of toast and even bicycle clips. Some families have placed a mobile-phone SIM card in their loved one's coffin so that he or she has the contact numbers of their friends and family to hand in the afterlife, while others have included phone cards or change in case the deceased can use them to make one last call from the afterlife to report having arrived safely.

If there is anything that you'd particularly like to be buried with, it's important that whoever will be organising your funeral knows your wishes, so don't forget to include them in your instructions. Also note that crematoria and even some graveyards have rules about what can, or cannot, be placed in their ovens or grounds. Mobile phones should not be placed in coffins that are to be cremated, for instance, because their batteries would explode and the chemicals then produced may be toxic. Other items that are potentially explosive, like bottles, are also banned (so make sure you place your last order before time is finally called). There may be ways around such bans, however, so it's worth investigating further.

PREPARING FOR THE GRAVE IN ANCIENT EGYPT

Preparing for the afterlife was a serious business for the ancient Egyptians, who believed that burial signalled the start of a perilous journey that would end in either annihilation or regeneration.

The first consideration was surviving the ferocious onslaught to which they would be subjected in the *Duat*, or underworld, while on their way from the grave to Osiris' hall of judgement. Amulets and protective symbols were tucked into their mummy wrappings and painted on their mummy masks and coffins, the most common being the *ankh* and *tiet*, both of which symbolised life; the *wedjat*, or eye of Horus, which denoted healing and well-being; the *djed*, which signified stability; and the heart amulet, which took the form of a symbolic scarab inscribed with text from the Book of the Dead. Indeed, papyrus Books of the Dead were counted among the most crucial items to accompany ancient Egyptians to the grave, for the images and hieroglyphic texts with which they were covered supplied vital spells and instructions for neutralising the malignant forces that would threaten the dead in the *Duat*.

If they made it that far, their ultimate fate would finally be decided by the weighing-of-the-heart ceremony in the presence of Osiris. A heart weighed down by sin would be devoured by the monstrous Ammut, but one that was judged worthy of eternal life would be restored to its owner's chest: a passport to paradise. Envisaging as they did the glorious afterlife as being an idealised version of life in Egypt, the ancient Egyptians imagined that they would require the same sorts of comforts that had served them on earth, which is why they were interred with as many useful and luxurious objects as their social standing allowed, including furniture, domestic utensils and jewellery. But perhaps the most important items to go to the grave with them – in ancient Egyptian eyes, at least – were the *ushabtis*, small figures symbolising human slaves who would volunteer to stand in for their owners should they be asked to labour on behalf of the common good in the heavenly "Field of Reeds".'

Contributed by **Clare Gibson**, symbols and artefacts expert and author of *The Hidden Life of Ancient Egypt*

Grooming and Dress

In many cultures, it is required that the body be prepared in a particular way before burial. For example, the bodies of Orthodox Jews and Muslims are cleaned and wrapped in shrouds, but embalming is prohibited.

Embalming is the practice of preserving the body to delay decomposition after death, usually with the addition of chemicals to the body, for a temporary period. It is often criticised, as research has shown that once the embalmed body is buried, these chemicals can seep into the ground and contaminate the soil for years. However, in one form or another, embalming has been practised since ancient times, as in, for example, mummification in ancient

Egypt, and sometimes as part of a religious ritual. In the Western world today it is mostly performed when a wake is planned (see page 103) or when funeral guests may be invited to view the body if they wish to; it is more likely to be done in preparation for a burial than before a cremation. Embalming is considerably more common in North America than it is in Europe. In the United States, a powerful funeral industry has largely been able to set the (elaborate and expensive) terms for what's seen as 'decency' in death – despite the satirical efforts of English writers like Evelyn Waugh and Jessica Mitford half a century ago. The morticians took a major hit in the 1960s, after Mitford's *The American Way of Death* hit the bookstalls, but they've been back with a vengeance for some decades now. The embalmer's art in particular is thriving in the age of the nip and tuck, the boob job and the facelift. It's taken as read that you'd want to 'look your best' (whatever that may be) in death. We may not have the historic notoriety of such famously embalmed figures as Lenin or Eva Perón, but – good Warholians – we can have our fifteen minutes of iconhood.

Argentinean writer Tomás Eloy Martínez devoted a whole novel to the international wanderings of Evita's corpse. For him, 'The art of the embalmer resembles that of the biographer.' Both, he says, 'try to immobilise a body or a life in the pose in which eternity is to remember it.' It's understandable, perhaps, that in a secular age in which so many of us don't have such great expectations of eternity in the traditional, religious sense, some of us invest in the hope that we can endure as an image of perfection. None the less, not everyone is enthralled with the notion of embalming, with some deploring the possible negative effects on the environment, and others just finding it plain creepy or ghoulish.

Presentation is key, and it begins with the basics: the mortician starts by positioning the body, massaging out the rigor mortis from stiff limbs. Embalming involves a cocktail of formaldehyde, methanol, ethanol and other solvents being introduced into our internal cavities and eased into our arteries to replace the blood as it is drained. The first thing this does is kill off bacteria, which would normally govern the putrefaction process. If this sounds unnatural, that's because it is. Not to be judgmental, but that's the whole point, given that the 'natural' thing for our dead bodies to do is to decay. Embalming literally denatures us, chemically converting the cellular structure of our blood and tissue into something inorganic, and thereby fixed. (Fixed, at least, for the time it takes for us to make a good appearance at our wake: once we've been buried, the body will decay, albeit more slowly.) Part of the skill in embalming is ensuring the effective circulation of the chemical solution, given that the heart is no longer functioning. While a pump is used to inject the fluid, the expert embalmer is alert to the presence of clots: often additional draining and injection points may be required. Where there's a highly localised blockage, fluid can be injected with a hypodermic syringe. Specific attention has also to be paid to internal cavities such as the stomach. Cuts are generally made so the contents can be pumped out and fluid introduced.

Attention is paid to external appearance too. The eyes are kept closed with special caps, whilst the mouth (which may otherwise hang open as the jaw drops) may be sutured or wired shut. Make-up is applied to take away the 'deathly pallor' that can come as such a shock to even the best-prepared well-wisher when they come to view the corpse. Cosmetic care may have to be more radical if, for example, the deceased was the victim of an accident: substantial reconstruction to the face may be required. A specialist embalming process will take place if the body is to be donated to science for anatomical dissection by medical students.

There are those who claim that a public-health benefit is achieved by embalming, because of the disinfecting effect of the chemicals, yet in most countries embalming is forbidden if the deceased suffered from certain infectious diseases. The environmental downsides of using hazardous chemicals and introducing them to the environment if a burial is planned (see also page

147) provide potent reasons for making more natural choices in preparing a body after death. It is also arguable that the practice of embalming – literally making the dead look as if they are still alive – only reinforces society's unhealthy denial of death.

Whether or not embalming is chosen, the body will generally be washed, and the eyes and mouth closed, before it is dressed. In Western cultures today there is typically no formal requirement for anything to be done to the body before its disposal, except in the case of cremation, when any implanted electrical medical device, such as a pacemaker, is removed to avoid it exploding during the cremation process.

There are no formal rules about how the body should be clothed either, although some feel that a simple shroud is the most appropriate attire for the grave. When there is to be an open-coffin viewing, families sometimes dress their loved one's body in his or her best formal clothes, or maybe a wedding dress in the case of a woman who was engaged to be married when she died. (And until relatively recently, there was a Scottish tradition that the first task of any new wife was to make grave clothes for her husband and herself.) Alternatively, they may choose an outfit that reflects the hobbies or affiliations of the deceased, such as a football shirt, the uniform of a youth organisation or a T-shirt displaying the logo or an illustration of a favourite rock band or computer game. For green burials, the body is typically covered with a simple, biodegradable shroud.

GREEN AND PINK

When Kevin Elliott, a private in the Black Watch, was laid to rest in a Dundee cemetery after a military funeral in 2009, one mourner stood out vividly: his friend, Barry Delaney, who wore a lime-green mini-dress with bright-pink knee socks. Prior to Elliott's final deployment to Helmand, Afghanistan, the two friends had promised each other that should one of them die, the survivor would wear a dress to his funeral. Delaney honoured his promise.

Waking the Dead

Another thing to think about is whether you would like your family and friends to hold a wake before your funeral, either at home or in a funeral parlour, as is customary in some cultures, and more common, for example, in the United States than the UK. In this context, 'wake' means to watch, rather than to stay awake, with the body of the deceased being watched over before the funeral. In Jewish tradition, for instance, the deceased's body must not be left alone between death and burial, and its care is the responsibility of a *shomer* (guardian) – generally a family member or friend – who recites psalms during the vigil.

Because some traditions encourage the consumption of alcohol, singing, loud conversation and other exuberant types of behaviour, it is possible that the original purpose of the wake – in the days before accurate medical confirmation of death was always possible – was to ensure that the deceased was really dead. The fear that he or she might not be is comically dramatised in the traditional ballad 'Finnegan's Wake', in which the drunken hod-carrier, apparently killed in an accident at work, is literally 'woken' by the raucous celebrations at his wake. In reality, while alcohol may feature at traditional Irish wakes, they are customarily both solemn occasions and celebrations of a dead person's life. Clocks are traditionally stopped, and mirrors are covered, while the family keeps vigil over its loved one. After viewing the body and paying their respects, guests may then gather in another room to have something to eat and drink and to share happy memories of the deceased.

The association between Irish Catholicism and the consumption of alcohol is of course firmly established in stereotype – one reason for the hostility of Presbyterian Scotland to the tradition of the wake. But there's more to Protestant objections than a po-faced puritan disapproval of excess. The very idea of praying for the dead was anathema to Reformation preachers like John Knox. For Catholicism held that only the most saintly went straight to heaven – or were 'saved', in Protestant terms. The Catholic Church taught that even good people went initially to 'purgatory', where they suffered torments, their sins being gradually burned away until they were fit to be received into paradise. The claim that their passage to salvation could be eased by the prayers of the living was a complicating factor – and a corrupting factor, indeed, given that the Church was soon handing out 'indulgences' (the promise of 'time off') in return for financial donations. If the moral impetus for the Reformation came from outrage that salvation should be for sale, its spiritual drive was towards a simplification of the relation between the believer and his or her God. Purgatory was seen as just another example of 'mumbo jumbo': God Himself would judge whether the dead were damned or saved. He didn't need any help from the living – and He certainly wouldn't be swayed by their intervention in the form of promises or pleas.

In fact, if the tradition of the wake has been enjoying a revival among Catholics (and in some Orthodox Christian traditions) in recent years, as well as beginning to feature in some Anglo denominations, this has arguably owed less to a literalistic interpretation of medieval tradition than to more modern notions – not least the pyschological one of 'closure'. Typically, the wake or vigil is justified in terms of the benefits for the living – who get to recollect and celebrate the departed one – rather than any dividend it may bring to the dead. Relatives and friends come together, at the funeral parlour or, increasingly, in the church where the funeral is to be held, and sit up all night in prayer in an atmosphere that is simultaneously solemn and informal. Readings and prayers are offered; there may also be reminiscences about the dead. Vigils like this are also becoming increasingly popular for mourners to gather and pay their respects without any religious context at all.

Way to Go

The next step, when imagining yourself on the way to the grave, is to consider how your body will be transported to the place where your funeral ceremony will be held, and maybe to its final resting place after that. In Britain's distant past, people usually walked behind the hearse as it was conveyed from the house of the deceased to the church or burial ground. This custom persists in some communities, but in most instances today, both the coffin and the mourners are conveyed by motorised hearse and limousines.

There is great scope for the personalisation of the hearse, particularly if the deceased was somehow involved with distinctive forms of transport. Fire engines have served as hearses, for example, particularly for the funerals of firefighters who died while on duty, while a fleet of bikers may follow a keen motorcyclist's funeral cortège, and it is not unknown for the coffin to be carried on a motorcycle's sidecar. Paul Sinclair, a Pentecostal minister from Leicestershire, unveiled just such a themed service at an open day at Kensal Green Cemetery in London in 2002. The Reverend Sinclair, who built a fully enclosed sidecar hearse for his Triumph Speed Triple motorbike, told the BBC: 'The service isn't just aimed at bikers, it's for people who are a bit different. People get carried off in horse-drawn carriages and they've never been on a horse'. Ray Biddiss, a Baptist minister from West Yorkshire and another biking believer, launched a similar service in 2008, having converted a Suzuki Cruiser into a trike with which to tow a bespoke hearse. He told the *Observer*: 'Launching a motorcycle hearse outfit is a dream I've had for years. Alongside God, my passion is biking. I wouldn't be seen dead in a car for my final journey'.

Horse-drawn hearses are popular in some parts of the country, often as part of an elaborate, Victorian-style funeral. Other possibilities include steam tractors, road-rollers or even a sturdy tricycle and trailer. Among funeral professionals, a hearse is more commonly referred to as a funeral coach, a description that funeral directors at the company Go As You Please took literally when, in 2009, the body of Ada Nelson, from Tyne and Wear, was transported to her cremation in the rear of a forty-nine-seater coach (the mourners also rode in the coach, above her wicker coffin).

Whilst elaborate or decorative modes of transport are relatively rare in British funeral arrangements, this is not true everywhere in the world. In Japan, for example, hearses are often converted to resemble small Buddhist temples.

Once at the site of the funeral service, the coffin will need to be carried into position for the ceremony. The pallbearers can be chosen from the relatives and friends (you may even want to specify them in advance), or the undertakers can carry the coffin.

Grace Notes

Until relatively recently, almost all of the funeral services in the UK were religious, being conducted in a church or its equivalent – maybe a crematorium's chapel – and being followed by a burial or cremation. The most popular funeral type today is a kind of hybrid service featuring a combination of religious and secular songs, readings and rituals. However, a growing number of people are opting for a a humanist or other non-religious type of service. A civil funeral is defined as one driven by the wishes and values of the deceased rather than of the person conducting the ceremony: see page 249 for information on the Institute of Civil Funerals (IOCF) and pages 110 to 111 for more on humanist funerals. Some brave souls are even choosing to conduct the service themselves, without the help of a religious celebrant (see pages 120 to 122). Whatever you decide on for yourself, it's important that your friends and family know your wishes before your death so that they can make the necessary arrangements and begin preparing for the ceremony.

Music is a common feature of most funeral ceremonies, so this is certainly something to think about. In a typical service, there will be music played while the mourners are entering the church or its equivalent, with another one or two pieces featuring as elements of the service, while a final piece will be played when the coffin is carried out of the church, or when the catafalque transports the coffin from the chapel of a crematorium. (Generally a raised platform that supports the coffin, in the crematorium context, the catafalque also acts as the device that automatically removes the coffin after the service, either through the back wall or by descending through the floor.)

People have chosen all types of music – from religious through classical to pop and rock music – for their funerals. Bear in mind that the music that is played as mourners file in can set the tone for the whole service, whether it is a cheery ditty associated with the deceased or a solemn, classical organ piece that suggests that the proceedings will be serious and sober.

Live music is another possibility, from a solo singer to a string quartet and anything in between. Members of the Guild of Funerary Violinists (which was founded in London in 1586), for instance, would give a deeply traditional ambience to your event with such pieces as The Noble March of Death, The Masque of Death, The Fleeting Panic of Death, Dirge in a Scottish Style and Great Funerary Sonata.

GOING FOR A SONG

Perhaps you already have a piece of music in mind for your funeral service, one that you feel sums up your personality, life, spiritual or religious beliefs, or how you would like to be remembered, or that you hope will comfort mourners, perhaps by sticking with a family tradition. If not, maybe some of the following suggestions will strike a chord.

If you are a traditionalist or a classical-music lover, you could opt for people to arrive at your funeral service to the strains of Chopin's Funeral March, or Nimrod, from Elgar's Enigma Variations. Or maybe the thought of 'Amazing Grace' appeals (this one is also popular with 'Trekkies' because it was played during Mr Spock's death scene in Star Trek III!).

Modern favourites include 'Wind beneath my Wings', sung by Bette Midler; Frank Sinatra's 'My Way'; 'Angels', by Robbie Williams; and John Lennon's 'Imagine'. And the following have proved popular, too: 'I will Always Love You', sung by Whitney Houston; Celine Dion's 'My Heart Will Go On'; 'Unforgettable', by Nat King Cole; and Simon & Garfunkel's 'Bridge over Troubled Water'.

If you would prefer something rather less solemn, however, how about Led Zeppelin's 'Stairway to Heaven'; Queen's 'Another One Bites the Dust'; 'Always Look on the Bright Side of Life', by the Monty Python team; or AC/DC's 'Highway to Hell'? You may even choose something as irreverent as 'Good Riddance (Time of Your Life)', by Green Day, or 'Going Underground', by The Jam. It's your funeral, after all...

For more ideas, the Co-operative Funeralcare website includes a listing, based on the company's own research, of the top 10 pieces of music played at UK funerals, separated into four categories: popular songs, hymns, classical music and 'quirky choices'.

Setting the Tone

Along with the choice of music, the tone of a funeral can also be set in part by the announcement that is usually placed in a local or national newspaper (or both). Some funeral announcements these days specify 'no black' alongside the more familiar 'no flowers', for example, suggesting that the occasion will be more along the lines of a celebration of the deceased's life than a solemn focus on the loss of a friend or relation. The answer – as just about always in these things – is to make your preferences explicit: come out and say 'Wear bright colours' or 'Formal mourning wear'. Don't leave it to chance: not everyone will see the paper: they'll be embarrassed (and other mourners perhaps unsettled) if they get things wrong. It might be said, indeed, that the newspaper announcement is on the point of turning into a tradition – done more because it always has been than because it's the best way of spreading news. Most of us these days communicate via email or social network sites, and it makes sense to use these for briefing friends and relations in advance of the funeral. That said, it shouldn't be forgotten that not everybody is in the online loop – among the elderly, most people, perhaps, are not. So the old-fashioned newspaper announcement still has a vital part to play.

If no guidance is provided by the funeral announcement, black (the colour of mourning) is the traditional choice for funeral clothes, but see pages 116 to 118 for colours preferred by various cultures. If the deceased was a member of a particular group, this may also suggest what some people wear to the funeral. Members of the armed forces, the emergency services, or another uniformed group may choose to show solidarity with a lost colleague by wearing the dress version of their work clothes, for instance. And those who are mourning a football fan may wear the colour, or colours, associated with the team that he or she supported.

Funeral flowers – or floral tributes, as funeral directors call them – can be just as varied as the mourners' clothing. (That said, although immediate family members generally arrange for flowers to be placed on the coffin, many funeral announcements ask guests not to spend money on flowers, and to make a donation to a specific charity instead.) Most suppliers of floral tributes offer flowers arranged in symbolic shapes – wreaths, hearts, teddy bears, crosses, pillows, the words 'mum' or 'dad', and so on – and if the florist is willing, a bit of imagination could applied to produce arrangements connected to the occupation or interests of the deceased. These might include football-club crests, cricket bats, whisky bottles, bowler hats, mobile phones, shovels, chefs' hats and a myriad of other forms and symbols.

A Religious, Humanist or Personalised Service?

At the heart of any funeral is the service itself, which, depending on your beliefs, you may want to be a religious, humanist or entirely personalised ceremony.

Religious funeral services follow a particular pattern, with limited scope for personalisation. This is often a great comfort, especially if everyone attending shares the same beliefs. For others, though, these relatively unvarying services can seem as though they have come off a sort of automatic production line, with the person leading the service sometimes seeming more concerned with the formal structure of the service than with the deceased or those present. Indeed, the celebrant delivering the eulogy may not even have known the deceased in life.

Humanist services, while being firmly focused on the life and experiences of the departed and his or her family, are also structured, and in a way that some would say recalls a religious ceremony. Alternatively, some people decide to dispense altogether with an outside organisation's ideas of what should be done and said at the service, and instead prepare their own ceremonies. In such cases, anything goes, the only restraints being the available time in the crematorium chapel or elsewhere.

In most instances, however, the service follows a familiar, traditional pattern, with only one or two elements having been changed to reflect the character of the deceased or the conventions of his or her family and friends. Some people may choose to have a singer or musician perform live rather than relying on recorded music, for example, and some may incorporate a tribute by a family member. Others may include the reading of the deceased's favourite poem, or one that sums up the feelings of those left behind. In the wake of the huge success of the film *Four Weddings and a Funeral* in 1994, the poem 'Funeral Blues', by W H Auden, has since been recited at countless funerals, with John Hannah's moving rendition, ending with the lines 'Pour away the ocean and sweep up the wood / For nothing now can ever come to any good', having even been credited with reviving poetry's popularity. Maybe it did – it certainly inspired its inclusion in funeral ceremonies, as well as that of a variety of other popular poems, such as Christina Rossetti's 'Remember', Mary Frye's 'Do Not Stand at my Grave and Weep' and Edward Guest's 'Miss Me, But Let Me Go'.

Some people have chosen to personalise a funeral by decorating the space within which it is held. They have projected videos of the deceased at work and at play on the walls, for instance; or they have created montages of photographs to exhibit; or they have made displays of objects associated with the person. Indeed, short films or a small group of their personal belongings can be powerful reminders of a person's life.

It is a good idea to discuss your funeral with your family and friends if you are going to ask them to personalise it extensively, and particularly if you are expecting them to organise and run the entire occasion themselves. You should also leave long and detailed instructions for them that include the locations of any films, photos or possessions that you'd like featured in your funeral, as well as the names and contact details of any technically minded people you know who may be needed to turn, for example, a canister of film into a digital display. If it's likely to be very elaborate, remember, too, to think about who would be paying for your funeral, and whether this would be feasible.

An outline of elements you might include in a personalised funeral service follows in The Order of Service (pages 112 to 114), but see also pages 210 to 214 in the Reflections section to help you make up a more detailed funeral plan if you wish to.

REMEMBER

REMEMBER ME WHEN I AM GONE AWAY,

Gone far away into the silent land;
When you can no more hold me by the hand,

Nor I half turn to go, yet turning stay.
Remember me when no more day by day
You tell me of our future that you plann'd:
Only remember me; you understand
It will be late to counsel then or pray.
Yet if you should forget me for a while
And afterwards remember, do not grieve:
For if the darkness and corruption leave
A vestige of the thoughts that once I had,
Better by far you should forget and smile
Than that you should remember and be sad.

Christina Rossetti

Recording for Posterity

Some crematoria offer the option of filming a funeral service, which may be watched live over the internet or recorded to DVD for posterity. This allows relatives and friends who are unable to attend it in person to watch the service as it happens, or to view it later at home. If you're worried about privacy issues, note that a user name and password can be given to specific friends and relatives allowing them to watch the service on the internet, but no one else.

It would be a good idea to include with your funeral instructions a note of any friends or relatives who you anticipate may not be able to attend the ceremony, but whom you'd like to be given access to your service or given a DVD recording. With the speed of changes occurring in this area, new modes of recording and broadcasting are likely to develop, so if you'd prefer to specify a relatively private occasion without any recording or remote access allowed, you should make a note to that effect.

The Order of Service

Most traditional funerals have the same basic elements in common. If you are planning your own, completely personalised event, you are free to do whatever you like, more or less; even so, the following guidelines should provide a good starting point. Remember that the celebrant, who leads the ceremony, can be a religious or humanist representative, or else anyone who would be emotionally prepared to take on this responsibility.

The main elements of a funeral are as follows:

1. The night before the funeral, there is often a wake, when family members or friends sit through the night with the deceased (see page 103).

2. There may also be a viewing, which is generally a more public event than a wake, during which anyone acquainted with family or deceased comes to offer their condolences and pay their respects (see page 103). (If you'd like a viewing before your funeral, remember to make a note of this.)

3. The funeral service itself often begins with entrance music being played for about fifteen minutes as the mourners arrive and take their seats. This is followed by a short welcome address by the celebrant, stating why the mourners have gathered together, along the lines of 'We are here to celebrate the life of our dear friend . . .' (see also pages 210 to 212).

4. A religious ceremony will typically feature a sermon, while a humanist funeral will generally incorporate a reading or music instead. There will usually be readings, whose nature will vary according to the individual and type of ceremony, but which may be pieces of prose or poetry, religious or non-religious.

5. The eulogy is normally delivered by the presiding member of the clergy in the case of a religious funeral. In other instances, however, one person may deliver a eulogy, or several people may share their memories of the deceased.

6. If the body is being transported to its final place of disposal after the ceremony, there will be a procession to the burial ground or crematorium, either on foot or by vehicle.

7. Just before the body is disposed of, the mourners will say their last goodbyes to the deceased. The celebrant will then thank those assembled for coming, after which music is normally played as they leave.

8. After the funeral ceremony, there is usually a reception (often a meal), a final gathering at which the mourners can remember the deceased.

Speaking of the Dead

Virtually every funeral ceremony includes a eulogy or some other public form of remembrance of the deceased. And while planning your own funeral is generally an act of kindness to those who survive you, it's a bit hard to plan your own eulogy. Although you could, perhaps, ask a close relative or friend to deliver one at your final send-off, you can hardly give them a list of nice things to say about you. Eulogy-wise, it is clearly more likely that you be called upon to deliver a tribute to someone else, in which case you'll no doubt be left wondering what to say.

The eulogy is an opportunity to remember and celebrate the deceased, something that you should keep at the forefront of your mind. This means that your eulogy is likely to be a mixture of grief and joy as you mourn your loss, while at the same time rejoicing in the deceased's life. A eulogy doesn't have to be a great work of art, but does need to come from the heart, and some starting points include a brief history of the person's life (you could also mention their accomplishments or hobbies) and any special memories that you may have of him or her. Despite your inevitable sense of grief and loss, affectionate humour is often both appropriate and welcome during a funeral service, especially when the person whose life you are celebrating was known for his or her own sense of humour.

Allow yourself plenty of time to prepare your speech, as well as to revise it (you may also want to ask others for their opinions, especially if there's a chance you may have inadvertently included something that could cause one of the mourners any offence).

Although you should know your eulogy well enough that you don't need to read it out word for word, it is essential to have a clear, well-organised written version to hand. This will not only be useful for your own reference: if you find that you are overcome by emotion and are unable to finish delivering your eulogy, or even to start, a back-up person can then use your notes to do so (and be sure to ask someone in advance if they would be prepared to step in and take over if necessary, and then make sure that they are sitting close by). It may also be that you are asked for a copy of your eulogy after the funeral service by someone who was moved by it, in which case you can then easily have one made. If possible, make sure that there is a glass of water nearby before you start speaking.

A EULOGY TO A PYTHON

When Monty Python actor Graham Chapman died in 1989, fellow Python John Cleese gave the only eulogy he could:

Graham Chapman, co-author of the 'Parrot Sketch', is no more.

He has ceased to be. Bereft of life, he rests in peace. He's kicked the bucket, hopped the twig, bit the dust, snuffed it, breathed his last, and gone to meet the great Head of Light Entertainment in the sky. And I guess that we're all thinking how sad it is that a man of such talent, of such capability for kindness, of such unusual intelligence, should now so suddenly be spirited away at the age of only forty-eight, before he'd achieved many of the things of which he was capable, and before he'd had enough fun.

Well, I feel that I should say: nonsense. Good riddance to him, the freeloading bastard, I hope he fries.

And the reason I feel I should say this is he would never forgive me if I didn't, if I threw away this glorious opportunity to shock you all on his behalf. Anything for him but mindless good taste!

Funeral Customs

We've described the basic elements of a modern British funeral, but every culture has different funeral traditions, of course, which have developed over centuries. Some of the major world religions' funeral customs are outlined below.

- All **Christian** funerals follow the general pattern described on pages 113 to 114, but the details vary from denomination to denomination. Protestant ceremonies tend to be simpler than Roman Catholic or Orthodox ones, for example. The Roman Catholic ceremony has a special mass, the Requiem, while for many years, the Catholic Church disapproved of cremation, believing that the entire body was necessary if resurrection was to be achieved. And although the option of an open or a closed coffin tends to vary in other Christian traditions, it is always open in that of the Greek Orthodox Church.

- **Jewish** custom insists on a quick burial, but this is surrounded by many traditions. First, there is *shemirah*, the vigil, for tradition dictates that the body should never be left alone. The body is not embalmed, nor is it displayed before burial. Prior to burial, mourners will tear their clothing (or, alternatively, a ribbon). The service consists of simple eulogies, after which the mourners help to fill the grave. Afterwards, the family will 'sit *shiva*', or observe the traditional seven-day mourning period. During this time, friends may bring them food, but no flowers. And because flowers are impermanent, small stones are placed on the grave instead.

- In **Islamic** tradition, a funeral also takes place very soon after death, and generally within two days. Muslims never cremate their dead, and the coffin is always closed as a sign of respect. The service itself is traditionally a short, restrained affair led by an imam, and, as in Christian tradition, black is the colour of mourning. Graves are oriented so that the deceased face the holy city of Mecca. (See also pages 224–26).

- A **Hindu** funeral occurs very quickly, too, but there the similarity between Islamic and Hindu funerals ends. In the Hindu tradition – one of the oldest in the world, dating back as it does 3,000 years – the body is always cremated. Because reincarnation is a central tenet of Hinduism, its followers view death as a natural part of a cycle of birth, death and rebirth. The Hindu ceremony is more colourful than its Christian or Muslim equivalents, with flowers being heaped upon the deceased's body, although the Hindu colour of mourning is white. The funeral is conducted by a priest and senior family members.

- **Sikh** funerals share many of their features with Hindu ones, although a notable difference is that the deceased must be buried with the 'five Ks': *kes*, uncut hair; *kanga*, a comb; *kara*, a steel wristband; *kachha*, a special undergarment; and *kirpan*, a ceremonial dagger.

- Like Hinduism, **Buddhism** holds that death is part of a natural cycle of reincarnation, and a death is not generally marked by an elaborate funeral, although monks will chant *sutras* (Buddhist texts). Emulating Buddha, many Buddhists opt for cremation. And as in other Asian traditions, white is the traditional colour of mourning.

- Despite modern China being officially atheist, **Chinese** funerals are governed by ancient traditions, and corpses are generally buried. The body of the deceased may be wrapped in textiles of various colours, but never red, which is the Chinese colour of happiness. And while white is the traditional colour of mourning in China, it is now acceptable to wear dark clothing or a dark armband. Ancestor veneration is also an ancient and important part of Chinese culture, being an expression of filial devotion.

NEW ORLEANS JAZZ FUNERALS

Drawing on New Orleans' mixed heritage of African, French and American influences, a New Orleans jazz funeral is a musical ceremony. During the procession to the graveside, a brass band plays dirges and somber hymns, such as 'Just a Closer Walk with Thee'. After the deceased has been interred, however, the mood changes to a joyful one as the participants and musicians (the 'first line') celebrate the deceased's life with lively music and dancing. Onlookers often form the 'second line' as they join in with the dancing, also twirling umbrellas and waving handkerchiefs. For many years, the jazz funeral was performed by Protestants only, for the Catholic Church frowned upon secular music and dancing being part of a funeral.

Refreshments for the Mourners

Once the funeral is over, and the coffin has been consigned to the grave or has been cremated, there is generally a gathering of the mourners for refreshments (usually known in Scotland as the 'funeral tea'). The tone of this event generally echoes that of the funeral service, so if the mood has been solemn and mournful, then the gathering will be, too. For more joyful ceremonies, a marquee may be hired and a real party held. A family member often makes a short speech at events like this, thanking the guests for attending, and for their kind cards and words.

Following on from the funeral service and refreshments, a third gathering generally takes place at the house of the bereaved family. There is usually a kind of social filter at work here, with the service being open to all, the post-funeral refreshments to an invited number, and a select gathering of family and close friends then meeting at the family home.

If there is a marked age difference or culture gap between the family and friends of the deceased, and the choices made by the family don't match the wishes of the friends – maybe the funeral service was religious or otherwise conservative – an informal gathering could be arranged to celebrate the life of the dead friend, perhaps a month or so after the funeral.

OPEN-AIR FUNERAL PYRES

In February 2010, the Court of Appeal ruled that open-air funeral pyres, which are required for Hindu and Sikh cremations (the open-air location is thought to allow the soul's migration to occur), were legal in Britain. The ruling followed a lengthy court battle on the part of Davender Ghai, who wished to be cremated on a traditional, open-air pyre after his death. Such pyres must nevertheless be situated within a building in Britain, which will either have a roof with an opening or no roof at all.

FINAL PASSAGES

Final Passages founder Jerrigrace Lyons never thought that she would be a 'death midwife', helping families to care for their dead. But when her dear friend Carolyn Whiting died, Lyons and other friends found that Carolyn had left instructions for a home funeral, and had specified no embalming or funeral directors. Although initially frightened, Lyons and the others found that preparing Carolyn's body was a healing experience, allowing them time to accept their friend's death.

The experience was also a life-changing one, and in 1995 Lyons opened Final Passages, a California-based centre designed to assist families to organise home funerals. She now helps survivors to prepare the bodies of their loved ones and to arrange funeral ceremonies. If the funeral has been planned well in advance of a death, many families – or even the individual concerned – also decorate the deceased's coffin.

DIY Funerals

Although it is rare in the UK, it is possible to hold a funeral at home, and there are signs that home funerals will increase. Most people who do this still use a funeral director's services, yet there is no law that requires it. All that is needed is the right paperwork: the death certificate, the certificate of registration of death (BD8) and the certificate for burial or cremation (see pages 87–88, and note that extra certificates are required for cremations).

There is a growing trend in the USA to return to the old practice of having a home funeral, in which the deceased's family or friends prepare the body for burial or cremation and, indeed, hold the entire undertaking at home. A do-it-yourself funeral is not for everyone: in view of the extreme modern emotional disconnection from death, there are many people who would find the very idea upsetting, and even abhorrent. Yet for thousands of years, this is how people bade their final farewells to their loved ones.

Once someone has died at home, the process of preparing for his or her funeral does not need to start instantly. For the first hour, many people will still be coming to terms with the death, and although it is advisable to close the deceased's mouth and eyes at this time, it is otherwise fine to do nothing.

The first thing to do then is to call for a physician to certify the death, and also to notify anyone who will be helping to prepare the body. Rigor mortis will set in between two and four hours after death, and it is easier to prepare the body at this time, although it can be done later. (Note that rigor mortis is not a permanent state, and that the body will revert to being limp at some point between twenty-four and forty-eight hours later.) Next, use vinegar to swab out the mouth before tying the jaw shut. Then, use a light weight to keep the eyes closed. Washing the body will require at least two people, for the body must be supported at all times. Because control of all bodily functions is lost at death, it's a good idea to place absorbent cloths under the body before washing it with warm water, which could be scented with such fragrant oils as lavender. After you have dried the body, dress it as the deceased wished or you think fit. Wherever you then choose to place the body, be sure to have plenty of dry ice to hand (20 kg/44 lb for the average adult) to keep it cool and prevent decomposition. Position the ice under the upper and lower back and on each side of the torso. Once in place, you can cover the ice with a blanket or another form of covering.

After the body has been prepared, the funeral process typically proceeds with family and friends coming to view the body, generally in a room that has been decorated to honour the deceased. Then, on the day of the funeral, a service is held, after which the body is either buried or cremated.

Many of those who have held home funerals have reported that caring for their dead had definite emotional benefits. They were often surprised that the process helped them to come to terms with their loss and to begin the healing process, for instance. Preparing the body and seeing the stillness and pallor of death helped them to accept that a death had really happened, and that their loved one had truly gone. 'But what about the children?' you may ask. Well, rather than being terrified, the adults reported that any children present were usually remarkably calm, and often came into the room where the deceased was lying, either to hold his or her hand or simply to sit quietly nearby.

For some, the idea of holding a DIY funeral might appeal partly as a reaction to recent trends in the business side of funeral-care service provision (as well as because of the sheer costs). Many independent, family-run undertaker businesses have been taken over by a small number of large groups during the last decade or so, in what is now estimated as a business worth around £2 billion each year in the UK. The publicly traded funeral conglomerate may seem quite an impersonal entity – perhaps reflecting the 'death of the high street' and the rise of a more corporate society, to which some may object on principle. If you want to make the DIY choice for your own funeral, though, be mindful of the task you'll be setting your loved ones, and discuss it with them in advance to make sure they understand what's involved and are willing to take it on.

The High Cost of Dying

Although the main motivation for having a DIY funeral is, for many, the psychological benefits, the reduced cost when compared to alternative options may also be a powerful motivator. According to a BBC report, the average cost of a funeral with burial in 2008 was £2,549, and as much as £3,424 in London. And an Oddfellows survey indicated that the equivalent cost was £2,048 in 2000, with the average cost of a cremation in that year being £1,215.

It is all too easy for funeral directors to sell grieving survivors expensive items or services that they don't really want, and it seems that their quotations either regularly underestimate funeral costs or are less than transparent. It is the high prices charged for unwanted and unnecessary services that are one of the factors cited by some who have chosen to take a more do-it-yourself approach to funerals (see pages 120 to 122). DIY funerals are still sufficiently rare in the UK that no statistics are available for them, but they often cost less than $1,000 in the USA.

Whether or not you opt for a DIY funeral for yourself or a loved one, you should be aware that the deceased's assets will be frozen and inaccessible until after the estate has been settled. Some banks will release funds for a funeral, and some funeral directors may allow time for payment, but there are no guarantees. This is one more reason to consider what you will need for your final send-off, and to set aside the necessary funds so that those who survive you will not have another stressful problem to deal with.

So what should you expect to pay for a funeral, in today's terms? There's no simple answer to this question, of course, other than to use the average figures quoted above as a guideline. Marketing men and women speak of certain items as 'grudge purchases': we get no obvious return in terms of pleasure for our outlay. Included can be anything from home insurance to gym-membership. And where's the retail-therapeutic thrill in getting our dry-cleaning done? Of all grudge purchases, though, you might imagine that none would be quite so deeply begrudged as that of the funeral: who wants either to die or to be bereaved? It's hardly surprising, then, that for all the families grateful for help given in their time of need, the funeral industry should also have so many dissatisfied customers – despite the best efforts of companies and their staff. As mentioned above, it's not necessarily all about the total cost – though that's important: there's been a sense that many firms might have been more transparent about the specifics of what they were charging for; that people were being asked to take too much on trust and end up paying for things they didn't want.

Even where money has been no object, there have been objections to the way some funeral directors do things. More affluent individuals or families who want to 'push the boat out' and show how much the late-beloved is going to be missed with a lavish send-off have often found themselves thwarted by an industry that hasn't been as responsive as it might have been. The feeling has grown that funeral directors have typically offered standardised, impersonal services geared more to their own convenience than the comfort to the bereaved.

But recent years have seen the emergence of a growing number of independents aiming to provide an alternative approach. It was dissatisfaction with his mother's funeral fifteen years ago that led Carl Marlow, for example, to start his own independent funeral company, Go As You Please, in Wallsend, Tyne and Wear (www.goasyouplease.com). Marlow's individual approach and frank discussion of costs are refreshing. While many funeral directors offer 'personal' touches, he is willing to provide whatever you want for a funeral – even fireworks. Marlow has also caused quite a few fireworks of his own by upsetting the wider funeral industry with his determination to be open about costs. (When asked for a quotation, the manager of one local branch of a funeral-services chain said, by contrast, that only the legal department of the head office could discuss prices.) Some accuse Marlow of being a cowboy, but he is as qualified as anyone to be a funeral director, given that no regulated qualification exists to become one.

Marlow acknowledges that the blame for the funeral industry's coyness doesn't lie entirely with it, but also with society. Even though nothing is more certain in life than death, there is still a great reluctance to talk about it, or to admit that no one actually needs a mahogany coffin. Fundamentally, Marlow wants society to accept death, and to use funerals to celebrate the lives of those who have died, with families talking about them, painting coffins, and maybe helping to dig woodland graves, for example. He has even performed a few 'living funerals' for those who feel that they should get to enjoy their end-of-life party, too.

So, what does a funeral cost? Clearly, there are many variables, but it helps to have a basic point of reference. For a typical cremation in Tyne and Wear at Go As You Please's 2010 prices, the cost was around £1,975 (regional variation was within £100). This included the fees and costs for any doctors required, the coffin and name plate, the hearse, one limousine, transfer of the coffin to the funeral home, the chapel of rest, pallbearers, the minister, cremation and the funeral director. Not included were flowers or death notices placed in newspapers. Most funeral directors have a mysterious category of charges called 'disbursements', which vary from one company to another, but which can easily add £800 or more to the advertised cost. (Another term to watch out for is 'hygienic treatment', which is another name for embalming – see pages 99 to 102.)

Marlow also gives average figures (based on 2010 prices, and note that they will vary by region) for some of the individual components of a funeral: a coffin: £300–£400; a hearse and limousine: £250; an officiant/celebrant: £150; crematorium service time: £410; a traditional grave: £1,000; a woodland grave: £500–£700. Go As You Please's increasingly popular funeral-coach option (see page 106) is £250, but transports forty-nine people, rather than the far smaller number that a limousine, which costs the same, can carry.

For those looking for a natural burial at an affordable price, Ken West's book *A Guide to Natural Burials* (see page 146) provides useful information and inspiration.

Children's Funerals

Those who have held home funerals often report that they are a better option for children to deal with than those arranged by funeral directors. For when a funeral is held at home, children have more time to accept that a loved one has died, and to say goodbye when they are ready (as opposed to being told, confusingly, that 'Granny's gone to a better place' while looking at a life-like, embalmed body lying in a funeral parlour). Children take their cue from the adults around them, and if you are able to mourn in a healthy, natural way, so will your children.

It is generally far more difficult to deal with a death when the deceased is a child, however. Although the general form of the funeral is the same as for an adult, burying a child is, emotionally, one of the hardest things that anyone ever has to do, especially a parent. For many families, it takes time to prepare for a child's funeral. And if you have lost a son or daughter, do not let anyone pressurise you into making any decisions immediately, and maybe enlist a close friend or relative to act as a buffer between you and anyone exerting any unwelcome pressure on you.

Home funerals are more common for children because parents typically cannot bear the thought of someone else looking after their child. Parents often want to be involved in taking care of their child – as they did in life – for the final time by dressing and perhaps washing the body. In the case of very young children, parents often make plaster casts of their hand- and footprints to keep as a reminder of their babies. And it may be that you decide that you want to have your child's body at home, where you, other family members, and his or her friends can say goodbye in private. Many families find it too difficult to have an open coffin or to invite mourners to a public viewing of their dead child, however, and it is perfectly acceptable to have a private viewing for the family only, and to display photographs of the child instead.

Whilst the extreme distress parents experience on the death of a child is universally recognised, the trauma caused by the loss of unborn children is sometimes underestimated, both in terms of the depth of grief and the sheer scale on which this occurs. Few debates have raged so strongly in recent years as that over when a baby's life begins: at the moment of conception? At the point of 'viability'? At birth? Some civilisations haven't been sure that their children have been fully accredited individuals even then: the Incas of the Andes didn't name their sons or daughters until they were a year old. Because so many infants didn't make it to that age, the less their elders invested in them emotionally before that time, perhaps, the better. And when the Spartans left their newborns on rugged hillsides to see whether they would survive, it could be said that they were simply acknowledging the realities of ancient life. They're not just ancient realities either: to this day, for example, an estimated 18.5 per cent of Angolan infants die within a year of birth – almost a fifth of the total number born, in other words.

In the developed world, the situation is very different, yet even the equivalent figure of 0.2 per cent in the European Union represents heartbreak for the mothers and fathers of the dead children. Stillborn babies must be given birth to just as living infants are, with all that that implies in terms of labour pains and hormone storms. A mother may already know that the baby that she is carrying has died when she goes into labour, or else may discover it only when the baby is finally delivered. If she does know, she may also have been aware of a period during which her unborn child was in distress. All in all, she is likely to be in considerable distress herself. Quite how deep the trauma goes will of course depend on the circumstances, the mother's individual temperament and time of life.

We don't know how successfully mothers in ancient times managed to maintain their detachment when their newborns didn't make it, but we do know that modern mothers aren't brought up the Spartan way. Yet even well-intentioned friends and relations can remain in denial, failing to see that stillbirths and, considerably more common, late miscarriages are quite simply experienced by the mother as a child's death.

Indeed, after twenty-four weeks of gestation, any baby is regarded as a child in the eyes of the law, which means that his or her death must be registered like any other. The same goes in cases of neo-natal death: the infant is a person, so a funeral must be held and a burial or cremation arranged. (The hospital at which the child was born will normally be able to help with this.) And while the mourning process may last a lifetime, more immediately, the need to hold a proper funeral can be beneficial to the bereaved parents, not least because it confirms the scale and significance of their loss. (See also "Questions of Medical Ethics and the Lessons of Experience" pages 216 to 220.)

A CHILD'S HOME FUNERAL

Massachusetts resident George Foy never considered using a funeral director when his one-month-old son died, he said in a radio discussion on DIY funerals. Instead, he took care of his son's body himself, and even made a small coffin for him. He decorated the coffin and filled it with mementos before placing it on the roller in the crematorium himself. His son's ashes now rest under a cypress tree at the family home.

Averting Family Friction

By discussing your last wishes with your family – and, even better, writing them down – you can help to avert a great deal of potential strife on the day of your funeral. Modern families tend to bring together people from a variety of cultural and religious backgrounds, and tempers can still flare even within the most homogeneous of families. Indeed, many families have ended up spending years, and even decades, not speaking to each other because of what did, or did not, happen at a funeral.

Interfaith families will usually already have gone through all manner of negotiating processes at weddings, births and other milestone events, and so, it is hoped, will have come to terms with their differences. But death tends to strengthen religious attachments, so if your religious beliefs differ from those of your family, it is important that you write down what you want for your funeral, and maybe appoint an executor to ensure that your wishes are carried out (see pages 38 to 39).

Another good reason for putting your last wishes in writing is if your significant other is a live-in partner or fiancé(e), with no formal legal status. Legally, there is no such thing as a 'common-law' spouse, and if you aren't married or in a civil partnership, you won't get a say in your partner's funeral (see page 52). And if you are contemplating your own funeral, remember that it is all too easy for a partner to be left out of funeral arrangements, especially if there is conflict between blood relatives and him or her.

On the subject of partners and funerals, many people will have to consider how to deal with an ex who was, or remained, close to their recently deceased parent. It is possible that everyone was on reasonably good terms following the breakdown of the relationship, but in the event of continuing tension, it is good to have a back-up plan. If the ex is the mother or father of any children who have been affected by a relative's death, it may be sensible to have them present at the funeral to support their children. You may want to specify that an ex or other potentially controversial guest is invited to sit in a prominent place for the service or be included in the family hearse en route to the ceremony, for example. If there is so much bad feeling that the presence of the ex might give rise to a great deal of tension, one compromise could be for the ex to attend the viewing (if there is one), but not the funeral. And in cases of extreme bad blood, a funeral director can be instructed to keep an eye open for any potentially disruptive people. Whatever the case, tension is more likely to be minimised if the deceased made his or her wishes plain in advance.

DEATH US DO PART?

In November 2009, Yu Liang married Zhang Jinying – at her funeral in Zhengzhou, China. Although the couple had already received their marriage certificate, Zhang had died before the wedding could take place. Such posthumous weddings are not as rare as you might think. In 2009, for instance, Magali Jaskiewicz, a French woman, became a wife and a widow at the same time when she married her deceased partner, Jonathan George, a year after his death in a car crash. Under French law, a posthumous wedding is legal as long as there is evidence that the deceased had intended to marry his or her posthumous spouse, and the couple (who had two children) had indeed already registered their intention to marry. According to reports, several such weddings take place each year in France.

Chapter Four
YOUR LAST
RESTING PLACE:

WHERE DO YOU
WANT TO END UP?

'After life's fitful fever he sleeps well', says Shakespeare's Macbeth of the murdered Duncan. That's the thing about the dead: they don't do much. Sure, you can have an impressive send-off, complete with mournful crowds, if you're a state personage, or be dispatched with full military honours if you've earned them. Or you can rebel against convention and maybe organise a cockney knees-up for after your cremation or opt for the high-rev racket of a biker funeral if that's more your style. Even so, once they've paid their final respects and the crowds have dispersed, the smoke has cleared, the beer's been mopped up and the sound of departing Harleys has faded, that's pretty much it: your remains are now set to rest where they are for ever more. In life, you may have strutted about in outrageous fashions; you may have been a high-profile blogger or the life-and-soul of the office at work; or you may have made a spectacular his-and-hers parachute-jump the centre of your wedding. Yet death, the mighty leveller, makes meek introverts of us all: however loud or boisterous you were in life, you'll be quiet in death.

Yet there is self-expression even in death, for if we're prepared to think ahead, we can have the option of deciding where we want to be buried or our ashes to be scattered. However passive we may be when we've passed away, we can make this active choice, which may well have an important bearing on the way we are remembered. If we're interred in a village churchyard, surrounded by our ancestors, for example, that says something about who we are, and about our values. The same is true (although the statement may be very different) if we're laid to rest with the rank and file in a city cemetery or have our ashes sprinkled on the slopes of the South Downs, or even donate our remains to medical science.

You only get one shot at body-disposal, of course: you can't be a stickler for tradition and be buried in a churchyard in the depths of rural Gloucestershire and also have your ashes scattered on the streets of Rome in homage to your love of Fellini films. So your scope is limited. On the other hand, it may be comforting to bear in mind that it seems unlikely that you're going to know what happens to your body after your death, or care too much about it. It only matters to the person you are now – and to those who are going to mourn you.

PLASTINATION – TAKING IT ON THE ROAD

During the 1970s, Gunther von Hagens applied for his first patent for 'plastination', a method of preserving living tissue after death involving fixation (embalming), dehydration and finally filling the body with epoxy resin or silicone rubber. Using this method, an entire human body can be preserved indefinitely.

Plastinated bodies and organs are generally used for anatomy courses, but in 1995, von Hagens took his models on tour in Japan. The exhibition was a huge success, drawing 3 million visitors, and von Hagens' exhibits have since toured several countries as BODY WORLDS. If you would like your body to be plastinated to help teach everyone about, well, the body, body donations can arranged through the Institute of Plastination in Heidelberg, Germany (see www.bodyworlds.com for further information).

BODIES MATTER

Not everyone wants their remains safely deposited at an eternal resting place. Some people feel that their death is an opportunity to give something back to society and would like to bequeath their bodies to help train tomorrow's scientists, or give another person a second chance at life.

Leaving Your Body to Medical Science

If you leave your body to medical science, it will most likely go to a medical school for the purposes of teaching medical students about anatomy, but different institutions accept different sorts of donations (human tissues and human brains, for instance). If you are thinking of leaving your body to medical science, it would therefore be wise to do some research into this well before your death, and then to leave detailed instructions, along with the required consent form. It may be helpful to know what sorts of criteria are used to accept or decline donations, for example, and note that if a medical institution rejects your donations, your family will be responsible for disposing of your remains.

The best source of information on the subject is the Human Tissue Authority (HTA, www.hta.gov.uk), which oversees all human donations in the UK. According to the Human Tissue Act of 2004, you must provide your written and witnessed body-donation consent for anatomical examination before you die. The necessary form is available from the bequeathal secretary of your nearest medical school, to which the completed form should also be returned; you should keep a copy of the completed consent form with your will, too. Don't forget to inform your nearest and dearest, the executor(s) of your will and your GP that you wish to donate your body to medical science.

Organ-isation

If you want to do it, but have not yet got around to it, this would also be a good time to register yourself as a organ donor. Some people have religious or other well-worked-out objections to do-ing so; others may simply be squeamish. That's fine – it's your body. But if you're happy enough to donate your organs, but haven't yet got your act together, then you should make the minimal effort required to add your details to the NHS Organ Donor Register. You can add them (and also amend or remove them) online at www.organdonation.nhs.uk or you can call 0300 123 23 23 (tel-ephone lines are always open) or text SAVE to 84118. Donating your organs will be worth it. Not so much for you (although when the moment comes, you may be surprised how comforting you find the knowledge that your death is going to help others) as for the family and friends that you leave behind. And most of all, of course, to those whose health you'll be helping to restore.

Not only is there a shortage of organ donors, there is a shortage of healthy organ donors. In 2008, British soldier Corporal Matthew Millington died after the lungs that he had received as a transplant developed a tumour. The donor had been a smoker with a habit of thirty to fifty cigarettes a day, and the immuno-suppressants taken by Millingon that had been necessary for a successful transplant had sadly enabled the tumour to grow more rapidly. About half of the organs available for transplant come from smokers. This is hardly ideal, but then health officials point out that if they rejected all smokers out of hand, we would face an even more serious shortage of donor organs, which would result in more people dying while on the waiting list for a transplant.

BURIAL OPTIONS

Being buried is the traditional method of body-disposal. If this idea appeals to you, would you prefer to lie in a country churchyard, a city cemetery or maybe a more natural, woodland burial site?

An English Elegy: Country Churchyards

'Fifty years on from now,' John Major – then prime minister – insisted, 'Britain will still be the country of long shadows on cricket grounds, warm beer, invincible green suburbs, dog lovers and pools fillers and, as George Orwell said, "Old maids cycling to holy communion through the morning mist"…' That was in 1993, and while the fifty years are nothing like up yet, that glowing vision already appears a little ragged around the edges. Just a year later, for example, the UK acquired its national lottery, as a result of which the football pools to which Major referred have been comprehensively marginalised. Labour's 'Cool Britannia' was no country for warm beer either, and from 1997, under Tony Blair's premiership, the UK reeled and swayed its way into the new millennium, drunk on alcopops, vodka shots and cider.

But then the Britain envisaged by Major was in any case a bit of political correctness on his part. For the prime minister was putting forward a view whose stereotyping scope encompassed only England (Scotland was never very big on cricket grounds, and nor was most of Wales), and an idealised England of white respectability at that, with its leafy suburbs and rural shires. This view, moreover, was already dated (the Orwell quotation that he cited dates from 1941).

Yet, like most stereotypes, John Major's vision was by no means an out-and-out falsehood, but touches on the truth in significant places. There are certainly still 'old maids', and some may indeed cycle to church for the morning service. And when they alight, wherever they are in the England conjured up by television staples like 'The Antiques Roadshow' and 'Midsomer Murders', they must lean their bikes against the churchyard wall and make their way through the lych gate, which is roofed to shelter waiting pallbearers, and often incorporates a shelf on which to rest coffins or shrouded corpses. And the path to the church door that our old maids then tread will be lined with monuments and headstones.

It was at Stoke Poges, in Buckinghamshire, in the summer of 1750, that Thomas Gray composed his famous 'Elegy Written in a Country Churchyard'. Its wonderfully atmospheric verses set the departed in their graves at the very heart of their communities, and their peaceful rest at the very centre of the village scene:

> *Beneath those rugged elms, that yew tree's shade,*
> *Where heaves the turf in many a mould'ring heap,*
> *Each in his narrow cell forever laid,*
> *The rude forefathers of the hamlet sleep . . .*

The forefathers buried in the churchyard would have been 'rude' because their social 'betters' would have been placed within the church itself, directly beneath the aisle-slabs or in special vaults set aside for their families under the floor. Minor members of the gentry or more affluent tradesmen might have had themselves buried outside, but close to the church door, and a lavish monument would have helped to raise their post-mortem profile.

Distinctions of wealth and status have been preserved in death in many, if not most, cultures, and class-ridden England has certainly been no exception. But Gray captures well the feeling, which we often still have in English villages, of the dead, regardless of rank, somehow persisting in the midst of the living, with all the sense of social community and cultural continuity that that implies. Conservatives are therefore generally attracted to the country churchyard for the same reasons that modern-minded liberals tend to look askance at them: it suggests a happily hierarchical country, class-bound, but completely untouched by class antagonisms and all the other changes of recent times.

A great many country-dwellers will feel that such a view is overanalytical, though, and overly negative as well. Indeed, if you have deep roots in a village – or a genuine love of the countryside and its age-old ways – what's so wrong with wanting to become a part of this tradition when you die by being buried in the local graveyard?

Pushed for Space

The country churchyard was traditionally called 'God's half-acre', and many are smaller still, with space being at a premium in the most picturesque. The rise of cremation's popularity in recent decades hasn't done enough to offset surging population growth overall, so the longstanding crisis of space not only in our urban cemeteries, but also in our churchyards, has only deepened. As of April 2010, a quarter of churchyards in Wales were completely full, for instance, whilst 43 per cent had fewer than twenty grave plots left. Even so, the situation varies enormously from place to place, so it's still worth approaching the clergy or church officials in the parish of your choice to sound them out about a particular churchyard.

Should you enquire about grave availability, you'll generally find that records of residence in the parish will determine your eligibility. (Bear in mind, though, that residence is typically noted in the parish's ecclesiastical records, and that this isn't necessarily the same as the ordinary – civic – electoral roll. So it's worth checking exactly what your status is.)

Don't forget to sound out your family and any other loved ones about a graveyard burial as well. A grave isn't just for the funeral and the few weeks that follow, and it won't be you who's left with what is, by definition, a lasting commitment. An unkempt grave is distressing to see, not only for the relations who visit it, but also for any other visitors to the churchyard. Yet maintaining a grave can be a demanding chore. The parish will look after a graveyard up to a point, but it can't take responsibility for individual graves. Most parishes are strapped for cash: congregations – and collections – have diminished in the past decades, causing churchyard maintenance to become a major headache for hard-pressed parishes. Most country churchyards are now maintained to a reasonable standard by a small army of older volunteer workers.

LIFE AFTER DEATH

Since St Francis preached his sermon to the swallows, wildlife and the Church have gone their separate ways, with little sense of any religious role in conservation. There was certainly no awareness that God's Half Acre might be Nature's too; that we owed a duty to the flora and fauna which flourished there. Graveyard humour had it that when we died we were 'pushing up daisies'. People believed that their mortal remains would be eaten up by 'worms'. But that was as far as it went: there was no real understanding of the churchyard as an ecclesiastically-administered ecosystem.

Increasingly, though, as towns and cities grew, and as the countryside itself was more intensively and intrusively managed, churchyards were becoming wildlife sanctuaries. These sacred spaces could neither be built over nor ploughed up: they were tended to some degree but for the most part left in peace. In the past few decades we've woken up to see how much of our natural heritage we've destroyed, but in our churchyards we still have places where wild flowers and trees can grow and birds can sing. From the bats in the belfry and the vole in the undergrowth to the moss on a tree-trunk or the lichen on a gravestone, all living things have their place in the place of the dead. This was the realisation that gave rise to the Living Churchyards Project. First promoted by the Alliance of Religions and Conservation (ARC), the scheme has been given government support and extended to city cemeteries – especially important in providing pockets of green in a wildlife-unfriendly urban context.

Today, over 6,000 churchyards and cemeteries are protected – along with the burial grounds of non-Christian groups, like Muslims. Typically, chemical weedkillers and pesticides have been abandoned, whilst mowing has been restricted to once a year to let grass grow. Work is done to optimise conditions in these special spaces. Helpers are drawn, not just from church congregations, but from communities at large and from school and youth groups: whilst the environment is supported, general consciousness is raised.

Cities of the Dead: City Cemeteries

What the churchyard is to the rural shires, so the cemetery is to our great cities; and like our great cities, it's a creation of relatively modern times. That's not to say that London didn't exist before the eighteenth century, but that it was incomparably smaller than it ultimately became. Nor did such conurbations as Liverpool and Manchester exist as such. The most significant urban centres then were those that we would now think of as market towns: places like Peterborough, Exeter and Lincoln. Yet even there, traditional churchyards were struggling to cope with increased population pressure. And as the seventeenth-century diarist John Evelyn noted on a visit to Norwich, 'most of the churchyards were filled up with Earth, or rather the congestion of dead bodys one upon another, for want of Earth etc to the very top of the walls, so as the Churches seem'd to be built in pitts'.

The centuries that followed saw an explosive expansion of our major cities. Driven off the land by 'improving' landlords, peasants flocked to the urban centres in search of the work that was becoming increasingly available as a result of the Industrial Revolution. And as urban populations soared, so smallpox, cholera and other infectious diseases ravaged the overcrowded slums, ensuring a free and bountiful flow of bodies into collective and anonymous paupers' graves. By the beginning of the Victorian period, late Londoners were bursting out of their burial grounds. An estimated 60–70,000 people had been interred in the churchyard of St Martin-in-the-Fields, which was only 18.5 square metres/200 square feet in area, for example. Things were easier in Islington's Nonconformist burial ground at Bunhill Fields, but even here, there were 2,323 bodies to the acre (an acre is the equivalent of 4,047 square metres).

It was clear to all that these overcrowded graveyards were by no means ideal. The theory of infection was as yet unknown, but doctors were convinced that miasmas (noxious mists) rising from places of dirt and corruption were inherently unhealthy. The same impulse that was to drive the construction of a sewer system for central London a few decades later led first to a horrified recoiling from burial grounds that were clearly effectively masses of rotten flesh.

The emergent middle class was, in any case, quiveringly alert to the dangers of a more figurative social contamination. They felt a fastidious distaste for the idea of being laid to rest with the hoi polloi in the promiscuous conditions of the old-established city churchyards. And if they didn't fancy keeping company with their inferiors in death, neither did their grieving relatives relish the thought of associating with their half-starved and shabbily dressed equivalents when it came to burying their loved ones and tending their graves. Affluent, and increasingly accustomed to making their own consumer choices, they were eager customers when the first commercial cemeteries began to open their gates during the 1830s.

Purpose-built complexes like the cemeteries at Kensal Green and Highgate were spaciously set out and elegantly arranged. You could have your own plot here, with whatever monument you pleased, subject, of course, to cost (but then if burial here was expensive, that had the advantage of ensuring the exclusion of the lower orders). Within the cemeteries themselves, there were subtle social distinctions, too. In death, as in life, the most affluent dwelt apart from the merely respectable. Parkland pathways, colonnaded walks and carefully landscaped rises set off the most prestigious tombs and monuments to their best advantage, and there were more modest plots for the petty bourgeoisie.

A MORTAL MERCHANT CITY

As in so much else, Glasgow got off the mark more quickly than London did when it came to burying its dead, with its necropolis ('city of the dead') being built in 1831. Admittedly, it wasn't the world's first: it was a deliberate copy of Paris' Père Lachaise, founded by Emperor Napoleon I in 1804. London's Highgate Cemetery may have Karl Marx, and Kensal Green Cemetery, great novelists like William Makepeace Thackeray and Anthony Trollope, but Glasgow's merchants and industrialists have the more impressive setting. For the Glasgow Necropolis stands high on a hill, overlooking St Mungo's Cathedral, with panoramic views of the spreading city and the hills beyond. The men who made Glasgow knew that they'd made it when they purchased their plots here, and their stunningly sculpted monuments testify to their personal and civic pride.

Cemeteries and Sprawl

The demography of death has always shadowed that of the living in strange, and sometimes eerie, ways. For the ancient Romans, for example, it seems that the dead had to be revered and propitiated – but kept at a distance. They were therefore banished beyond Rome's city limits, being laid to rest outside the built-up area of the day. Archaeologists Jon Coulston and Hazel Dodge have described how, as the centuries wore on and Rome kept on expanding, a 'bow-wave of cemeteries flowed ahead'. Many were built along the Via Appia – the Appian Way – the main route running south out of the city.

Something similar could be seen in Victorian England. London was the most striking example of this, with cemeteries springing up around the outer edges of the built-up sprawl. First, during the 1830s and early 1840s, came the 'magnificent seven' (Kensal Green, West Norwood, Highgate, Abney Park, Nunhead, Brompton and Tower Hamlets), fanning out around the then periphery of the capital in an arc that, with hindsight, can be seen as a sort of separate territory for the dead.

But this pushing outward of burials was not the result of religious belief or superstition (however sceptical modern medical science may be of some of the assumptions of the time). Rather, it was driven by what was seen as a purely rational desire to give the departed the space they needed in which to rest in civilised fashion, and to create healthier conditions for those who mourned them. At a time when the middle classes were drifting out from overcrowded city centres to settle in open and leafy suburbs, something similar was happening to their dead. The departed were no longer being crammed in cheek by jowl with generations past, but were now being given ample room in the new cemeteries, not just for themselves, but also for the magnificent monuments that were becoming *de rigueur*.

ROMAN FUNERARY RITES

The ancient Romans revered the dead, and the nobility drew inspiration from their famous ancestors. At the same time, though, they seem to have suffered serious heebie-jeebies at the thought of death. This was why the dead were allotted their own territories beyond the realms of the living: outside the city.

Whilst the dead who had been laid to rest with all the requisite rituals were worshipped as a sort of collective deity, called the di manes ('ancestral gods'), the offerings that the Romans made to them seem less loving than propitiatory, as though they feared the spirits' vengeful anger more than they hoped to please them.

It seems that the worst of all were the spirits of people who had died without the appropriate ceremonies being performed, these being fitting funerals, and also regular visits thereafter with offerings of oil and wine. (These liquid offerings were typically poured on to the ground atop the grave, but some tombs had special tubes built into them so that poured libations would pass straight down to the body beneath.) It was believed that those unfortunates who missed out on such ritual tributes following their deaths were condemned to roam the earth restlessly as ghosts. The Romans would go to just about any lengths to avoid this fate for themselves, with childless people often adopting sons so they would have someone to arrange their funerals and tend their graves.

Commuting Corpses

The establishment of suburbia was made possible by the coming of the railways, and the cobweb of commuter lines that consequently radiated from central London. What had once been far-flung village settlements were now brought into the orbit of the capital, one of these being Woking, in the depths of Surrey. And it was here, in 1854, that the Necropolis and National Museum Company opened Brookwood Cemetery, the burial facility to end all burial facilities, spilling out impressively as it did across over 2,000 acres (about 8,000 hectares) of rolling parkland. This would be enough, it was proposed, to accommodate all of London's dead in perpetuity.

For despite its Surrey setting, Brookwood was intended as a London cemetery. It had its own rail link with London, with regular services running to and from Waterloo Station. There were separate hearse cars for Church of England and Nonconformist coffins, and there were also different classes of carriages (first, second and third), so that the elite didn't have to mingle with the hoi polloi. And for the convenience of those movers and shakers who were too busy to make the trip to Surrey themselves, a mortuary chapel was built at Waterloo. You could attend a funeral service there and still slip back to the City in time for lunch, leaving the undertakers – and the train – to take the strain.

Altogether, then, Brookwood would appear to have been the ultimate suburban dream cemetery, being not so much a necropolis as a dormitory town for the dead. Like a busy banker, broker or lawyer unwinding in the garden of his suburban villa after a hard week's labours, the deceased could enjoy a sort of rural retirement at Brookwood. You could lie here in perfect peace in what appeared to be open countryside, just a short commute from the hustle and bustle of the capital.

Although the trains kept on running until 1941, in the end, the cemetery never fulfilled its founders' (admittedly ambitious) plans. The Victorians' solemnity regarding death and its rituals is widely known; less often noted, however, is the extent to which undertaking became an industry, with people taking an ever more consumerist approach to funeral arrangements that, over time, became quite shockingly fashion-focused. The essence of consumerism is choice, and the fact is that many people chose to be buried somewhere other than Brookwood. So today, although a quarter of a million people have been laid to rest at the cemetery (which remains open and in use to this day), this vast burial ground is nothing like full.

Woodland Ways

So big is Brookwood Cemetery, and so open is so much of its rolling parkland, that it can, in places, be a surprise to stumble upon a grave at all. In that way, it can be seen, at least in hindsight, as anticipating the modern trend for 'woodland burial', in which the body is laid to rest in what approximates as far as possible to a back-to-nature, wilderness setting.

For hundreds of years, the basic model for burial grounds was the garden – an artificial creation, in which culture and nature are in equipoise. Now, though, the balance has tipped decisively towards nature, however artificially such apparent woodland wildernesses have to be maintained. In part, this shift can be seen as the final triumph of a post-Romantic sensibility – all that Wordsworthian stuff about solitary walks and daffodils – that's been with us for around two hundred years.

As we've seen, the now traditional cemetery can be compared to a suburb in which graves and handsomely built and carefully maintained monuments are set out in neat and orderly rows. This has a certain dignity; there's also room to breathe; and there's a bit of greenery. But the suburb was always a compromise between urban convenience and country quietness, and it also had discontentments of its own: the need to keep up with the Joneses, for instance, along with disputes over hedges and so forth. Most of all, perhaps, it was characterised by an iron grip of respectability, of conformism. This may have been supportive for some, giving them a code by which they could order their lives. Increasingly, however – and exponentially, in the aggressively individualistic age of the baby-boomer – it came to be seen as both imprisoning and profoundly naff.

Soon, free spirits were asking themselves why they should settle for a suburban compromise in death when they could actually be laid to rest in nature's very bosom. That option became available in England in 1993, when Ken West, who had just retired as manager of Carlisle's city cemetery, received permission to start an experimental woodland-burial ground on an unused area of land. The following year, a private facility of this type was opened at Lilbourn, outside Rugby, while the United States got its first woodland-burial ground at Ramsey Creek, southern Carolina, in 1998. Today, Britain has more than two hundred such sites. Providers have their own code of practice, as well as an umbrella organisation, the Association of Natural Burial Grounds (which maintains its own website at www.naturaldeath.org.uk, should you wish to learn more). Ken West's 2010 book, *A Guide to Natural Burial,* has become the movement's indispensable reference, covering as it does every aspect of this topic, from social responsibility to digging graves and the rights and wrongs of mowing.

AT REST WITH THE ROSES

When Dame Barbara Cartland died in 2000, you might have expected that one of the world's most famous novelists and socialites to have been buried in a high-profile cemetery such as Highgate in London. In the event, she was buried simply in her own garden, beneath a tree.

Although garden burials are more usually associated with a plot on an aristocrat's country estate, it is actually possible (and surprisingly easy) to be buried on any piece of private land, including a suburban back garden. The Burials Laws Amendment Act of 1880 requires that the person's death first be registered with the Registrar of Births, Deaths and Marriages and the local authority should be notified. The body must be buried at least 30 metres from any running or standing water and at least 50 metres from any well, borehole or spring that supplies water for any use. The whereabouts of the grave should also be recorded, though planning permission for a headstone is only required if it is near a highway or is over a certain height. For more information about the rules governing garden burials, see www.naturaldeath.org.uk

Despite the relative lack of red tape involved, there are other issues that need to be taken into account if you are seriously considering a garden burial. If the house is sold, how would family be able to visit the grave? On a different note, would it even be possible to sell the house once there's a body in the back garden? And what on earth would the neighbours think?

Earth to Earth

It would be quite wrong to put the whole woodland-burial movement down to a Reggie-Perrin-type rebellion on the part of the middle class. The element of lifestyle (or 'deathstyle') choice is just a part of it. At least as important has been the enormous rise in eco-consciousness over the past two decades, with concern genuinely growing about the natural environment at the micro-level, and global warming at the macro.

And the conventional funeral industry consumes frightening amounts of materials, all of which come at a significant environmental cost. Rare hardwoods are used for prestigious coffins, for instance, and even cheaper timbers have to come from some wooded hillside somewhere; steel is required for casket frames; and concrete is needed for any vaulting. Then there's the carbon footprint that the funeral industry leaves in the form of the greenhouse gases generated by the manufacturing and transportation of coffins and other supplies. Add to all of this the insertion in the ground of human remains that, during the embalming process, have been steeped for days in chemicals that are not only environmentally harmful, but believed to be carcinogenic and thus a real and present danger for the workers involved, and it's clear that conventional burials are hardly environmentally friendly.

'All flesh is grass', says the Old Testament Book of Isaiah. For generations, this was really just a cliché: things are transitory, it meant, and not a great deal more. In recent decades, however, this dead letter has taken on an entirely new significance as we've come to see our own place in what could be a better, and simpler, ecological scheme. 'Natural burial' is now more than just a vogue, with the dead being placed in biodegradable coffins or shrouds and interred at lower depths to allow air to penetrate and facilitate the natural process of decomposition. And once our bodies have been completely composted within the earth, then yes: we may come back as blades of grass. Other green body-disposal options can be seen on pages 158 to 160.

ALL AT SEA

While none of the major religious traditions of the West has been wild about burial at sea, Orthodox Judaism prohibits it entirely (but then there is no history of Jews being among the seafaring peoples). Christianity and Islam, by contrast, although preferring land burial, acknowledge that there may sometimes be no alternative to burial at sea.

For a burial at sea, the body is first typically weighted down: iron bolts may simply be lashed to the feet or the entire body may be tied up in sailcloth or placed in a wooden casket and ballasted with bolts or shot. The ship is then generally hove-to (stopped), and special prayers are said before the body is pushed over the side and allowed to sink.

In the Royal Navy, centuries of history have led to the establishment of set traditions for sea burials, which are conducted with a certain amount of pageantry, featuring firing parties and bugle calls.

CREMATION CHOICES

Maybe you'd prefer cremation to burial. Indeed, not only is cremation generally a cleaner, greener option, but disposing of someone's ashes offers more possibilities than disposing of his or her body.

Ashes to Ashes

The understanding that we'll 'moulder' in the grave; be eaten by 'worms'; and generally decompose doesn't seem to have worried people too much in times gone by. As long as the body lay undisturbed, it could be felt, in some sense, to have kept its 'integrity', even if it had completely ceased to be in any normal sense. That it should be dismantled or destroyed by human agency was an altogether more alarming prospect, however: how would the pieces be put together again on the Last Day, when, in Judaeo–Christian belief, we must all be resurrected in order to be judged by God?

This partly explains the practice of hanging, drawing and finally 'quartering' convicted traitors in medieval, and occasionally even early modern, times. Cutting up the bodies of those found guilty of treason and displaying the different bits on sharpened stakes set up in different corners of the realm was the ultimate punishment for what was seen as the ultimate crime. Hence, too, the dread of dissection in the early days of modern medical science, and the only too real problem posed by the 'resurrectionists', or body-snatchers. This is why those that could afford to had themselves buried within safe-like iron coffins in fortified tombs, and why armed watchmen were charged with guarding many churchyards.

The same deep fear also underlay the longstanding resistance to the idea of cremation. What would the doctrine of the 'resurrection of the body' mean if that body had been reduced to dust? In some symbolic way, the body mouldering in the ground could be seen as staying intact; exposing it to fire, by contrast, seemed irreparably destructive, perhaps also suggesting hell.

Gradually, however, theological thinking and social attitudes changed (although which process drove the other is far from clear), and mainstream Christians increasingly began to move away from the idea of bodily resurrection, which was not so much a 'place', or a literal state of being, they argued, but rather a 'state of mind'. Consequently, the taboo on cremation started to lose its hold. And whilst Catholicism still officially insists that the body is resurrected, it no longer sees cremation as in any way impeding this. (It does, however, consider the dispersal of the remains as destroying the integrity of the body; ashes should be stored in an urn or another receptacle, it says, and should not be scattered. Neither should the urn be taken home, but should instead remain within the cemetery or columbarium.)

DOVECOTES OF DEATH

One point in favour of cremation is completely practical: the space that it saves (just compare the size of an urn to that of a full-sized coffin).

For all their fears about death, the Romans seem – at least in later centuries – to have been relaxed about the burial versus cremation question. It's not too difficult to understand why cremation made sense, given the burgeoning size of their empire's capital: with over a million people occupying a comparatively limited area, the arguments in favour of it are obvious. And even then, steps were taken to economise on space, with special columbaria (literally, 'dove houses') being built. These contained row upon row of little niches (or, as we'd now call them, 'pigeonholes'), in which urns containing the ashes of the dead could be placed. The remains of hundreds – and in some cases, thousands – of people could thus be housed in a limited space, but could still be easily located by any visitors wishing to renew funerary rites.

Similar structures have been built in modern times. They are generally preferred to gardens of remembrance in Catholic cemeteries because it is a Roman Catholic requirement that the ashes of the dead be kept together rather than being scattered.

Cranks and Cremation

It's tempting to wonder whether cremation would have caught on more quickly had it not been for the sheer eccentricity of so many of its pioneers. Had Dr William Price not been prepared to put his freedom – and even, arguably, his life – on the line to promote the cause of cremation in 1884, there's really no knowing when it would have become legal. At the same time, though, this self-declared descendant of druids was not necessarily the poster boy that the practice needed.

Price left it late to catch the public's attention, but catch it he most certainly did when, at the age of 83, he fathered a child by a young servant girl he'd moved into his Llantrisant home. So far, so sleazy, but the wagging tongues of mid-Glamorgan were really stopped short in shock when the doctor announced that the baby had been given the name of 'Iesu Grist'. The unfortunate infant dying soon afterwards, Price took him to the top of a hillock in Caerlan Field, close to his home, where he built a pyre and placed poor Iesu's body on it. He then proceeded to cremate the baby, to the utter outrage of the local villagers, who were only narrowly prevented from lynching Price when the police constables arrived. Price was taken off to stand trial, but, to the amazement of all, was acquitted. This effectively meant that he had made cremation legal. And when, ten years later, he himself died, he was cremated in turn in Caerlan Field.

It would be unfair to tar radical thinkers like H G Wells, Marie Stopes and Sigmund Freud with the same brush as the frankly loopy William Price. At the same time, though, cremation was long associated with writers, artists, actors and other 'bohemians'. Indeed, a procession of the famous-named deceased has passed through the crematorium at Golders Green, north London, in the decades since it opened its furnace doors for the first time in 1902. Some of those who have been cremated saw an important principle at stake. When he died in 1970, the philosopher Bertrand Russell, for example, was cremated at Colwyn Bay, in North Wales. He had insisted that there should be no ceremony of any sort after his death. For him to have been buried would have been seeming to endorse what he considered the mumbo jumbo that he'd spent his life attacking. Instead, he wanted his ashes simply to be scattered, as though he'd never existed.

THE TIBETAN SKY BURIAL

The Bön religion of Tibet has the same sense of *samsara*, or death and rebirth, as the great Indian creeds, and so also the same easy acceptance of the body as being entirely disposable after death. Up here on the 'roof of the world', there's very little in the way of wood, though, and anything there is can hardly be spared for burning bodies; in addition, the soil is only a few inches deep, making burial impractical. Hence the tradition of the *jhator*, or 'sky burial', in which bodies are left on rocky outcrops for the vultures, which come down to deal with the dead in nature's way.

America's Lakota Sioux people traditionally took a broadly similar approach to disposing of their dead, even though there was no shortage of timber in their case (in fact, they laid out the bodies on platforms fixed high up in the trees). And in Zoroastrian belief, dead bodies are unclean and should not come into contact with either earth or fire (fire being sacred in the Zoroastrian tradition). Bodies were therefore traditionally placed atop 'towers of silence', where birds and the elements would consume everything but the bones. The bones would then be removed and placed in ossuaries.

A BURNING QUESTION

Why is it that cremation was so hard for the modern Western world to come to terms with, yet so easily accepted by the great religions of Indian antiquity? In Hinduism, Buddhism, Sikhism and Jainism, cremation is considered essential after death. Ideally, it is conducted outdoors, so that the soul can be carried off by the rising smoke.

Judaism, Christianity and Islam, the three great monotheistic creeds of the modern era, are also monomortal: they believe that we die just once before embarking on an afterlife. So it was natural enough that, historically, despite drawing a clear distinction between the 'body' and the 'soul', they believed that our physical forms were somehow 'us'. That being the case, it was felt that these forms should not be destroyed by human agency, but should instead be allowed to decompose naturally, in their own way.

In the Indian tradition, however, it is assumed that each soul is likely to keep coming back in repeated reincarnations, in human or animal shape, in a usually never-ending sequence of samsara: death and rebirth. That being the case, the living body is just something that we are 'passing through': once we die, it has no further relevance to the soul. The practice of cremation is perfectly logical, then, because it banishes the body altogether: it is the integrity of the soul – with its successive reincarnations – that has to be preserved.

Keeping It Clean

Some people embraced the idea of cremation for what might be described as aesthetic motives. Their distaste for burial may have been less clearly articulated than by people of principle like Bertrand Russell, but was just as strong. The early to mid-twentieth century was hygiene-obsessed: germ theory was not only understood, but had been emphatically taken on board. Technological advances had only heightened people's concerns, as well as setting higher standards for personal hygiene and housekeeping. More and more people consequently had baths and lavatories in their homes; they were, moreover, also being bombarded with ads for vacuum cleaners and for white goods – fridges, washing machines and cookers – run by 'clean' electric power. To this mindset, fire suddenly seemed akin to a purgative and therefore a good thing. And for many people, the fear of their bodies being burned away was now as nothing beside the dread of being laid in the dirt and damp of the ground and becoming a gooey mess as their dead bodies suddenly became 'alive' with bacteria.

The new sensibility was therefore starting to see cremation as the clean and modern option for body disposal. It was 'streamlined'; it was manageable; it dispensed with mess; and it was also exciting.

GOING OUT WITH A BANG TO THE FINAL FRONTIER

When Joanna Booth's husband, James (a vintage-shotgun expert), died in 2004, she had his ashes loaded into 275 shotgun shells and blessed by a Church of Scotland minister. Then she and her husband's friends went out shooting on a Scottish estate. The late Mr Booth now holds what must be a one-day record for a deceased person: 70 partridges, 23 pheasants, 7 ducks and 1 fox.

Star Trek creator Gene Rodenberry also went out with a bang when his ashes were launched into orbit in 1997. By 2004, the capsule's orbit had deteriorated, and the capsule then burned up on re-entering the earth's atmosphere. But like the many spin-offs of his original work, Rodenberry will return to space, for more of his ashes will be going into orbit in 2012.

Spread a Little Happiness

Cremation was exciting in another, much more important and positive way than simply being a modern and efficient method of body disposal, in that it offered wholly new possibilities for self-expression after death. For while some people preferred to have their urns buried in cemeteries (or in the specially landscaped memorial gardens that were becoming increasingly common), others wanted their ashes scattered in particular places that had significance for them. Places where they'd loved to walk with their families; places where they'd holidayed year after year; places where they'd met their partners or become engaged.

Alfred Wainwright, the walker and writer who'd done so much to interest people in the beauties of the Lakeland fells, for instance, had his ashes scattered on his favourite mountain, Haystacks, above Buttermere. The fashion designer Alexander McQueen, who committed suicide in 2010, left instructions that his ashes should be scattered on the Isle of Skye, which he considered his ancestral home. Although London-born and celebrated in Paris, Milan, New York and elsewhere, McQueen felt a close attachment to the Scottish island, making this clear with this final wish. And after Norman 'Phil Archer' Painting passed away in 2009, his ashes were scattered in a Warwickshire wood that had been planted in his honour. In real life, the actor had been vice president of the Tree Council, so this was a way of honouring his enthusiasm and work. By contrast, Roy Hughes, a railway engineer whose ambition had been to build an underground loop linking Liverpool's mainline stations, creating a fully integrated system, had his ashes placed within a subway wall at Liverpool's Moorfields Station after his death in 1994. 'He was born and he died within sight and sound of the Railway', says the plaque that commemorates his life there, where his remains still lie.

Ashes can be easily divided up, too. In April 2010, more than half a century after he had conquered Mount Everest, some of Sir Edmund Hillary's ashes were taken back to the Himalayas. The mountaineer had died two years before that, and while most of his ashes were tipped into the sea off the coast of New Zealand, his beloved homeland, some were kept back to be sprinkled on Everest's upper slopes. And a gonzo to the last, journalist Hunter S Thompson had his ashes placed in a rocket that then blasted off to send his remains into space.

Ashes are often sprinkled on to running water. This is a requirement of the traditional Indian religions (for Hindus, it should ideally be the sacred river, the Ganges), but it's something that seems to strike a chord with Western humanists as well. Whilst many people would like their ashes to be scattered at sea, others prefer favourite rivers, lakes and streams.

'THANK YOU FOR NOT SCATTERING'

The Environment Agency has issued a code of conduct for those with loved ones' ashes to scatter, as follows.

- Don't scatter ashes on mountain summits. If you must leave ashes in these places, then bury them.
- Don't scatter ashes on rivers, close to known fishing or bathing spots or buildings.

- Don't pour ashes from a bridge above water used by canoes or boats.
- Don't scatter ashes anywhere under a kilometre upstream of where water is extracted for drinking. If you don't know, take what steps you can to find out.
- Don't leave plastic wreaths floating on water or on riverbanks: your heartfelt tribute is someone else's litter.
- Don't scatter ashes in windy conditions, where they're going to blow up and affect people who live or work nearby. For the same reason, always sprinkle the ashes from as close as possible to the ground or water surface.

For the most part, ashes' etiquette isn't so different from any other kind of etiquette. All that's really required are common sense and the imagination to see other people's points of view.

Keeping Company

'That's Beatrice, you know', the socialist Sidney Webb would say to horrified visitors at his home in Passfield, Suffolk, as he pointed to the urn of ashes on the mantelpiece in his living room. Always a team in life, as husband and wife, the founders of the Fabian Society would ultimately be buried together in their own back garden. But while Sidney still lived, Beatrice remained with him in their house.

More recently, it's become possible to have your loved one's ashes transformed into glass or incorporated into other materials that can then be fashioned into ornaments, or into jewellery that can be worn on the person at all times. While this may seem macabre and morbid to some, to others, it may offer the prospect of priceless continuing contact with a deceased loved one.

Post-Mortem Manners

So is the world our ashes' oyster? Up to a point, perhaps. The possibilities are pretty amazing, that's for sure. Whereas you're boxed up in a confined space for burial, when your ashes are scattered, in a sense you're free (well, at least your inert ashes are) to inscribe yourself into a beloved place or piece of landscape, rather like a graffiti artist's tag that no one has to see.

But your options aren't limitless: there are places where you shouldn't scatter ashes, and other places where it may be alright on some occasions, but not on others. And however strong your sentimental motives may be, they shouldn't be seen as somehow trumping others' needs. Being dead is no excuse for bad manners.

Sometimes, it's a question of degree. It was fine for Alfred Wainwright to have his ashes scattered on his favourite mountain, but what happens when the remains of the two-hundredth walker are thrown across the top of a popular peak like Snowdon? One consideration is that high phosphate concentrations in human ash change the nature of the soil, encouraging the growth of some plants and suppressing others, and consequently overturning the natural balance in highly delicate eco-systems.

And when so many Liverpool Football Club fans want their ashes scattered on the Anfield turf, how is the club going to keep the pitch halfway decent? All flesh may be grass, but as we've seen, human ashes play havoc with growing plants. The American musician (and baseball fan) Meat Loaf announced as early as 2006 that he had plans in place for his ashes to be scattered from a helicopter across the diamond in the Yankee Stadium in the Bronx. He freely acknowledged that what he intended doing was illegal, and refused to name the helicopter charter firm that had agreed to take on the task. This sort of egotism is, well, egotistical, especially when the institutions concerned are often happy enough to meet us halfway. When it moved to a new stadium at Eastlands, Manchester City Football Club opened a memorial garden, for instance, where fans can lie in perpetuity with their fellow sky-blues.

Moving from one type of hallowed turf to another: in 2008, staff at the Jane Austen's House Museum at Chawton, Hampshire, had to ask visitors not to bring human ashes, heaps of which they were finding in the gardens, not biodegrading and looking unsightly. If, as is illustrated by these cases, our ashes are going to compromise the character of the places that we so love, then it's hard to see what the advantage is of them being scattered there.

There are other factors to be considered as well. While it's an offence to drop anything on private property, a sprinkling of ashes on a cliff top or in a corner of a field may not matter much. Yet sometimes it may, for reasons that you can't yet envisage. In any case, private land can be sold for development, so that a fondly remembered coastal walk may end up being covered with caravans or chalets, while a football team may move to a new stadium, outside town. And where would your scattered ashes be left then?

Resomation, Cryomation and Other Green Options

People who live their lives with an awareness of green issues are usually keen to discover fresh applications for their eco-values. On every front, from domestic recycling to business processes, those who want to live a planet-friendly life tend to embrace the opportunity to follow best practice as soon as it becomes a practical possibility. And many are therefore considering green body-disposal options.

Commonplace burial practices may seem innocuous, but their carbon impact can often come as a surprise. Cremation – currently the preferred body-disposal option of 75 per cent of UK residents – had, by the late twentieth century, come to be seen as the modern, 'cleaner' route. The UK Carbon Trust refuted this myth, however, by flagging up how traditional cremations are harming our environment. Its report, published in 2010, pointed out that every cremation results in the release into the atmosphere of close on 150 kg of carbon dioxide (CO_2). Given that around 600,000 people die in the UK per annum, that adds up to a lot of CO_2 – 72,000 metric tonnes each year, which translates globally into 6,840,000 metric tonnes from an average annual death count of around 56,000,000. These statistics show why the subject is starting to be taken seriously. Indeed, there never was a more obvious application of the old Friends of the Earth mantra, 'Think globally, act locally'.

Of at least as much concern are the toxic chemicals created by cremations, a subject that has come under very little scrutiny until recently. Now research has shown that 1 cubic metre of crematorium emissions contain around 200 micrograms of mercury, from dental fillings, as well as dioxins and other environmental pollutants. In fact, around 30 per cent of mercury emissions globally can be attributed to this source. The UK government's response has been to bring in new legislation making it mandatory for UK crematoria to install mercury filters by 2012.

Greener alternatives to cremation lie just around the corner. The technique of resomation, pioneered by a Glasgow company of the same name, by which a body is decomposed, results in less than half the CO_2 emissions of a cremation. The process involves the use of sodium hydroxide heated in a gas-fired steam boiler to a temperature of 180°C (356°F). Resomation has been endorsed by a number of US states, and looks like becoming available in the UK before too long, particularly once an understanding of its green benefits has spread and demand consequently rises.

Cryomation is emerging as another strong contender for the title of one of the most eco-friendly techniques for body disposal. Here, a freeze-drying process involving liquid nitrogen is used that renders the body brittle, allowing metals to be removed (and, potentially, recycled). The Carbon Trust's analysis of this procedure shows that its carbon footprint totals around 100 kg, which includes transporting the liquid nitrogen. The powdery remains can then be buried, scattered, or even used as fertiliser. But as Ian Hanson, a forensic archaeologist at Bournemouth University, remarked in a New Scientist article on the eco-ethics of body disposal: 'Space would not be an issue if the powder was put to use, but is our society ready for our mortal remains to be used as fertiliser or harrowed into crop fields?'

A more conventional and simpler option adopted by a company in Melbourne, Australia, has been to offer 'upright burial' within a biodegradable bag in a cylindrical hole about 60 cm (2 ft) wide and 3 m (10 ft) deep, with a tree being planted on nearby Mount Elephant to 'offset the carbon footprint in the collection, storage and delivery of the body to the cemetery'. Other options that have been suggested include upright burial around the base of trees or a tree being planted on each burial site. The thought of entering into an intimate symbiotic relationship with such a beautiful life form as a tree holds a certain attractions.

DIAMONDS (AND TITANIUM) ARE FOREVER

If you want your mortal remains to become immortal, why not have your ashes transformed into a diamond? LifeGem Created Diamonds (www.lifegem-uk.com) specialises in creating diamonds from deceased people's ashes (although they can alternatively use a lock of hair if you prefer), using the same techniques of carbon collection, heat and pressure with which other synthetic diamonds are made. The company offers the same service for pets, too (a case of man's best friend being turned into a girl's best friend?)

You could even have your body recycled – or your 'spare parts', anyway. OrthoMetals, a Dutch company, recycles metal implants, such as hips, from cremated human remains, and the metal is used to make anything from cars to wind turbines.

TO INFINITY... AND BEYOND!

It may sound extreme, but perhaps the ultimate solution to green body disposal has been proposed by artist Jae Rhim Lee, who suggests that our bodies should be eaten after death by mushrooms!

Fungi usually grow on wood and decaying forest material but, as part of her Infinity Burial Project, Lee had the idea of training mushroom species to break down human remains instead, by feeding them on her own discarded body tissue, such as hair, nails and skin. The artist has even invented a 'Mushroom Death Suit' - a cotton body suit that is embedded with spores of the new species of Infinity Mushroom - which transforms the deceased into a 'Decompinaut'.

Although her method has not been perfected, she has argued that it is more environmentally friendly than popular funeral practices and would help us embrace our own inevitable demise and decay, thus helping society to get over its death denial.

PRESERVATION?

For some, the prospect of any form of decay and disposal is completely intolerable, perhaps because they believe that after their demise, scientists could devise new routes to eternity here on earth − or maybe simply because they can't come to terms with their mortality. Eccentric as these ideas undoubtedly are, and unhealthy on many levels, there are people who, for a fee, can help you pursue such goals.

Chilly Prospects

There are those whose faith in science is such that they live in the 'sure and certain hope of the Resurrection to eternal life' − not in heaven, but on earth. As well as arguably having more money than sense, believers in 'cryonics' believe that they can be flash-frozen at the moment of death, and then kept intact until they are restored to life at some future point when the medical technology exists to keep them alive indefinitely.

If its supporters are right, a body subjected to cryonics doesn't have a final resting place, but is instead resting in long-term cold storage. The theory is that by maintaining the body at a super-low temperature − −196°C (−385°F) − the body can be preserved until medicine is sufficiently advanced to heal whatever problem resulted in the person's legal death. According to leading cryonics company Alcor (www.alcor.org), an individual is not completely dead until their brain is incapable of restoring their memories, personality and all of the information stored in the brain that makes a person who they are. Alcor is a bit sensitive about the popular notion that it 'freezes heads': instead, it says, it uses a neuropreservation option that focuses on preserving the brain, which is where our individuality, our personhood, resides.

Improbable? Perhaps. But how many times, supporters ask, has medicine made astonishing breakthroughs? And what new scientific revolutions are in store now that we've cracked the secrets of DNA? It's hard to argue with this point of view, given the incredible strides that have certainly been made, even if one can't help feeling that the defeat of death may be a frontier too far.

Yet however absurd it may seem, cryonics seems sensible beside the suggestion that we can conquer death by cloning ourselves anew. That we may be able to reproduce our physical bodies this way hardly seems like sci-fi any more, but in what sense would a clone be 'us'? Identical another body may conceivably be, but it would not be the same. And in any case, 'we' are surely the sum of our genetic inheritance, and also of our experiences in life, including the telling-off we got from a teacher in primary school, our first kiss, our disappointing GCSE results and our weekend in Paris in 2003.

DEATH ON DISPLAY

While most people – in the UK, at least – are embalmed after their death before being removed from others' sight forever, some embalmed bodies are intended to be viewed in perpetuity. The most famous example is that of Vladimir Lenin, the Russian statesman who died in 1924. Lenin's embalmed body still rests in state in Moscow, where it undergoes constant maintenance to ensure that it remains well preserved.

Become a Mummy

At the time of writing, Summum (www.summum.org) is the only company in the world that offers to mummify your body. This US outfit will perform a 'mummification of transference' rite on your remains, this apparently being a blend of mysticism and chemistry that will, it is said, preserve you for all eternity.

The process involves immersing the body in a chemical bath (it is unclear what the chemicals in the bath are, although it is claimed that some are used in genetic engineering), before wrapping it in layers of gauze and silk and covering it with a polymer and then a fibreglass resin. Next, the mummy is taken to a pyramid, where the rites of transference are continued. Afterwards, the body is placed in a coffin, which is filled with a mixture of amber resin and quartz crystals before being welded shut, the mummy inside now being all set for eternity.

Summum claims that the mummification that it performs is the only permanent form of body preservation, which may explain way the process results in a bill fit for a pharaoh: it costs $67,000, not including the cost of the mummiform coffin.

RESTING ASSURED

When it comes to what happens to your body after your death, the important thing, as ever, is to think ahead, and to talk it through with those who are going to be your mourners. What practical considerations may there be? What financial constraints can you envisage? Is your heart's desire realistic? And if not, can any sort of compromise be found?

It may be that these questions answer themselves: you may have a spot in your village churchyard already earmarked; or you may want to join your partner or parents in a particular cemetery. If you do have such arrangements in place, make sure that you know where any relevant paperwork is, and that your loved ones or executors know, too.

If you're the prospective deceased, then this is your gig, and it's you who gets to decide what you want. But you should also consider how far your choices will suit those likely to survive you. If your ashes are to be scattered on the shores of Islay, for instance, do you mind that your family may not often make it up there to 'see' you? You won't know whether they do or not, of course, and you may well feel that none of this makes any difference anyway: when you're dead, you're dead, and that's all there is to say about it. Yet there are still practicalities to be decided, however dispassionate you may feel about your death, and however low-key you want the arrangements arising from it to be.

You should recognise, too, not only that you yourself may not always feel the same way that you do now, but also that others around you may want regular access to a place where they can 'visit' you, especially to help them through the grieving process. Again, the more you can talk things through, the better it will be all round. With a bit of imagination, sympathy and give and take, it should be possible to come up with a lasting solution that makes the thought of death and bodily disposal, if not quite appealing, then at least not quite as daunting.

Chapter Five
IN MEMORIAM:
HOW DO YOU WANT

TO BE REMEMBERED?

We shouldn't really want to be remembered after we're dead: we shouldn't be so narcissistic. Why should those who love us have to have their grief prolonged? As for those who don't, why should they be reminded of us? And what use is it going to be to us once we're dead anyway?

Rationally, we understand that we're not going to know whether or not others remember us. So surely it's better for us to be forgotten? Shakespeare put it beautifully in his Sonnet 7:

> *No longer mourn for me when I am dead*
> *Than you shall hear the surly sullen bell*
> *Give notice to the world that I am fled*
> *From this vile world, with vilest worms to dwell.*

Yet there's something that doesn't smell quite right here, and it's not the worms, unpleasant as the thought of them may be. Rather, it's the odour of sanctity. Could anyone truly be this unselfish? The gentleman doth protest too much, perhaps. Let's read on:

> *Nay, if you should read this line, remember not*
> *The hand that writ it; for I love you so*
> *That I in your sweet thoughts would be forgot,*
> *If thinking on me then should make you woe . . .*

And there we have it, unmistakably: almost four hundred years before the term was in common usage, passive-aggressive behaviour cringes and manipulates its way on to the stage. Of course we're going to read it and not remember the hand that wrote it; of course Shakespeare wanted his reader to forget him – a likely story.

But then immortal memory is an odd thing. In sonnet after sonnet, Shakespeare writes about how the young man he's addressing is going to live forever in his lines. So it's strange that within only a few years no one had any real idea as to the young man's identity (it's a debate that rages furiously to this day). And then there's Keats, whose epitaph famously reads 'Here lies one whose name is writ in water', and yet everyone knows that it's him lying there. Although the young Romantic poet's name wasn't actually 'writ' on his gravestone in Rome, his friends knew that his fame was such that it didn't need to be. What mattered was the mark that he'd made in life, albeit as yet with only a small group of readers. But then they were in no danger of forgetting who he was.

GOING OUT IN STYLE

While most humans have been laid in nondescript, forgettable final resting places during the course of history, some have had considerably more fuss made over their bodies. The ancient Egyptian Great Pyramid of Giza is probably the most famous tomb in the world, but others are equally impressive.

Another of the Seven Wonders of the Ancient World, the tomb of Mausolus, king of Caria, at Halicarnassus, has given us the word 'mausoleum', meaning a large, grand tomb. Qin Shi Huang, the first emperor of China, lies undisturbed in his tomb in the world's largest underground mausoleum, surrounded by his terracotta army. India's Taj Mahal, in Agra, is the mausoleum of Mumtaz Mahal; it was built by her grieving husband, the Mughal emperor Shah Jahan. The former North Korean dictator Kim Jong-il had the entire presidential palace in Pyongyang turned into a mausoleum so that his embalmed body could be displayed next to his father's.

Each of these tombs was constructed specifically for the individual that lies within it, but some equally stunning buildings also host tombs. Rome's Pantheon, the Vatican City's St Peter's Basilica and London's Westminster Abbey are all are home to the great, and sometimes also to the good.

A FITTING MEMORIAL

Thinking about how you'd like to be remembered after your death is much more fun than thinking about dying. What would your epitaph be? If you're opting for burial, what should your headstone look like? Would you like to be remembered in a certain place, or through the use of a combined memorial and gift to a community group? Or maybe you'd like money to be donated in your memory to a chosen charity? You won't usually have a say in them, but death notices and obituaries are also forms of memorials, as are the memories of the deceased that friends and acquaintances often share with bereaved families in letters of condolence.

Here Lies . . . All Lies?

A craze for comic epitaphs swept the English-speaking world during the eighteenth century, and many of the leading poets of the period queued up to try their hand at them. John Gay hit the requisite note of rueful waggishness in the epitaph that he scripted for himself:

Life is a jest and all things show it
I thought so once but now I know it.

His friend, Alexander Pope, wrote Gay a witty epitaph as well:

Well then, poor G— lies underground!
So there's an end to honest Jack.
So little justice here he found,
'Tis ten to one, he'll ne'er come back.

In the event, though, neither of them was used. People still preferred their epitaphs to be a bit more serious, although Pope managed to combine wit with reverence in his thoughts on scientist Sir Isaac Newton, who died in 1727:

Nature and nature's laws lay hid in night;
God said 'Let Newton be' and all was light.

But the death of a young couple at Stanton Harcourt, Oxfordshire, on being struck by lightning in the course of a thunderstorm, found the poet striking an irreverent, even ribald, vein:

> *Here lie two young lovers, who had the mishap*
> *Tho very chaste People, to die of a Clap.*

This one was strictly for circulation among his friends, though, and Pope also wrote a far more respectful, 'official' version, which was actually used to commemorate the pair.

We are starting to see something of a pattern here. The 'epitaph', although supposedly written specifically to be inscribed on the subject's headstone, was fast becoming a free-floating phenomenon. Indeed, many of the most famous epitaphs written in this, and succeeding, centuries were never destined for a grave. The result was what amounted to a literary genre, and to this day, it seems that every anthology of comic verse to be published comes with its own little section on epitaphs. This is fair enough: many are wonderfully quirky and amusing, and it's always nice to have the chance to laugh at something as frightening as death. Surf the web awhile, though, and you'll find apparently endless quantities of these comic epitaphs, with the same ones cropping up over and over again, often in the same sequence and with the same framing text – transmitted virally, like so much knowledge on the net. You'll also find that, for the most part, there's very little photographic evidence for these epitaphs' existence. And whilst it's true that many gravestones end up being lost and damaged, it's hard to avoid the suspicion that a great many of these sallies were never actually set in stone.

Most of the actual epitaphs that we do see are solemn, and although some are undoubtedly bleakly funny, it isn't always certain that the humour is intentional. From a tomb outside the kirk in Durness, Highland, comes this celebrated example, for instance:

Here doth lye the bodie
Of John Flyne, who did die
By a stroke from a sky-rocket,
Which hit him in the eye-socket.

Yet these verses often appear to have been composed by an unsophisticated writer, and in an English that is no longer our own. How can we tell if they are bleakly witty or just inept?

Some people are lifelong clowns, of course, and they'll crack their jokes come what may. Like the one-time Goon Spike Milligan, who died in 2002, and, at his own request, was interred in the churchyard of St Thomas's, Winchelsea. His chosen epitaph was 'I told you I was ill', but a killjoy cleric wouldn't let him have this on his headstone, and his family was forced to settle for the blander 'Love, Light, Peace' instead. The offending line was still smuggled in, however, to be hidden in plain sight in Irish (*Dúirt mé leat go raibh mé breoite*). Now everyone's happy: Spike gets to enjoy his eternal rest sleeping with a smile, while his English-speaking neighbours can slumber on unaffronted.

LET MY WORDS BE MY EPITAPH

The last words that you speak don't have to be your final message to posterity. For those that sum up your life will be your epitaph. So why not enjoy planning them in advance lest someone else gets to choose what goes on your memorial? Here are some notable examples of epitaphs inscribed on people's headstones.

HURRAY, NO MORE COUNCIL TAX

Brian Cawley

HERE IS EDWARD I, HAMMER OF THE SCOTS

King Edward I of England

MAN MUST ENDURE HIS GOING HENCE

Writer C S Lewis

HE LIES HERE, SOMEWHERE

Werner Heisenberg, the physicist responsible for
quantum theory's uncertainty principle

HERE LIES THE BODY OF RICHARD HIND
WHO WAS NEITHER INGENIOUS, SOBER, NOR KIND

Richard Hind

MURDERED BY A TRAITOR AND A COWARD
WHOSE NAME IS NOT WORTHY TO APPEAR HERE

The outlaw Jesse James, by his mother

174517

Writer Primo Levi (his epitaph was his Auschwitz number)

ROB ROY MACGREGOR, DESPITE THEM ALL

Scottish outlaw Rob Roy MacGregor, whose family name had been banned

GOOD FRIEND, FOR JESUS SAKE FORBEARE
TO DIG THE DUST ENCLOSÈD HERE.
BLESSED BE YE MAN THAT SPARES THESE STONES,
AND CURST BE HE THAT MOVES MY BONES

William Shakespeare (who is still resting peacefully)

LÚTHIEN. BEREN.

Writer and academic J R R Tolkien and his wife, Edith Tolkien
(FROM TOLKIEN'S STORY, THE TALE OF BEREN AND LÚTHIEN)

I TOLD YOU SO, YOU DAMNED FOOLS

Writer H G Wells

TOMORROW, I SHALL NO LONGER BE HERE

Nostradamus, the French author of a book of prophecies,
correctly foreseeing his death

SHE DID IT THE HARD WAY

Screen icon Bette Davis

Set in Stone

If you are going to have a headstone (or a memorial tablet in a church or elsewhere) – and there's no reason why you shouldn't – the wording can be as simple as you like. Indeed, less may well be more: you don't have a duty to entertain posterity (and even if you try to, there's no guarantee that it'll get the joke). A gravestone's look is also likely to be at least as important as any wording.

So what material do you want your headstone to be made from: marble or granite? And what colour? Just a headstone, standing at the 'head' of the grave, or a horizontal slab or 'kerb-set' stone? (Remember that you can also have smaller versions of any of these for buried ashes.) How about the shape (marble, in particular, can be elaborately carved)? Would you like a picture or design to be incorporated? (Inset photo-portraits have been introduced for gravestones in recent years; for some, they provide a much-needed sense of personality to an otherwise relatively anonymous grave; to others, they appear to be in quite excruciating taste.) In theory, you can also have sculpted reliefs or freestanding figures on your grave, ranging from angels through animals to cartoon characters. (Again, beware: this is a potential minefield because people really do differ in their tastes, and this sort of thing can provoke reactions of violent dislike. Commissioning such a memorial sculpture is therefore not something to be embarked on unthinkingly.)

As ever, it's important to think of those who'll be mourning you, and to talk to them to find out what their feelings are. When we consider questions of death and dying, we constantly seem to learn that issues that would seem to be about us are, in fact, as much about others. Certainly, once you've died, 'your' memorial will mainly be for those who survive you. Not only will it be their link with you, it will also, increasingly, be the means by which they characterise you and what you meant to the world at large. You, of course, will be well past caring by then: whether you've slipped into dark oblivion or have entered eternal life in another world, you'll no longer be concerned with managing your image in this one.

FLYING HIGH: THE SHAMAN

In many older cultural traditions, the question of commemorating the dead does not arise. How could it, when they're assumed to be there, still living all around us? Ancestors, it is believed, are a continuing influence upon our lives, for good or for ill, according to their mood. Mortals attempt to keep them sweet with ceremonies and offerings, also appealing to them for assistance and advice.

They contact their ancestors through the medium of the shaman, a holy man (or woman) who journeys to the spirit dimension on their behalf. Typically, shamans do this in a trance, brought on by furious ritual dancing and/or drumming, perhaps artificially boosted by the use of some naturally occurring, psychoactive drug. Siberian shamans traditionally used entheogen, from the fly-agaric mushroom, for example, while in Mesoamerica, it was the peyote cactus. Whipped up into a frenzy, the shaman would then take figurative flight and travel to the world beyond, whence he or she would return with instructions for herbal cures, guidance for hunting ventures or thoughts on crops or livestock issues.

NOT YOUR AVERAGE TOMBSTONE . . .

When asked to describe a graveyard, most of us would probably come up with a similar vision: lines of headstones with sombre epitaphs amid manicured lawns, or rows of memorials within a memorial garden. Yet quite a few individuals have had rather more unusual, more memorable memorials, like Paul Lind, whose tombstone in Portland, Oregon, features a Scrabble mosaic (the designer even included blank tiles). The Knights of Malta also went in for equally elaborate, if less cheerful, tombstones: in Valletta's St John's Co-Cathedral, hundreds of knights await Judgement Day within marble tombs bearing realistic portraits of skeletons. And the entire cemetery of Chichicastenango, Guatemala, appears the opposite of the traditional, solemn cemetery of our imagination. Indeed, its brightly painted tombs feature architecture that is more suited to a cheery, sixteenth-century village than a necropolis. But the prize for the most bizarre monument probably goes to that of Gerard Barthelemy, in Paris' famous Montparnasse cemetery. For Barthelemy's tomb features several exotic plants and a large, reddish bird (which appears to be a roseate spoonbill), all carved in stone.

In Them-Oriam?

You could have an epitaph or gravestone to be remembered by, but don't have to, or even a memorial of any kind, for that matter. If, like so many people these days, you're thinking of being cremated and of having your ashes scattered somewhere, that place itself could then be your memorial, as long as those you love associate it with you. (As Sir Christopher Wren's epitaph in London's St Paul's Cathedral says, *Si monumentum requiris, circumspice:* 'If you seek his monument, look around'.) The same applies if you (or your ashes) are buried in your garden or a public natural burial ground, although it might be nice for your family or loved ones to plant a tree to remember you by. Not that it has to be a tree, of course, or, indeed, any other living thing, although the symbolism would be appropriate if it were a growing plant.

Another type of memorial that's been tried and tested over generations is the endowment of a bench in a park, or some other public patch of green or location with a view. A bench would certainly assure you of a place at the very heart of community life. By day, it could be used by mums or dads out with their toddlers, or by oldsters out for a stroll; by night, it could be sat on by smooching couples. Bear in mind that not all of the uses that it's put to might be quite as edifying as you would wish, though: key beneficiaries may be gaggles of teenagers handing around vodka or cheap cider, for instance. But then you may shrug your shoulders and take the view that all human life is then represented, and in any case, you're only young once (as you yourself should be ideally placed to know by the time you're contemplating death).

But why stop at a bench? Depending on how you're fixed financially, you might want to give a piano to your local primary school, for example, or a pool table to the youth club; or how about a water-cooler for a community centre or a hospice lobby? Even a far smaller combined memorial and gift is likely to be gladly accepted at a time when all of our public services are starved of cash. Obviously, when you endow something for public use, you'll be expecting it to be used, unlike a marble plaque that will endure for centuries (rather than it being a case of *in* me-*moriam*, your memorial could be described as *in* them-*oriam*). Indeed, for many of us, it's likely to matter more that we'll still be making a continuing contribution to the life of our community when we're gone, and that our surviving loved ones have the comfort of knowing that, too.

THE BASRA MEMORIAL WALL

In 2006, British Army engineers built a brick wall in Basra, Iraq, as a memorial to the 179 Britons who had died on combat operations in Iraq since 2003, each being commemorated with a brass plaque fixed to the wall. The Basra Memorial Wall was subsequently dismantled and rebuilt in England as it had been in Iraq, albeit covered in marble to protect the original mud bricks from the destructive effects of the damp British weather. It now stands in the National Memorial Arboretum in Staffordshire

www.thenma.org.uk.

SKULLS AND BONES

The world's largest ossuary (technically, a container or place in which bones are buried) is the famous Paris catacombs. As Paris grew and its cemeteries filled, officials decided that the bones of the deceased should be moved into old quarries beneath the city.

And as construction progressed, they realised that if the bones were arranged carefully, they could create a popular tourist site.

One of the most stunning collections of bones is at the Sedlec Ossuary in the Czech Republic. After a thirteenth-century century abbot brought back soil from the Holy Land and sprinkled it over the cemetery of Sedlec's Cistercian monastery, it became a popular place for burial. As in Paris, the cemetery eventually ran out of space, however. The exhumation and removal of the skeletons to a nearby chapel began during the sixteenth century, but it was not until 1870 that a local carpenter arranged the bones into the patterns that can be seen today. The centrepiece is a massive chandelier that contains at least one of each type of bone in the human body.

While the catacombs were intended for tourists, and the Sedlec Ossuary was meant to inspire meditation on the transitory nature of life, the Skull Tower in Serbia was built to inspire terror, but is now a memorable memorial. Following an unsuccessful Serbian uprising against the Ottoman Empire in 1809, Ottoman soldiers placed the skulls of 952 Serbs on a tower to warn the local population of the consequences of rebellion. Most of the skulls were later removed for burial, so that in 1892, when a memorial was built to protect the remaining skulls, there were only fifty-eight left. Today, the Skull Tower stands as a monument to the Serbs who fell in their battle against the Ottoman oppressors.

An Electronic Afterlife

We saw in the introduction to this book (see page 18) that some people are uploading 'last wills and testaments' of a sort to Youtube and other websites, and that these personal online testaments can go far beyond divvying up property and possessions: indeed, there can be a corner of cyberspace that is forever you. There's lots more scope for imaginative thinking here, too: could your Facebook wall become a memorial, for instance? Tribute and memorial pages on social-networking websites like Facebook are becoming increasingly common. However, a tribute page is not immune from the rows, insensitivity and even hate that freely erupts on the web, and there have been instances, for example, of distressing comments and photographs being posted on tribute pages for dead children. Police advice is consequently either not to set up such tribute pages or else to make them private (such as on Facebook, where memorial pages are only open to people that have been confirmed as 'friends'; see also page 192).

Alternatively could you organise a tribute page for someone you've loved and know that others will miss after his or her death? Or do you have enough material (and aptitude) to establish a memorial website? If not, but you'd like to endure online – or, perhaps more likely (unless you're something of a narcissist), to commemorate a loved one – various companies now offer such services, many of them at relatively reasonable prices. Either you could have your own website designed specially for you, for example, or you could have your own niche in what amounts to an e-columbarium, where your portrait, family photos, biography, favourite poems and thoughts – whatever you like – are displayed.

In a digital development of the old idea of the death notice, a lot of local newspapers similarly now allow you to create and customise your own 'remembrance album' on their websites. Again, you can choose the words and photos that you want to upload and have a say in any soundtrack and other effects that may feature on it. And once it's been established, your friends and loved ones can access your online memorial and maybe light virtual candles or make commemorative comments.

Sometimes inspired by the film *P.S. I Love You* (2007), people are increasingly considering leaving posthumous messages for their friends and family (and possibly their enemies, too). Because the writing of letters has fallen out of fashion, services have sprung up to fill the gap offering to send e-mails to anyone you specify after your death – for a fee, of course. Such systems often rely on a set of advisors, as well as contact with you, to ensure that your messages are not released while you're still alive. Moreover, your message is not sent directly to a recipient: rather, they receive an e-mail notifying them that you have left a message and instructions on how to access it.

If you know that your end is near, arranging to send a final letter, or a birthday or anniversary e-card, may seem like a good idea. But would receiving a message from beyond the grave upset the recipient? And consider this: if you have the time to open the necessary account, arrange for at least two advisors to confirm your death, and to provide e-mail addresses, not to mention messages, don't you have the time to tell your loved ones how you feel about them now, and in person?

A DATE WITH THE DEAD

The feast of All Souls is celebrated around the Christian world on 2 November, during the autumnal 'dying' of the year. Perhaps most famously, it's a highlight of the festive calendar in Mexico, where it's known as the *Día de los Muertos*, the 'Day of the Dead'. In the Mexican tradition, the Day of the Dead is a happy and festive celebration of loved ones who have died, and is an opportunity for families to gather to remember and welcome back their spirits. The whole country therefore congregates at its cemeteries, to weed and tidy them up, but also to make a great party of the occasion by bringing picnics for themselves and offerings for the dead. Drinks of beer and tequila, little skull-shaped sweets and cakes, cigarettes . . . the departed don't mind if these are consumed mainly by the living. And when night falls, gangs of teenagers charge up and down through the darkness, wearing skull masks and trailing clacking chains of seashells that sound like bones (and that are noisy enough to wake the dead). As well as visiting the graves of the deceased, families set up festive altars in their homes, with flowers and offerings being placed around them to encourage the deceased to return. Some of the traditional elements of the festival include sugar skulls, pan de muerto ('bread of the dead', an egg-and-sugar-enriched bread, often in the shape of a skull) and Catrina dolls: skeletal figures dressed in fine gowns.

That there could hardly be a livelier, more manic celebration is perhaps the point of the *Día de los Muertos*. The Day of the Dead goes back to an ancient Aztec summer festival, a similarly cheerful affair in honour of an Aztec death goddess called Mictecacihuatl, the 'Lady of the Dead'. On their arrival in Mexico, Spanish priests were appalled by this impious celebration, and moved the date from 2 to 1 November – All Saints' Day in the Christian tradition – in an effort to make it a more sombre religious festival. The shift of date was the only change that endured, however, and today the Day of the Dead remains a time to recall happy memories of those who have died. So, in Mexico, the pagan spirit of the ancestors lives on. The nearest equivalent of these festivities within the British context takes place two days earlier on 31 October, and is also pagan in origin: this is Hallowe'en, which literally means the 'eve' of All Hallows' or All Saints' Day, and whose roots can be traced back to the Celtic festival of Samhain.

Making a Difference

When you're considering a conventional headstone or memorial, cost is, of course, an issue: the price can be anything from a few hundred pounds to . . . well, subject to churchyard rules or local planning law, you could probably have a priceless Great Pyramid if you wanted to. And you may well feel (or may come to feel, as you start to go through the practicable options) that this is money that would be better spent on something else.

As with the 'No flowers, donations instead to . . .' requests that are often made before funerals, many people these days take the view that any money that would have been spent on a memorial should go to charity instead. And they can get quite moralistic about it: it's one of those subjects that seems to divide the world, with people's ideas of what's fitting in this respect being highly personal, and generally non–negotiable. Those who think that you should give the money to Cancer Research or Oxfam tend to take a brisk, pull-your-socks-up attitude to sentimentality: in their view, commissioning a carved and polished piece of stone with an inscription is just a waste of money. But those who feel that they, or their late parent or partner, have to have a tangible memorial can't really explain that conviction, or its strength.

In the end, it has to be up to you. And you have to think about what you – and your family or loved ones – are likely to be comfortable with in the longer term. But if you'd rather like your memorial to be in the difference that you make to the world, whether it be to medical research, to the developing world or to the church-roof appeal, you'll certainly find that your contribution is welcome. The government, moreover, encourages such gifts by making them tax-exempt. The bigger charities are all geared up to handling this sort of thing, too, with Barnardo's receiving 60 per cent of its voluntary funding from bequests, to take just one example.

Leaving a bequest to charity could hardly be easier. Lots of charities have links on their websites to explain exactly how it's done, and to ease the way. Or your solicitor will be able to help. Briefly, you can make bequests in a number of different ways. A 'residual' bequest, for example, stipulates that your executors first have to pay out to all of your creditors and other appointed legatees (family, etc), after which whatever's left – or whatever percentage of it you've decided on – goes to the charity of your choice. This bequest might amount to a higher or lower figure, according to how your affairs are resolved. A 'pecuniary' bequest, on the other hand, involves a set sum of money being handed over to the charity of your choice by your executors, so this type of bequest doesn't vary: what you've promised the charity is what it'll get. A 'reversionary bequest' is a sort of temporary legacy: someone has the use of it for a while, but then it 'reverts' to some other beneficiary that you've appointed. You could, for instance, allow your child to receive the interest on a capital sum for as long as he or she lives, while stipulating that the capital goes to a charity upon your offspring's death.

And you don't have to leave money, either: you can make a 'specific' bequest in which you gift a particular thing, which could be anything from a piece of land to a pick-up truck. You can attach conditions to a specific bequest: your local art gallery will get your original El Greco, say, but only if they display it – they can't just sell it for the money that it may realise. Which takes us to an obvious caution: a bequest like this has to be thought through. To save everyone from administrative headaches and embarrassment, it's important to be realistic. How kind is it to leave Uncle Arnie's watercolours to the Tate, for instance? Or, being practical: is your lock-up garage really suitable for redevelopment as an orphanage? You will also have to be decent, or, at least, legal: you couldn't donate a pony to your local city farm on the condition that only white children get to ride it, for example.

With any charitable legacy, moreover, you will have to think about the impact of your bequest on your family. Not, of course, that you're obliged to leave everything (or anything) to them. But if they're going to be able to make a convincing case that you've passed over them out of malice or caprice (and there's plenty of precedent for that), then you may also be bequeathing your chosen beneficiary a great deal of legal trouble.

Going Public

One of the first things that a bereaved family or partner has to do when a loved one dies is decide how they're going to announce the death. The death notice doubles as a type of memorial. Read by all sorts of people in the local community (if it is placed in a local newspaper, and in the wider community if it appears in a national newspaper), it's a way of breaking the news to those who may not be in our immediate circle of acquaintances – who'll have heard already – but who may still be interested, and, in all probability, moved.

In a sense, the death notice is really just a classified advertisement, of the sort that you might take out if you wanted to sell your car, although the content – and the tone – are very different, of course. Like other such ads, these notices are generally found online these days, as well as in conventional newspapers, and may be accompanied by photos or images (a white rose or suchlike). The essence of the message hasn't changed too much, however, typically starting 'Peacefully . . .', or 'After a short illness . . .', or whatever, followed by the where and when of the death, and then by the name and details of the person who has died (for instance, 'beloved wife to George and mother to James and Mary'). It's generally rounded off with brief details of when and where the funeral is going to be held. Because newspapers are archived, whether in libraries or online, these announcements endure as a permanent record of who we were.

Such death notices are sometimes called obituaries, which isn't incorrect. But most people understand the word 'obituary' to refer to the rather fuller life summaries prepared unprompted by the press. A big newspaper or news magazine will have a full-time department employed in putting these mini-biographies together in advance so as to not to be caught napping when an important person dies. *We* don't get to decide whether we're given this kind of obituary: *they're* the ones who judge whether we make the grade. Some papers take this duty extremely seriously: the *Daily Telegraph*, for example, regards its obituaries as being pretty much a rolling record of modern Britain, its life and times, and publishes regular anthologies of them in book form.

In an increasingly interactive age, however, there's been a great deal of interest in singing the praises of previously unsung heroes and heroines. One response to this trend has been the *Guardian's* 'Other lives' feature, in which readers send in their own obits of friends or loved ones, who maybe weren't obviously members of the 'great and the good' elite, but who nevertheless had an important impact on their professions or communities during their lives.

PREMATURE OBITS

'The report of my death is an exaggeration', said Mark Twain notoriously in 1897, although, in fact, reports of this episode were exaggerated, too. No obituary had yet been printed, as is widely believed, even though a reporter had been dispatched to see the author of *The Adventures of Tom Sawyer* in what he felt was indecent haste, given that the individual at death's door was actually his cousin, not himself.

But a great many people have had the strange experience of being able to read their own obituaries – or, at least, of knowing that their obituaries have been written before their time was up. The poet Samuel Taylor Coleridge, for example, heard his own obituary being discussed. It was in 1816, and he'd apparently committed suicide: a man had been found hanged in London's Hyde Park in what appears to have been the poet's stolen shirt.

Author Ernest Hemingway's obituary appeared after he and his wife were lost in a plane crash in the African interior in 1954. And when it comes to premature obituaries like these, they're often down to chaos and confusion, although there may be a measure of wishful thinking, too. During the years of fighting that followed the Russian Revolution of 1917, Lenin's death was reported pretty much weekly by the Western press.

It could be assumed that much the same, hopeful sentiment prompted the American television news channel CNN to report Cuban dictator Fidel Castro's death on its website in 2003: the Comandante wasn't exactly a favourite with the US establishment. But this was really an instructive example of how new technologies afford new scope for fouling things up. In an age of instant communication, one would have thought that premature reports of death would have become less common, not more. But this instant communication means that an internet rumour or tiny technical error can quickly result in the premature announcement of someone's death, particularly in the case of celebrities, for whom news outlets often have draft obituaries ready and waiting. As had always been customary in the print media, CNN had prepared obituaries in advance of their subjects' death and had stored them away. By an oversight, though, they'd allowed open access to a collection of obituaries of not-yet-dead worthies, including not only Fidel, but also Dick Cheney, Nelson Mandela and Pope John Paul II.

Bob Hope's obituary was there, too. A premature obituary written about him had previously been made public a few years earlier, in 1998, but the CNN one, as yet a work in progress, was based on one already written for HM the Queen Mother, and informed readers that the US comedian was the 'UK's favorite grandmother'. The practice of using earlier obituaries to provide the framework around which new ones could be constructed was clearly habitual on the CNN writers' part. Indeed, Castro's was based on the former right-wing US President Ronald Reagan's; it's hard to guess which of the two men would have been more insulted.

Although embarrassing for CNN, such obvious errors prevented the obituaries from being taken too seriously. It was a different story for Jamaican national hero Marcus Garvey in 1940, however, who suffered a stroke and died after reading his premature obituary in the *Chicago Defender*, which described him as 'broke, alone, and unpopular'.

Acknowledgements and Anniversaries

It doesn't begin to offset the loss, but in the aftermath of their loved one's death, it can still be really heartening for the bereaved to read other people's messages of sympathy and good wishes – and even some of their cherished memories. The senders of such messages may have known the deceased only slightly, or may not have seen them for a long time. But just because somebody wasn't a firm or lifelong friend of him or her, doesn't mean that the deceased didn't make a strong and lasting impression on them, or that it didn't give them a jolt, or stir an emotion, when they heard that their acquaintance had died.

Conversely, when people take the trouble to get in touch, it's only courteous to offer some appreciation in return. In many cases, the recipient of messages of condolence will want to write to thank the senders personally, perhaps a few weeks later, after things have settled down a little. Some people even find this therapeutic.

Alternatively, it may make sense to take out an acknowledgement advertisement in the same place (or places) where the original death notice appeared. That way, those who responded first time around have the satisfaction of knowing that their good wishes were appreciated by the grieving family.

Bereaved relations often like to take out further ads in ensuing years, for example, on the deceased's birthday or on appropriate recognised occasions like Mothers' or Fathers' Day. That way, the memory of the person is regularly brought back. Some people find this comforting; others may not. Whether or not to place a notice in a newspaper in this way therefore has to be a personal decision, although one in which it would be sensible for all of the close family members to have a say.

A TIME TO MOURN

If you're the one that's left behind, you will inevitably mourn your loved one's death. It may even feel as though you've put your own life on hold for a while. But for how long? Is there a correct, expected or optimum mourning period? Will we be accused of wallowing in grief if we seem sad for too long? Or will we be considered heartless if it appears that we've 'moved on' too quickly?

Memory in Mourning

What is mourning if not (painful) remembrance? While the sufferings of the dead are over when they die, those of the living may just be beginning, especially if a death was unexpected, but even if it wasn't. The immediate shock of bereavement can be paradoxically energising as the system initially receives a massive jolt of adrenaline. First, that bolt from the blue, and then – well, there's just so much to do! It's in the weeks and months that follow that the world really starts to feel bleak and dreary and the bereaved become the most vulnerable – it's a cliché, but no less true for that.

It's a good thing, surely, that we've long abandoned the Victorian code of mourning, given the iron grip that it established over the lives of men and (especially) women. If truth be told, it was always in large part driven by commercial interests: it wasn't just the wall-to-wall crepe and carriages of the typical Victorian funereal excesses, but also the prescribed mourning period after a death. The respectable Victorian wife, for instance, had to go into 'deep mourning' when she was widowed, according to historian Catharine Arnold, the author of *Necropolis: London and its Dead*. She hardly left her house, and, if she did, she went out dressed and veiled in black. This state of affairs was only the beginning:

Once a widow had completed her first year, she dressed in 'secondary mourning'. This had a less rigorous dress code, and white collars and cuffs, reminiscent of a nun's habit, were permitted. After nine months came 'ordinary mourning', a three-month stretch during which women were permitted to wear shiny fabrics such as silk and velvet, trimmed with lace or beads, and also gold and silver jewellery, with appropriately somber precious stones like amethysts, garnet and opals. Finally, a widow entered the six-months of 'half-mourning', when muted colours such as grey, purple and lilac were permissible. Black evening dress was accessorized with a black fan, trimmed with ostrich feathers . . .

With hindsight, we can see how much of this was driven by sheer consumerism, for each of these stages of mourning called for a complete wardrobe overhaul. It was terribly restrictive, too: life was never exactly free and easy for the Victorian wife, but the bourgeois widow was practically imprisoned in her home. (Working-class widows had a more rational response enforced by economic necessity: they had to go straight back to work after their husbands' deaths, and couldn't even contemplate keeping up with this sort of dress code.)

But has the pendulum swung too far the other way today? Are we fast-forwarding our feelings at a rate that they don't want to go? Many funeral announcements specify that no black should be worn by mourners. It's one thing not to want to wallow in doom and gloom, but no black at all? At a funeral? How can this not be a case of denial? It's easy to see that the Victorian widow must have been climbing the walls by the time that her confinement ended, but at least she wasn't being told within a few weeks of being bereaved that it was time for her to 'move on'. Surely there has to be a happy medium?

The existence of a prescribed period of mourning, restrictive as it may be, does have the virtue of ring-fencing some time when we have permission to be sad. Even the most sympathetic friends and colleagues can't be expected to feel our grief as intensely as we do. Whilst they'll bend over backwards to accommodate our melancholy at first, there comes a point at which it slips from the forefront of their minds, after which our sadness may seem to rain on their parade at times. Then, of course, there's the guilt that they feel when they remember that they forgot that we are grieving. Having a clearly signalled mourning period can therefore be a help all round. We don't have to wear black for months (or at all), but there can surely be no harm in being upfront about the fact that we're going through a difficult chapter of our lives in the aftermath of a loved one's death.

MOURNING JEWELLERY

Although *memento mori* jewellery and jewelled tokens of remembrance date back far earlier than the nineteenth century, mourning jewellery became hugely popular during the Victorian period, encouraged by Queen Victoria's prolonged mourning of her beloved husband, Albert, who died in 1861. It was sometimes a gemstone's colour that was the significant feature of such pieces of jewellery, with the most commonly used black 'stone' (it is, in fact, a type of lignite) being jet. Black symbolised death and 'deep mourning', but purple amethysts and white pearls (alluding to tears) were also acceptable, and had the advantage of matching the grey, purple and lilac shades that signified 'half-mourning'. Many pieces of mourning jewellery also bore symbols of death and bereavement, such as the letters 'IMO' ('in memory of'), as well as engraved names, dates or messages of remembrance. A lock of a loved one's hair might in addition be placed inside a locket, to be worn close to a bereaved person's heart, or might be made into hairwork jewellery, so that that a surviving part of the dear departed was always visible, and sometimes even touchable.

Jewellery is not the only form of body adornment that can be used as a way of remembering someone who has died. It is not uncommon today for bereaved person to have a loved one's name tattooed his or her body, for example, along with, perhaps, the deceased person's birth and death dates and an appropriate symbol, such as a heart or flower. And when Mark Richmond's toddler, Ayden, died of a rare disorder in 2009, the tattoo artist from Herefordshire decided to have some of his son's ashes mixed with ink with which to have a portrait of Ayden tattooed on his chest.

Contributed by **Clare Gibson**, symbols specialist and Twitter's @talkingjewels.

In Mourning for My Life

Mourning is all about us: not necessarily because we're selfish or self-absorbed, but because, in the end, we're the ones who experience and have to come to terms with our bereavement.

A book like this can't hope to map out how it feels to lose a loved one – apart from anything else, everyone experiences it differently. How we're affected depends not only on how close we were to the departed, but also on how complicated our feelings about him or her were. How much 'unfinished business' did we have, for example? We may feel the loss of a bad parent much more forcefully than we do that of a good one because we know that the opportunity for any sort of explanation or reconciliation has now passed. Similarly, we may miss a partner more if we feel that we left any quarrels or tensions unresolved. We expect bereavement to be sad, but it can be utterly bewildering, too, when our own lives are abruptly presented to us in a new perspective.

Where we're up to in the story of our life makes a difference as to how we experience bereavement, too. Is our marriage or partnership rocky, perhaps, or our employment situation insecure? Are we yelling at our teenage kids the way we remember the departed bawling us out? Do we look at our children's shortcomings and see ourselves? Or do we feel that they've seen, and judged, our own shortcomings as parents, and as people? Did we dump our problems on our children, or, conversely, disappear and not see them for years on end? Do we feel that we disappointed them, or let them down? These sorts of issues often have a bearing on how greatly someone's death affects us.

Science and What Works for You

Today's problem-page psychology, with all of its talk of a scientific-sounding 'grieving process', sets out clear stages for mourning. These are based (at least loosely) on the work of the Swiss psychiatrist Elisabeth Kübler-Ross, who came up with her model for mourning in 1969.

As far as Kübler-Ross was concerned, the sequence was liable to kick in before death, when a terminal illness was diagnosed. It could also be applied to other losses (and events experienced as such): anything from a partner's infidelity, for example, to the birth of a child with a disability. The sequence, as she saw it, went from denial to indignation (anger), after which came bargaining (subconscious attempts to make some deal with fate). Then there was depression (basically, just giving up), and finally came acceptance. Kübler-Ross acknowledged that these different stages could be experienced differently by different people, and that they might not always occur in exactly the order she'd set out.

Was the Kübler-Ross model for mourning a bit vague? A bit woolly? It could be thought so. It's interesting, moreover, that her stages are at odds with those suggested by the English psychoanalyst John Bowlby. A specialist in the structures of loss and grieving, he had been working on his attachment theory since the late 1950s at least, although his most influential work in this area was published during the 1970s. Bowlby suggested a four-stage sequence of his own, beginning with a period of numbing, perhaps punctuated by outbursts of anger. Next, he said, came a sometimes protracted period during which the afflicted mind yearned, or 'searched', for the lost person, primarily through recollection. After that, they fell apart, in a phase of 'disorganisation' and despair. And finally, they got themselves together again – what Bowlby called organisation – and were then ready to resume something like an ordinary life once more.

The two theories clearly have a certain amount in common; there are also obvious differences between them. And neither commands anything like uncritical acceptance in the academic literature. But does that matter, if we're not professional psychologists? After all, we have to do whatever it is that gets us through. Most of us will recognise aspects of what Kübler-Ross and Bowlby are talking about as we try to come to terms with our bereavement. If it helps us to know that this is a well-worn trail, in which established stages have been identified (even if there's some disagreement about what they are), then that surely can't be such a bad thing, can it?

In the end, maybe, it's just a matter of muddling through. Each of us finds our own way of mourning the one we've lost.

DEATH DUTIES

The Virgin Mary cradling Christ beneath the cross; war widows wailing; stage Irishwomen keening: mourning has stereotypically been seen as women's work. Not that men don't grieve, but throughout history, women have borne the brunt of the duty to mourn the dead.

'So what?' some may ask. Women have borne the brunt of all sorts of duties in the domestic sphere: not just the cooking, cleaning and childcare, but also the duty to provide unlimited TLC as and when required. Then there's what researcher Pamela Fishman notoriously described as the 'interactional shitwork': the hard conversational labour needed to keep dialogues going and things functioning within the family. This responsibility, too, has traditionally rested with the mother (and she's traditionally been rewarded with accusations of 'rabbiting').

One explanation for why women have traditionally been the visible faces of mourning is because, at just about every time in history, men have, on average, died before their 'better halves', so that there have tended to be more widows than widowers. It surely goes deeper than this, though. Is it because it is through women that we come into the world that it seems natural for them to see us out, too? Then there's the fact that men, as the family's public face, have had to present an image of strength and assurance, which has called for stoicism in the face of death.

Wealthy women have, moreover, always been walking, talking advertisements for the success of their husbands and families. The Victorian widow's subtly changing mourning costumes were examples of conspicuous consumption, even as her loyal show of bereavement seemed to proclaim her husband's moral worth. The widow's withdrawal from life, its interests and its pleasures in some sense represented the enormity of her husband's loss to the world at large: look what a difference this man's death has made!

In some cultures, this sort of self-abnegation has been carried to extremes, as with the ancient Indian practice of *sati*, or *suttee*, according to which high-caste women were expected to fling themselves on to their husbands' funeral pyres, with thousands dying agonising deaths this way down the centuries. Other widows have had to subject themselves to what might be seen as a form of semi-*sati*. Anthropologists Richard Huntington and Peter Metcalf found one example in Borneo during the 1970s. Living for a while among the Berawan people (as described in *Celebrations of Death: the Anthropology of Mortuary Ritual*, 1991), they found that a newly widowed woman there was 'cooped up for as many as eleven days in a cage next to the corpse'. In addition:

She may not bathe, and may ... eat only the poorest foods which she 'shares' with the deceased ... She suffers because of the vengeful soul of the deceased. Its envy of the living, caused by its own miserable state, is softened by the spectacle of the hardship visited on those it formerly loved.

Well, you know what they say: a problem shared is a problem halved.

SAVING FACEBOOK

Who ever really had 300 friends? Where's the social value in swapping kitten videos, wordlessly 'poking' people or sending them electronically prompted birthday greetings? How does telling the world your bra-colour raise breast cancer awareness? The absurdities of social network sites have been often (indeed, well-nigh interminably) rehearsed by the older among us. Yet they wouldn't be used if they didn't have a function. The last few years have seen young accident- or murder-victims' Facebook pages turned spontaneously into commemorative shrines – and into forums for their bewildered friends to talk through just what they have lost.

Chapter Six
A HAPPY ENDING?

Death brings our story to its conclusion. It's the ending that gives our life an outline and a shape: from being just one damn thing after another, it starts to assume the form of a narrative, with ourselves at the centre. Only at the end of our life does it become clear what, and who, we were. Popular psychologists may refer to our acceptance of death's inevitable approach as 'closure', but we may be more at home with Aeschylus' tragic vision of the dénouement that defines us, or, staying with the theatre, with the 'final curtain' of which Sinatra sang. Even as we approach our end, we can't help but sense that something's starting: the 'Once upon a time . . .' of our life story *as* a story, if you like.

MAKING SENSE OF DEATH

After the initial shock of someone's death has passed, we are often left pondering some rather philosophical questions – particularly when that death was sudden or unexpected – not least about our continuing place in the world.

Mortal Metaphysics

'In my end is my beginning', observed T S Eliot in characteristically cryptic style. Yet his comment still resonates intuitively, and not only with those of us who, nearing our end, can't help but feel that there's a start of sorts in prospect as we anticipate (whether in fear, hope, curiosity or sceptical amusement) whatever it may be that is, or isn't, going to come next.

It also stirs a thought in those of us who are going to be left behind: those who are trying to imagine a future without the soon-to-be-departed, a time when this still living presence will have been consigned to an irrecoverable past. Who they were – and who we were with them – has become an aspect of what we ourselves are, and they will therefore play their part in shaping where we go from here. No wonder we find ourselves getting our tenses in a twist. Or, as Eliot puts it more aphoristically in 'Burnt Norton':

> *Time present and time past*
> *Are both perhaps present in time future,*
> *And time future contained in time past.*

One objection to this observation – which is obvious to anyone who's seen someone die or has experienced any kind of bereavement – is that we don't actually experience the end of life in this way. Whether it's our own or someone else's death, it doesn't generally present itself as the metaphysical poser that these lines seem to suggest. On the contrary, there can hardly be anything so obdurately *physical* as the body of one from whom life's spirit has departed. The better we've known and loved them, and the more accustomed we've become to their animated presence, the more stolid and inert their lifeless body seems. And then there are the thousand and one practical concerns that we must immediately address when a loved one dies. As a result, there's little leisure time in which one can muse on what it all might mean.

Soon enough, though, as the dust slowly settles and we start to have odd moments here and there for reflection, we often find ourselves trying to compute exactly what we've lost and where it leaves us. However old the deceased may have been, they've left us facing a new situation. We may not think of ourselves as thinkers, but these are philosophical questions that go right to the heart of who we are and where in the world we see ourselves as being.

Rewriting the Script

Al Alvarez wrote his study of suicide, *The Savage God,* in 1972, just under a decade after his friend and fellow poet Sylvia Plath took her own life. Himself prone to bouts of deep depression, Alvarez had first-hand experience of the suicidal frame of mind. One point that he noted is its tendency to envisage a certain narrative and then stick to it: the sufferer who's determined to throw himself under a tube train will ignore the paracetamol bottles in the bathroom cabinet and will walk across high bridges without a sideways glance, single-minded in his intent to reach the underground station. Is this a way of asserting some sort of control?

Committing suicide can clearly be seen as the ultimate act of taking charge: what more emphatic way do we have of demonstrating that we order our own destiny? In lesser ways, though, as Australian psychologist Dorothy Rowe has noted, we all tell ourselves stories and buy into myths of various sorts to get ourselves through the challenges of existence. (Our politicians know this, she suggests, and are happy to feed us further lies.)

But it's not just a matter of finding feel-good fantasies more palatable than harsh truths: it seems somehow enabling when we can create narratives around our lives, and around those of others. Alarming as it may seem on the face of it, we may, in fact, find it much easier to imagine our father dying of a heart attack at sixty-five the way *his* father did, for example, than to accept the possibility of more painful ends – or, perhaps worse, the sheer anguish of simply not knowing how or when death will come.

Sudden-Death Denial

When life – or, rather, death – departs from the script that we've written for it, it only makes the shock worse for those left behind. Bereavement is bad enough when we lose a loved one as the natural conclusion of a long and predictable decline, but when it comes, as a double-whammy, with complete surprise, it can be that much harder to bear. And when a loved one's murder brings violence and hatred irrupting into our lives, or we're emotionally ambushed by the loss of someone to a terrible accident, it can seem impossible even to take the fact on board.

Because what's happened makes no sense to us, the temptation is to struggle on as though nothing *has* happened – by definition, we're unprepared for a sudden death like this. We won't, then, have made the sorts of arrangements that we might otherwise have done for taking adequate time off work, nor will we have thought about the type of support that we might need from family or friends. Caught unawares like this, people typically self-medicate with drugs or alcohol – this is understandable, but it's a very bad idea. Grief counselling is a much better one. Not only can it do a great deal for anyone who's been bereaved, but it is also especially helpful when we're struggling to get our heads around a tragic ending in which we can see no sense at all.

A DEATH ABROAD

A sudden death is always a shock, but can be particularly difficult to handle when someone was abroad when they died. If the deceased was away on business and you're at home, the news will very likely be broken to you by your local police, who will typically have been contacted by consular officials on the spot. If not – if you're told by the deceased's travelling companions, tour operators or someone else, for instance – you should contact the British Foreign & Commonwealth Office yourself to be sure that they are aware of the death. Officials around the world know the ropes in the event of the sudden death of a British national: they've done it all before and can make sure that all of the formalities demanded by the authorities locally are attended to. They can also advise on making arrangements for a funeral to be held in the place of death or for having the body brought back home.

The same applies if the death took place while you were with the deceased on holiday, with the first thing to do being to alert the British consulate without delay. If you're on a package deal, the operator may take care of this on your behalf, but it can't be left to chance. The country in which the death occurred will have its own strict rules about the registration of deaths and associated obligations, and you will therefore need the help of someone who knows the system inside out: this is not an area that you can realistically deal with yourself.

The World Turned Upside Down

A loved one's death upsets us, and rather more literally than we may think: indeed, it can completely overturn our psychological equilibrium. Our self-confidence, so long in the construction, may well come crashing down, for example. We're at a loss: we don't know what to do or where to turn. For most of us, it isn't just a matter of being the same, but sadder, but of our entire sense of self being thrown into doubt.

Even the most solitary of us are social beings: we live in relation to those among whom we live. Take any individual out of that nexus of relationships, and the emotional pattern of our existence will be changed. If it's just a nodding-acquaintance neighbour or colleague who's died, the shift may be so subtle as scarcely to signify, but if it's a partner, parent or child, our existence will be transformed. For every day of their lives in our interactions with them, they reflected back to us a sense of who we were.

There's no *ego* without others: 'I' may be an individual, but much of what makes 'me' I draw from those around me – not just companionship or moral support, but affirmation of every sort. How likeable, appealing or trustworthy we are, for example; whether our opinions are to be taken seriously or our jokes to be laughed at: we need unending reassurance from others that we're the people who we think we are.

'I' and Others

John Donne observed in 1623 that 'no man is an island'. When he wrote this, the poet–preacher appears to have had a moral and spiritual solidarity between human beings in mind, but it seems to make just as much sense with the sort of psychological spin that we're liable to give it today. For we are not just influenced by, but to a considerable extent also formed by (and, in a certain sense, even 'created' by) our relationships with those among whom we spend our lives.

The very idea of the 'self' is now said by many theorists to be a social construct. Who we are is a product of our culture and the community – familial, local and national, for example – of which we are a part. Even big, impersonal structures like those of class, state organisation and the economy shape our subjectivities at the most intimately private level. Who we find attractive; how we see our gender roles; the sort of food we like; the films that move us . . . our most apparently personal desires, tastes and emotional assumptions are arguably all moulded by the prevailing culture.

You don't need to carry the argument anything like that far to see that each of us can easily be seen as the product first of our families and, after that, of a succession of carers and then of a widening circle of friends, acquaintances and colleagues. For better or for worse (and sometimes for much worse), we wouldn't be what we are today if it hadn't been for how we were brought up by our mothers and fathers, or for the interventions of key teachers, sports coaches and other adults in our early years. Old friends and long-forgotten lovers have left their mark, too.

BREAKING RULES

'Survivor's guilt' may have become a cliché, but there's no doubt that for some people, in some circumstances, bereavement prompts a complex of feelings to develop for which a label like 'grief' or 'mourning' seems far too blunt.

While we may pride ourselves on having left the rule-bound rigidity of Victorian mourning far behind us, we still have a clear sense of what's 'appropriate' and what's not. That can be too restrictive a regime for men and women who feel all at sea emotionally following a bereavement, however, and can result in rule-breaking behaviour, sometimes on an awe-inspiring scale. The drowning of sorrows in alcohol may feature, but also the doing of drugs, as well as the indecorous spectacle of (deeply unmerry) widows or widowers cruising bars for dates. Yet the proprieties say that they should be above such things.

The reality is that like most people who go off the rails to this extent, the 'badly behaved' bereaved are usually acting out profoundly negative feelings of self-rejection. If not actually to blame for what's happened, they may feel that they somehow haven't merited the gift of their departed loved one's continued life. What's left for them, then, but this spiral of self-destruction? And all that those who know and love them can do is resist the instinct to recoil and instead offer support and encouragement to find the help that they need.

Less anarchic, although potentially equally damaging, may be those romances that grow out of bereavement-bonding, when a partner falls in love with a sibling or close friend of the deceased. Both are typically in the grip of a grief that seems to bring them together, even as it sets them apart from the rest of the world. They feel a deep understanding: there's something special that they share, and before they know it, they're in love, in a pure and meaningful way (it could hardly be further from the reckless one-night stands of their badly behaved brethren in bereavement). At best, however, this feeling's likely to be premature, and they should ideally wait for a year or so to see how they feel about each other under more normal conditions before taking their relationship further. And at worst, if one party's married or attached to someone else, a beguiling, but catastrophic, path to an affair beckons.

Through the Eyes of Love

'What joy', wrote Pedro Salinas in one of the twentieth century's most celebrated love poems:

That there's another being through whom I see the world,
Because she's loving me with her eyes.

This is an extravagant claim, to be sure, born of the all-transporting rapture of romance. Had those eyes got used to falling on his dirty underpants strewn across the bedroom floor, or on the parts of his dismantled bike on the kitchen table, it seems safe to assume that they would have been a bit more jaundiced. Yet even within the workaday reality of the relationships that we lesser mortals tend to have, we learn to see our world in subtly different ways through the prism of partnership.

Even our more prosaic partnerships are tested by their ups and downs, and if they're not actually broken by these, they're strengthened. We're brought ever closer by years of shared experience. And, inevitably, we're changed by what we've gone through and by the years that we've spent gradually coming to rely ever more upon another's judgement. How we see our 'better half' doesn't just affect how we see ourselves: it also leaves its imprint on all of our attitudes and views.

One of the great virtues of a relationship that's proved enduring is that the endorsement it provides is enduring, too. Knocked sideways though we may be by the loss of the one we love, we are also often left with the resilient confidence that their affection, trust and loyalty gave us, which helps to equip us to face the lonely times ahead.

DEALING WITH THE UNEXPECTED

Following someone's death, it may emerge that they had a completely different side to the one that they showed to their family and friends. In which case, how does one deal with the sense of hurt and betrayal that may come from discovering that a loved one had a secret life, or that someone whom you idolised was not so perfect after all – far from it, in fact?

Another Story

What if it turns out that we didn't see the one we loved as clear-sightedly as we thought when he or she was alive? What if their life story, as we knew it, was fictional? We've read of such stories in the more excitable newspapers: of the grieving widow who was upstaged at her husband's funeral by the histrionics of the next-door neighbour, who, it turned out, had been having an affair with him for several years, for example, or of the decent guy who was the last to know that his late partner had been revisiting her lost youth in the arms of an old boyfriend who had found her again on Facebook.

Death can be the conclusion that makes all things clear, but then some of those things may not be wholly to our liking. The credit-card bill showing the payments that a husband made to an escort service, for example. Or the letters tucked away in a wife's drawer revealing that what she felt for her best female friend from college wasn't quite as innocent as it seemed. Indeed, it could be anything, from a stash of drugs to a cache of particularly extreme pornography on the computer. Or maybe something altogether softer's discovered – something quite inoffensive to many decent people, yet somehow at odds with the image that you had of your deceased loved one. A secret gambling habit, perhaps, or continued contact with someone with whom you fell out badly a couple of years before. At a time when, bereft and vulnerable, you've been drawing on the love that you thought you'd banked, any such discovery will be unsettling, and perhaps profoundly so. Indeed, the dissonance that it suggests between the person that you were so sure you knew and the person that you're beginning to see revealed calls into question every other certainty that you may have.

When we're relying on the relationship that we had with the deceased to be our rock of stability in the years ahead, it's not too encouraging to see it crumbling away before our eyes. Many psychologists consider the discovery of a living partner's infidelity as constituting a sort of bereavement in its own right, so when it's discovered at the posthumous stage of a relationship, it can amount to a sort of double death.

The Best-Laid Plans

The emotional impact of unwelcome revelations about a deceased loved one's 'secret' life aside, there can be hell to pay in practical terms. There's no generally accepted bullet-point list for what to do when, all grown up now, the baby that your wife had adopted and never got around to telling you about before she died turns up at her birth mother's funeral, for example, or your late husband's other widow and family fly in from Adelaide in order to be present at his burial. But if this happens to you, try to stay as calm as you can and to talk things through – again and again, if necessary – with the friends and relations that you trust the most. If necessary, you should also take legal advice.

'It's not so much the affair itself, but the lying that's so painful', we're half-expected to say about an infidelity, but then lying can have consequences that are all too real. Being wounded by the 'principle of the thing' is all very well – and it's true that we're likely to be personally outraged if we discover that our partner set up his secretary in a flat or fed the last six months' mortgage payments into a slot machine. But addressing our moral disillusionment may have to wait, for example, if our financial situation is at stake and it's necessary to take steps immediately to secure what's ours. By all means be shocked and shaken, but also get a solicitor and take action.

Not that action always guarantees results, however. An octogenarian father's last-minute marriage to a Thai nightclub hostess may have been every bit as ill-advised as we believe it to have been, but it was his life and his prerogative to screw it up. As for his young widow, we may take as dim a view of her motives as we like, but unless we can prove badly failing mental powers on his part or some sort of coercion on hers, the law will uphold her rights as next of kin. If he hasn't left a will – or has, however foolishly from our perspective, amended an older one in her favour – then she's going to inherit his estate. There *are* principles at stake as well, though. And if the law sides with the individual's right to make mistakes, we have a responsibility to respect that right ourselves. Maybe Dad at last found the love that had previously eluded him down the long and lonely years – stranger things have happened, after all.

If the emotions can be messy in such situations, the ethics can also be tangled, with the hardest thing to accept possibly being that we don't get to decide what's best. We can judge away to our heart's content, but can't necessarily expect to dictate how things pan out. If the Battersea Dogs' Home can be proven to have sent heavies around to her house, or to have employed brainwashing techniques to sway the vulnerable old lady's decision-making, then we have a legal basis for objecting when our aged mother leaves it her whole fortune. But if it's just that Mum was fonder of dogs than she ever was of us, then, unpalatable as it may be to come to terms with, that's simply tough.

MIGHT MAKES RIGHT

When world conqueror Alexander the Great died without an heir in 323 BC, his generals fought among themselves for his empire. According to custom, burial of the king was the right and duty of his successor. So the general Ptolemy hijacked Alexander's funeral cortège and took the body with him to Egypt (which was easy enough to do as it in any case had to travel from Babylon to Macedonia). Given that Alexander's body was laid in a golden sarcophagus, which was in turn placed in a golden coffin, it seems appropriate that his final resting place should have been in the land of the pharaohs, whose burials typically also featured gleaming gold.

Challenging a Will

By definition, it's difficult to know what was in the mind of someone who's no longer here to tell us. The law works on the assumption that what they meant was what they said. So unless there's conclusive proof that they were of radically 'unsound mind', or that there was clear coercion when they signed it, the courts are reluctant to accept that someone's will does not express their will. Legal proceedings aimed at overturning wills tend to be long and accordingly expensive. And their outcome is notoriously unpredictable.

How can you prove that the nurse who tended your dying mother forced her to leave her her fortune, for example? How can you prove that your sometimes confused or forgetful father was actually of unsound mind? An exhaustive process of evidence-gathering will be needed to build a case, and expert witnesses will, in all likelihood, have to be assembled. This all takes an enormous amount of time and money.

It's not as though your challenge is likely to go unchallenged in its turn either. For you to benefit, the existing beneficiary has to lose. And if they're the ruthless vulture that you think they are, they're not likely to give up without a fight; they have nothing to gain by making things easy for you. They'll assemble evidence and expert witnesses as well. If you think that a charity will fight fairer than an individual, think again, too. In fact, under the terms of its charitable registration, it's bound by law to do its best to protect any funds that come its way.

So by all means take legal advice if you feel badly done by, but don't expect your solicitor to take a gung-ho, up-and-at-'em attitude. A correctly witnessed will is a difficult document to find a legal way around. After all, that's the point of it.

THE KOSTIC CRISIS

When Belgrade-born businessman Branislav Kostic died in 2005, he left behind a fortune of over £8 million, but not a penny of it to Zoran, his surviving son. Not a penny of it to anyone, indeed, who he associated with the 'dark forces' that, as he had become convinced, had taken over the world and schemed daily to bring about his destruction.

The only people who weren't in the pocket of these sinister forces, in his opinion, were members of the Conservative Party, to which he accordingly left the lot. That the Conservative Party may pretty much be the definition of a 'dark force' to many people cut no ice with the law, nor should it have done. That the Tories themselves could apparently see no evidence to show that Kostic had been incapable of making rational decisions is, perhaps, odd, but understandable, given the sum involved.

When the case came to court, the Conservative Party's lawyers argued that while Kostic had clearly suffered from delusions, these had not been so comprehensive as to invalidate his will. In the end, however, Zoran was able successfully to overthrow their claim, especially because his father had left everything to him in an earlier will.

IN THE END . . .

Ultimately, whether it's your own death or another's that you find yourself confronting, you will have to steer your own course as courageously and sensibly as you can. Both elements of this approach are important: whilst it's tempting to dramatise the drawing-near of death as some sort of heroic date with destiny, it's as well to remember the practical challenges, too, and if there are things that you can do to make the situation easier, make sure that you do them. (See pages 233 to 237 for some thoughts on supporting your loved one through their last days.) But you have to know your limits as well – and you're about to be reminded of them in no uncertain terms – so control what you can, but accept what you know you must.

Some say that you shouldn't accept the inevitability of death: 'Do not go gentle into that good night', as poet Dylan Thomas put it. And respectable medics did, for a time, suggest that patients who showed a fighting spirit might have a better chance of holding off – or even reversing – the advance of cancer. This was a pleasing and emotionally persuasive view to a generation brought up to celebrate feisty individualism, also, no doubt, being a useful counter to an older ethic of quiet resignation that might have been seen to have been barely distinguishable from despair. It was argued that those of the sick who slipped too easily into a deathbed role shut down their lives long before it was necessary to do so, and far sooner than was maybe good for their mental health. Sadly, as research proceeded, the statistical evidence needed to support the 'fight and beat it' theory wasn't forthcoming, any more than it was for any relentlessly upbeat attempts to stick a smiley face on sickness. American author Barbara Ehrenreich has written witheringly on what she sees as the 'sugar-coating' of cancer, the view that suffering and loss can be buried beneath a mountain of flowers, hearts and cheery optimism. By contrast, all of the evidence appears to show that the disease goes on its biological way pretty much regardless of whether we accept it, reject it or pretend that it isn't there.

If it doesn't make much difference to a disease how we respond to it, it can obviously make a big difference to us. Yet what 'works' (in the sense of making things halfway bearable) for one individual will be completely inappropriate for another. It's hardly surprising that a strong-willed, intellectual woman like Ehrenreich would opt for anger: 'Damn braces, bless relaxes', in the words of William Blake. But it's likely that someone else, coming from a different background, and with a different temperament, would find herself feeling that 'bless' lends comfort, whilst 'damn' destroys.

This book doesn't claim to have all of the answers – or maybe even any. (Now we tell you, as you reach the final pages!) What it *has* done, we hope, is to raise some of the questions surrounding death that you may want to ask yourself and those you love, so that you can try to come up with some of the answers for yourselves. That way, you can at least hope to sort out the issues that matter to you from the issues that don't, and to take the steps that you can without getting too down about those that you can't. And if, in the immediate term, you're expecting to be a mourner rather than the deceased, then talking through these questions should enable you to be a real support to the person who is facing death, rather than a bystander, feeling helpless and guilty, when the critical time comes.

When we think about it, we know that we wouldn't really want to live forever, although that doesn't seem to make the thought of dying any easier. The only thing that does is feeling that we've done our best to manage things so that our exit is as smooth and dignified as possible. For some of us, as for the medieval monk or the seventeenth-century alderman, that will primarily mean making our peace with God. Most of us, however, will be content if we can make our peace with our family and friends. It also makes sense to spare them as much administrative grief as we can at a time when they'll have plenty of real grief to deal with. And if there are things that they can do to help us feel better as we face our final moments, then we should say so.

In the end, it's your ending. You have to die, just as you've lived, in your own way. But there's really no reason why the end should have to be unhappy.

REFLECTIONS

In this section we throw things open, admitting a variety of different voices. Men and women with a wide range of expertise and experience share these in their own words and their own way. Practical advice; therapeutic suggestions; philosophical musings; personal experience: this is a kaleidoscopic collection designed to be read in any order, each reflecting the particular viewpoint of its author.

A Funeral Service for People With no Church Connections

Dr James Russell is an Edinburgh-based Unitarian who has conducted hundreds of funerals, many of them for people who have no church connections. Based on his experience, he suggests the form that a non-religious, humanist or secular funeral service prior to a cremation might take.

1. The service could begin with an appropriate introductory statement, such as the following quotations:

     IF YOU WOULD INDEED BEHOLD THE SPIRIT OF DEATH, OPEN
     YOUR HEART WIDE UNTO THE BODY OF LIFE. FOR LIFE AND
     DEATH ARE ONE, EVEN AS THE RIVER AND THE SEA ARE ONE.

     Syro–Lebanese poet Kahlil Gibran

     TO EVERY THING THERE IS SEASON,
     AND A TIME TO EVERY PURPOSE UNDER THE HEAVEN:
     A TIME TO BE BORN, AND A TIME TO DIE;
     A TIME TO PLANT, AND A TIME TO PLUCK UP THAT
     WHICH IS PLANTED.

     Ecclesiastes 3:1–2

     NO [WO]MAN IS AN ISLAND, ENTIRE OF ITSELF.
     ANY [WO]MAN'S DEATH DIMINISHES ME BECAUSE
     I AM INVOLVED IN [HU]MANKIND.

AND THEREFORE NEVER SEND TO KNOW FOR WHOM
THE BELL TOLLS; IT TOLLS FOR THEE.

English poet John Donne

I WAS NOT, I HAVE BEEN. I AM NOT. I DO NOT MIND.
THERE IS NOTHING TERRIBLE IN LIFE FOR THE [WO]MAN WHO
HAS TRULY COMPREHENDED THAT THERE IS NOTHING
TERRIBLE IN NOT LIVING.

Epicurean motto

DO NOT SEEK DEATH. DEATH WILL FIND YOU.
BUT SEEK THE ROAD WHICH MAKES DEATH A FULFILMENT.

Swedish diplomat Dag Hammarskjöld

2. After welcoming the mourners, the officiant should state the
    name of the person who they have come to mourn, then say-
    ing that he or she has touched all of their lives in some way
    and will be missed.

3. If appropriate, speak of the deceased's age at death, how he or
    she died, and of the grief and sadness that those who are left
    feel at the loss of this person. Give some words of comfort,
    maybe:

    Inevitably, you will find the world a poorer place without [the
    deceased's name], but it will always be a richer place because
    [he or she] was once in it. So the joy of having [the deceased's
    name] in your life may indeed be lost, but the joy of having
    had that relationship [or friendship], the delight and comfort
    of its memories, is never lost. There never has been, and never
    will be, anyone in the world like [the deceased person's name],
    and [he or she] will live on in your memories, not just at special
    times like birthdays, but always. [He or she] will remain a part
    of the family and circle of friends.

4. Speak of the deceased's personality and life, and of how he or she touched and enriched the lives of others.

5. Introduce the singing of a song, or the playing of music, maybe with the following poem by **Joyce Grenfell**:

> *If I should go before the rest of you,*
> *Break not a flower, nor inscribe a stone,*
> *Nor, when I'm gone, speak in a Sunday voice,*
> *But be the usual selves that I have known.*
> *Weep if you must:*
> *Parting is hell,*
> *But life goes on*
> *So . . . Sing as well!*

6. An appropriate reading could follow, such as, perhaps, the following extract from the Tibetan *Book of Living and Dying*:

Death is a vast mystery, but there are two things we can say about it: it is absolutely certain that we will die, and it is uncertain when or how we will die. The only surety we have, then, is this uncertainty about the hour of our death, which we seize on as the excuse to postpone facing death directly. We are like children who cover their eyes in a game of hide-and-seek and think that no one can see them.

The pace of our lives is so hectic that the last thing we have time to think of is death. We smother our secret fears of impermanence by surrounding ourselves with more and more goods, more and more things, more and more comforts, only to find ourselves their slaves. All our time and energy is exhausted simply maintaining them. Our only aim in life soon becomes to keep everything as safe and secure as possible. When changes do happen, we find the quickest remedy, some

slick and temporary solution. And so our lives drift on, unless
a serious illness or disaster shakes us out of our stupor.

7. The mourners could now be invited to reflect, meditate or
   pray for a few minutes as the officiant maybe gives thanks
   for the life of the deceased and offers some words of solace.

8. A tribute could follow, given by a relative or friend of the
   deceased, or by the officiant. This could include the chrono-
   logical 'story' of the deceased's life, from birth to death.

9. In the case of a cremation, the mourners could now be asked
   to stand as the body is committed for cremation and the officiant says some appropriate words, such as these from the
   British Humanist Association:

   Here, in this last act, in sorrow, but without fear, in love and
   appreciation we commit the body of [the deceased's name] to
   its (natural) end; its transformation into the ultimate elements
   of the universe, through the purifying process of the fire, which
   is itself one of the great forces of nature. Amen.

10. Having asked the mourners to be seated and to meditate or
    pray for a few moments, the officiant may prepare them to go
    back to life without the deceased, perhaps leaving them with
    some words to reflect on, such as this Native American thought:

    When I am dead, cry for me a little.
    Think of me sometimes, but not too much.
    Think of me now and again as I was in life,
    At some moment it is pleasant to recall,
    But not for too long.
    Leave me in peace and I shall leave you in peace
    And while you live, let your thoughts be with the living.

11. A reading or song could then be followed by some parting words by the officiant, such as this Celtic blessing:

> *The deep peace of the running water to you;*
> *The deep peace of the flowing air to you;*
> *The deep peace of the quiet earth to you;*
> *The deep peace of the shining stars to you;*
> *And the love and care of us all . . . to you.*

12. Finally, before the closing music is played, and speaking on behalf of the deceased's family, the officiant could invite the mourners to join them for refreshments.

Giving Comfort to the Dying

Stewart McGregor, chaplain at the Royal Infirmary of Edinburgh, Scotland, for over twenty years.

My experience as a hospital chaplain for twenty-eight years has made me very wary of generalisations about death and dying, circumstances being so various and individuals so different. In a general hospital, unlike a specialised hospice, death comes in many different ways. People may have to deal with still-birth or perinatal death; the death of a child; the trauma of sudden death through accident, violence, suicide, heart attack, stroke or after surgery; or death following prolonged treatment for incurable illness. Each individual circumstance and need calls for an appropriate response from carers, both for the dying person and for their relatives and friends.

Yet while generalisations about individual deaths are inappropriate, death is an inevitable personal experience, and we must all live with our own mortality. It was the philosopher Heidegger who said that the knowledge that we must die is the background music that plays faintly throughout our lives, and though we may blot it out, there are times when the music increases in volume and tempo and we cannot be unaware of it.

Attitudes to communication have changed radically since I first worked in the NHS. There was a time when you might hear consultants state that they had never told a patient that he or she was going to die, but nowadays doctors seek to open up a conversation on the subject, while respecting the wishes of those who prefer not to talk about their demise. Most of us, however, will know that we are going to die when our time comes.

A chaplain in a hospital setting is not imposed on, but available to any patient, of whatever faith or none. We are not there to proselytise. A patient has a right to see a chaplain or a leader of their faith community if they wish; they also have a right not to do so. The chaplain is available, too, to minister to relatives and friends, and, as a member of the ward team, to hospital staff. A chaplain who has a long-standing relationship with a person who is reaching the end of their life may already have spoken with them about death, but when called, may sometimes be visiting a person for the first time. If the person were beyond speech, their relatives might indicate whether it would be helpful for me to offer some ministry of prayer or blessing. While people with a religious affiliation may die in the context of the beliefs, values, liturgies and practices of their religion, since each individual is unique, his or her spiritual needs must form the agenda of the chaplain's care. Chaplains always try to stay open to the wishes of the individual and their relatives. Sensitivity to the particular set of circumstances sometimes means knowing the right time to leave.

Death is a journey that we all make alone as individuals, but a loving, caring presence with the dying right up to the point of death is often highly desirable. The frail and dying are the better for knowing that they're loved and cherished and will be missed. They need to feel that their lives have been significant.

Giving comfort to a dying person is something that each of us is likely to be called on to do. How communicative dying people are depends on their level of consciousness. Hearing seems to be the last of the senses to go, and so kind words might be a comfort, even if there is no detectable response. One of the main things I've learned is how much presence matters – not just being in the room, but being truly attentive, and knowing that simply holding a hand can say more than words.

When they're dying, people sometimes want to speak; sometimes they may not. If they're not at peace with themselves, they may share their regrets. They may want to talk about life after death. Some people are frightened of dying; others are eager to go. Some grieve the prospect of parting from loved ones here; some relish the prospect of reunion with those who have already departed this life. Death can be faced as an adventure; or as a homecoming. Religious belief can help us to die well. I will never forget one fourteen-year-old girl – her faith so straightforward, so incomparably strong – who faced death with a serenity that few of us will ever equal.

Questions of Medical Ethics and the Lessons of Experience

Hazel McHaffie, author of medical-ethics novels
(www.hazelmchaffie.com)

I originally trained as a nurse and a midwife, and after having my own children, I spent most of my working hours in a regional neonatal unit: a very challenging environment, at the forefront of major advances in medicine. Many sick and premature infants still die; many are seriously damaged. It was there that my interest in medical ethics was really honed. I found myself questioning so many things. The opportunity to take up a research fellowship enabled me to start seeking answers, and to obtain a doctorate. At first, I concentrated on issues like how do mothers feel when taking tiny babies home after months in a high-powered unit? Who supports them? Where do grandparents and friends fit in?

But gradually, bigger questions prevailed. For example: When is enough enough? When should we stop treatment? Are there circumstances where we shouldn't even start to treat? By this time, I was deputy director of research at the Institute of Medical Ethics, based at the University of Edinburgh, and in a position to design and sustain a programme of research. I undertook to interview 176 doctors and nurses about their views and experiences of withholding or withdrawing treatment, and then to interview 108 parents whose babies had died, carrying out all the interviews myself. What a privilege. The results have influenced the way that these situations are handled in clinical practice in the UK and abroad.

Intuitively, one might think that parents would shy away from making huge life-or-death decisions for their infants, and, indeed, many professionals think that they should be protected from doing so. But in reality this is not the case. Parents do want to be given the opportunity to be involved in the decision-making process. Many of the ones to whom I spoke believed that they had indeed been involved. Perhaps more importantly, only one father felt that it was too burdensome for a parent, yet even he believed that decision-making should rest with the parents. It should be noted that there was, in fact, a sort of screening process operating that parents did not necessarily appreciate: they weren't asked even to consider cessation of treatment unless the medical team felt that the prognosis was very poor.

There are essentially two scenarios in which these questions are discussed: firstly, when the baby will die anyway, and it's a matter of how long its life should be prolonged; and, secondly, when the baby might survive, but with an extremely poor quality of life. The second case involves a harder decision and a bigger weight of responsibility, but the parents clearly demonstrated that they felt that they were the ones who should make this decision, and none expressed subsequent doubt about the choice that they had made.

Parents inevitably went over and over the events, both during the experience and afterwards. Few harboured doubts or regret, and this was very much related to how these situations were managed. Excellent communication is paramount: full and frank information should be given, with no false reassurances. And the other key factor is that when the parents are told that the prognosis is very poor, they should be shown concrete evidence of the truth of this fact.

Certain scenarios and developments may give rise to particular anxieties, although they may be unavoidable. Perhaps the hardest is when the dying process is protracted, perhaps over many hours, or even days, when parents may start to fear that they, and the doctors, have made a mistake. In such cases, they need to be constantly supported by the professional team, and to be given ongoing explanations about exactly what is happening and why, with reassurances that the baby is not suffering.

Some may question the wisdom of involving such parents in research. Without doubt, the families to whom I talked found the whole experience of reliving the pregnancy, birth, death and bereavement cathartic. Couples were interviewed together so that they could support each other, and in every case, they learned things about their partner's emotions and reactions that helped them to understand what was happening. Fathers, outside of the interview situation, were often reluctant to share their emotions with anyone else at all, which is not a healthy way to resolve deep grief.

Resuming 'everyday' life after such a devastating loss is not easy. Most friends and acquaintances never knew the baby who died. Many people react with platitudes and false reassurances, which seem to the parents to deny the enormity of their grief. Few 'lay' people understand the importance of taking their cue from the parents, and of listening, acknowledging and empathising sincerely. At this stage, the parents welcome opportunities to talk to the healthcare professionals who have known and cared for the child, for whom he or she was a real person. With them, they can relive the experience and try to make sense of what has happened. Interestingly, very few of the parents that I interviewed found a bereavement group helpful in these circumstances.

Having other children in the family forces the parents to get up in the morning, helping them to lurch through each day with a semblance of normality. But surviving twins or triplets from the same pregnancy carry a special kind of pain. There is a sense of constant comparison: the other baby should have been doing the same kinds of things. Becoming pregnant again after the loss can bring renewed hope, but the appropriate timing is very much an individual decision.

Overall, the kinds of support that these parents find most effective can be summed up concisely as caring, sharing and remembering.

- Caring means valuing the life of the baby and acknowledging the parents' loss. This includes the father's (there's a tendency for him to be overlooked).

- Sharing involves responsive, empathetic listening: listening without diminishing what has happened or giving false reassurances, and not imposing one's own assessment or perceptions.

- Remembering includes gathering and treasuring tangible mementos of the baby (clothes, a lock of hair, photographs, or footprints, for instance) that reinforce the reality of the lost child, and sharing memories of its short life. When others – relatives or staff who knew the child – show their own genuine grief at the death, this has particular significance for parents: their baby was valued and loved as a real individual.

Working in the field of ethical dilemmas around deciding how far to go, and when to stop treatment, has a personal resonance for me. My own first baby collapsed unexpectedly at three weeks of age. We were told that there was no possibility that he would survive. When he did, the medical team said that he'd be severely mentally and physically impaired. Back then, parents weren't consulted, but if I had been asked, I'd have said, 'Just let him die with dignity'. We would then have missed out on the joy of a son who grew up normal in every respect. This experience taught me the fallibility of both medical prognoses and parental instincts.

Forty years on, medical knowledge has expanded greatly. Parents are involved closely. There is, of course, still a margin for error, but where doubt exists, clinicians always err on the side of life. Time often provides a clearer answer. I am confident that both decision-making and managing the dying process are infinitely better because we have listened to the lived experience of those most intimately involved.

Shiatsu for Those who Are Close to Death
Tamsin Grainger, director of the Shiatsu Centre in Edinburgh (www.tssed.org).

Shiatsu has its roots in the theory of yin and yang – put in the most simple terms, it is about balancing the ki, or chi, usually translated as 'energy', although the word literally means 'steamed rice' (the rice being the yang, the actual form; and the steam, the yin, the energy that arises from the steamed rice). Shiatsu is a form of 'listening' with the hands, and that's exactly what I do. My approach with a person who is close to death is essentially the same as with anyone else: I am as present, open-minded and open-hearted as I can be. It is vital that the person wants me to be there, and I first need to be sure of that.

I see the person in terms of body–mind, and believe that change on any level – physical, mental, emotional or spiritual

– will affect the other levels. My training and experience mean that I know the subtle physical signs that imply that someone is becoming more relaxed. I have a developed awareness of ki energy: where it is accumulated, where it is less present and when it changes. Shiatsu training involves a good deal of medicine and pathology so that we can properly understand the physical situation, disease processes and the effects of specific medications. Through touch, we focus on the spirit of the person.

Having shiatsu practitioners working in hospitals and hospices is gradually becoming more common. The therapy was notably central in the establishment of the Bristol Cancer Help Centre during the 1980s, where counselling and body work were introduced to complement conventional Western medicine in order to address the complex needs of individuals. Shiatsu belongs to a Chinese tradition in which the Hun (part of the soul) will go forwards after death. I'm not a practising Buddhist, but my own belief is that we are all working towards some form of enlightenment through our lives, and that death can be seen as a threshold.

People approaching the end of their life usually want to cope as well as possible, and I will work with them at whichever level they are seeking. I'll often work with them on a practical level, aiming to help with flexibility and mobility. When they report that they are ready – not only physically, but also psychologically – this is often the point when they want to enter into a dialogue about preparing to die, or perhaps voice their concerns about others. My experience is that as they grow closer to death, people tend to focus on making things good: they may remember keenly things that haven't been resolved, and may want to resolve them; they may want to repair, or at least acknowledge, relationship difficulties.

Talking might not be easy. While sitting with someone who is dying, focusing on their breath tends to bring that person's attention to their own breath, resulting in a slowing and calming of their breathing, an overall relaxation. It's not true that people who are close to death don't want deep touch. They often do, but it depends on the individual. What most people need is for others to be really present with them, and that is something that the shiatsu practitioner's touch specifically does. It's different from an aromatherapist's touch, or a healer's touch, in that what we develop more than anything else is absolute presence in the moment. If you touch someone with that awareness, having built up that skill, it brings up that awareness for the receiver, in that moment.

It has often been observed that people can seem to hold off death for a while, even though they are ready to go, perhaps because they are waiting for someone to arrive at their bedside. It's possible that they are being held back by concern for family members who can't bear to see them go. In that situation, I might also support the soon-to-be-bereaved, knowing that their loved one was ready to go. In this, or any other scenario, I need to be saying with my whole self: 'Whatever you come up with, this is fine'. If the dying person is going through the 'I've got to be jolly' phase, I work with that. If they say, 'People tell me to be positive, but I simply can't because I'm having nightmares', then I'll be with them in that place. Being absolutely present is key to what shiatsu practitioners do.

Telling Your Life Story
Jean Edmiston, storyteller and storymaker (www.jeanstoryteller.co.uk)

Like most storytellers, I am not a therapist, although some therapists are storytellers. However, in my twenty years as a professional storyteller, I have often seen storytelling having a therapeutic effect. During storytelling workshops with older people, I have seen this demonstrated again and again. People facing bereavement, isolation and the various challenges of old age have wanted to talk about their lives, both for themselves and for the younger generation.

Telling their own stories allowed them to explore specific themes and sometimes opened up a way of resolving issues. For example, there was a very frail gentleman with poor sight who had been coming along to a storytelling group for a few weeks. He was so frail that he was brought along by a carer and had said very little. Then, one day, he said that he wanted to tell a story about something that had happened during the war. We all had the feeling that this really mattered to him, and you could have heard a pin drop.

Everyone listened intently. He had written down the story he wanted to tell and read it out with extraordinary passion, given how frail he was. He told us that during the Second World War, he had been a member of a military band. For him, the band was like his family. They were crossing the Atlantic in a troop carrier when the ship was attacked and sunk, with huge loss of life, including every one of his fellow band members. Ever since, he had carried the guilt of being the sole survivor of the band. This man died two weeks later. His wife sent the group a letter saying how much it had meant to him to have told that story, which he had never before told in detail until that day. After telling it, she said, he had seemed much more contented and settled in himself.

Storytelling is a very deep, natural way of uncovering such 'hidden material'. Its beneficial effects are becoming more widely recognised, and I myself have been called in to work in hospital and hospice settings. Of course, for storytelling to be helpful, the focus doesn't have to be on difficulty. I remember at a storytelling session at the hospice attached to Salisbury Hospital, asking the group what they'd like to do, and one man saying, 'Tell us stories about life, we're still alive'. The visualisations that come out of stories work powerfully on the imagination and can have a very positive effect on mood.

I have led storytelling workshops for people whose employment means that they have to deal with death on a frequent basis.

Some were concerned that they were becoming hardened to death through being exposed to it so often. Several voiced regret at never having talked to certain people who were dying, even when they could see that they did want to talk. They explained that they didn't have the time to chat, or were wary that such conversations would trigger a sense of loss in them. The outcome was that some group members decided to try to spend the time listening to dying patients and making a deeper human connection with them. They discovered that they felt better about themselves and the job, and came to see that this was a better way of working.

So many folk stories deal with death. These can be a good starting point in dealing with the subject – there's so much in them that's common to human experience. Traditional tales have a universal quality, and in that sense, an inclusiveness. One I like is this version of the story of the hare, who, on hearing about death, decides to wrap himself in his blanket and hide. The other animals come and ask the hare why he isn't out in the open air with the rest of them, enjoying the beautiful world. The frightened hare says he's hiding because death's out there. But the other creatures explain that since there's no real hiding from death, he might as well live life to the full.

There's an old African proverb: 'When an old person dies it's like a library going up in flames'. You could say that we are all made of stories. I think intergenerational work is a great thing. Everyone wants to be remembered, for others to know what their life has meant. I always say to people, 'Get that photograph album out!' Storytelling is a very natural way of passing down the fruits of a life to a young person.

Attending a Muslim Funeral

Suleman Nagdi MBE is the founding member and chairman of the Muslim Burial Council of Leicestershire (MBCOL, see www.mbcol.org.uk and page 245) and is a leading promoter of inter-faith understanding through his work with government, local authorities, police and media.

Britain is now indisputably a multicultural and a multi-faith society. As such, it is important that we learn about the different customs that are practised by the many religious groups, including what happens at funerals. The Muslim Burial Council of Leicestershire has created this brief guide to help familiarise non-Muslims with the process that occurs when a Muslim dies. Of course, within Muslim communities, grief and the way it is handled can vary according to different cultural influences, so the advice below should be treated as general guidance. Nonetheless, we hope that it will help those who want to pay their respects to a Muslim friend who has passed away or may want to attend the actual funeral, but do not know what to expect and what is considered appropriate.

When a Muslim is near death, those around him or her are called upon to give comfort, and for all to be reminded of God's mercy and forgiveness. They are encouraged to recite verses from the Holy Qur'an, and the dying person may also recite words of prayer. It is recommended for a Muslim's last words to be the declaration of faith, that is, 'I bear witness that there is no god but Allah'. However, there should be no coercion to recite this statement. Beyond this, efforts should be made to make the last moments as comfortable for the individual as possible. Offering water and physical comfort is recommended.

When the death occurs, those with the deceased are encouraged to remain calm, pray for the departed, and begin preparations for burial. Grief is normal, and it is natural and permitted to cry. Muslims are encouraged to strive to be patient and to remember that God is the One who gives life and takes it away – at a time He decides – and that it's not for us to question His wisdom.

A loss of an individual is not just as a loss to the family but to the whole community. For this reason, it is common for people who may not know the deceased personally to attend the funeral. In fact Muslims are encouraged to attend any Muslim's funeral, due to the profound personal, social and spiritual significance of such an event.

Muslims strive to bury the deceased as soon as possible after death; therefore it is not unusual for burial to take place within 24 hours of a death. The main steps involved are washing the body of the deceased, shrouding it, performance of the funeral prayer and finally, burial. The first two steps are performed only by selected relatives and community members due to the intimate nature of the tasks. The funeral prayer is a Muslim ritual that must be performed by Muslims, though observers are welcome.

There are also some matters regarding etiquette that everyone should be aware of when attending the funeral. Women from the Muslim faith commonly do not attend the funeral; however, should non-Muslim women wish to attend, it is important to remember that a headscarf is essential. The dress code for both men and women should be modest. This means a shirt and trousers for men and an ankle-length skirt, which should not be tight or transparent, together with a long-sleeved and high-necked top for women. As shoes must be removed before going into the prayer hall, it is a good idea to wear clean and presentable socks, stockings, or tights.

The congregation will line up in rows behind the coffin to perform the funeral prayer. It should be noted here that the funeral prayer is performed for the deceased and not to the deceased. Following its completion the congregation will form two lines and pass the coffin from shoulder to shoulder, taking it towards the grave site. Visitors are welcome to follow the congregation as they move the coffin towards the grave, but they should keep a short distance away so that there is enough walking space for the congregation to carry the coffin. Once at the grave, the coffin will be lowered, usually by family members, and the gravesite filled. The Imam will then say a few final prayers at the graveside, and following this, the congregation will disperse. The immediate members of the family will most likely remain at the graveside for a short while longer; this may be an opportune time for visitors to convey their condolences if they so wish.

In Her Best Interests?

This account is written by the sister of a woman undergoing compulsory treatment in the wake of a car accident that left her with profound brain injury. Despite having expressed strong views about not wanting her life prolonged in such a situation, she had not prepared a legally binding Advance Decision. Her fate is subject to 'best interest' decision-making: her prior wishes must be taken into account, but they do not determine her treatment.

I thought it would do me good to get away from the hospital, to escape from the 'family room' – a bleak space accessed from a stairwell, away from public view – assigned to those of us who wait. This room is an improvement on sleeping in the chair beside Hannah's bed, or crouching in the toilet at the end of the ward, writing up notes and trying to make calls to family and lawyers. But it is also a trap. I want to escape – from the noises, from the acrid smell of my unwashed clothes and my own stress, from the ceaseless shifts of trying to keep Hannah calm, trying to make her feel safe. But for her there is no escape. She must wait for the operation she always said she would refuse.

Each time I go back to her bedside I am confronted by her shocked expression. Now that the nasal gastric tube is in, she looks like a bull with a ring through its nose. She has ceased to resist, which is a relief – and yet I can't ignore the look in her eyes: confusion and what I imagine is a deep-down comprehension that they can use force on her now if they wish; minimal restraint, meticulously calibrated. The judge ruled that they will have to stop short of using a bridle on her. For that, at least, I am grateful.

For the first night here we were able to comfort her, Jessie and I, until at 2.30 a.m. we surrendered to exhaustion. Until then we stayed – talking to her softly and trying to explain to the nurses why attempts at brisk efficiency with Hannah are counter-productive, and why they would need to allow for the possibility of her lashing out – a kick in the stomach, a sudden claw to the face or twisting of their fingers, wrenching at ligaments. In spite of her lying like this for over two years since the car crash left her in a coma, then a 'minimally conscious state', and now in this shadow-land that is deemed 'recovery', Hannah's physical strength remains. She still has muscles, even though, apart from under the dedicated care of her physiotherapists, they are exercised only in spasmodic fury.

The transfer from her care home had gone OK, despite our anxieties. After days of rage, ripping out her feeding tube and subcutaneous lines and resisting all touch, she had finally fallen into an exhausted sleep. Awoken during the journey, she was calm while we waited in Accident and Emergency, at least for a while. But once on the ward, it all broke down again, as we had feared.

It didn't help that the nurses appeared to have no experience of profound brain injuries. One briskly poked the thermometer in Hannah's right ear, startling her into trying to squirm away. The nurse then simply switched to Hannah's paralysed side – an ear she could not defend. I took her hand in mine and she squeezed back, so tight that her fingernails cut into me (faeces were still ingrained beneath her nails, and I made a mental note to disinfect the little wounds she left – rubbing the hand-cleanser fluid outside each ward door into the skin to make it sting).

We protected her as best we could, Jessie and I, her two sisters. Jessie reassured Hannah as a look of terror contorted her face, as if she thought the blood-pressure cuff would expand indefinitely until her arm was severed. We tried to turn the placing of the oxygen monitor clip into a game – placing it on our own fingers, and then toes, showing Hannah the red glow, cajoling her. It worked, for a moment, holding her in an illusion, but then she savagely shook her hand and the clip spun off, exasperating the kind but busy nurse. She picked at the tube into her hand, tugging at the cannula, tightly bandaged in, while I tried to connect the dripping rubber tube back in place.

Hannah would not be comforted. She stared at her hand, holding it out with a pleading look, like a lion holding out its paw. I stroked her arm and tried to explain to her that the IV was there to help her feel better – the truths unsaid tasting bitter in my mouth. But Hannah glared and rubbed her 'good' hand against her 'bad' in an effort to dislodge the tube. Her distress escalated until she became frantic, yanking at the tube, moaning, shouting inarticulate, slurred, repeated syllables. She knows what she is saying, but her world has gone mad. We, her familiar strangers, must seem to mock her with our useless incomprehension.

Jessie lowered the cot sides and rolled into the bed with Hannah, offering a restraining embrace. Hannah paused and I grasped the moment to distract her, reaching for the dog-eared poetry book that has gone with us everywhere for the last two years and two months. Unable to find it, I had to rely on my internalised repertoire. '*April is the cruelest month*', I began, recalling the poem we learnt by heart as children. We knew the lines back then, but now I searched for the next one. '*April is the cruelest month*', I repeated, '*breeding lilacs out of the dead land, mixing memory and desire, stirring dull roots with spring rain*'. I paused, and stuttered, '*feeding a little life with dried tubers*', before drying up completely. I turned to a safer standby. 'Daffodils' is innocuous enough, and not pregnant with new meaning. '*I wandered lonely as a cloud*', I recited, hoping to lull her into 'vacant or pensive mood', to take her somewhere else where flowers dance beneath trees. She gazed at me, still in Jessica's arms, and sighed. Her eyes smiled at me for a moment, and then her expression changed to fear, fury, and then a sneer. One eye, drifting to the left, stared sightlessly into the far distance, while her other eye focused on me, seeming to glare accusingly at the betrayal of our play-acting.

That was last week. We are entirely defeated now. After Jessie and I left Hannah's bedside in the early morning she ripped out the cannula three times, and kept the whole ward awake with her distress. We went back to the care home to collect the much-needed volume of poetry and her shawl, and the manager approached us, grim-faced, ushering us into the 'quiet room'. The hospital had rung saying they needed someone with Hannah at all times to help control her. 'It's not your job', the manager advised. 'You need to look after yourselves for a while, we'll send in one of our staff for the morning.' That worked for a few hours, but not for long. The clinicians have by now precisely clarified the degree of restraint they can deploy against Hannah, and the system has systematically worn us down ever since.

All three of us sisters are exhausted now, no reserves left. Jessie and I are tetchy, beyond caring. We leave Hannah and seek respite away from it all. We get into the heavy Kangoo vehicle, with its ramp and electric winch and wheelchairs straps, and drive to a nearby pub that looks across to distant hills. Jessie had promised me a break from the hospital, a place to pause. She has chosen well; the old alehouse has heavy wooden tables, cushioned benches, an inglenook fireplace, curved walls, and ceilings that drop low so that I must duck into the snug.

The comfort food looks good. I worry about Jessie's diabetes, but we have two cardinal rules now: 'don't fuss', and 'fit your own oxygen mask before helping others'. We find a tucked-away table and try to talk of other things than Hannah's plight. The cider is sweet and strong, softening my edges, blurring my conscience. I feel the buzz of others' easy conversation. I relish the aliveness of it all, connectedness, and I feel my own existence in three dimensions. Then I'm shocked back to the reality of my sister, who will never leave an institution. Dragged back repeatedly from the jaws of death, she must accept the perverse umbilical cords that tether her to life; she must endure surgery and invasions into every orifice.

This texture of life that we can escape to will never be hers again. For now, all we can do is look forward to getting her back to the 'rehabilitation' centre, where her room has natural light and overlooks a field and has been carefully 'personalised'. Her own paintings hang on the wall, one, painted after her visit to Africa, showing a herd of zebras in the Serengeti, another depicting a gloriously fierce dragon, steam hissing from its nostrils. We have filled the room with photos of her garden – sweet peas in bloom, the raised bed of cabbages and potatoes – and Jessie has made sure that Hannah's favourite shower gel is on the shelf in the bathroom: her sense of smell is finally recovering, and the carers say she cooperates and sometimes smiles when they shower her.

It is time to leave the pub. We have already left her too long. A numbness is creeping in. We drive back, and as we walk into the hospital lobby and fluorescent lighting, the automatic doors hiss shut behind us.

An Instinct for Kindness

Chris Larner is an actor and playwright whose powerful, award-winning play 'An Instinct for Kindness' conveys the stark realities of assisted suicide. His experience in a supporting role at Dignitas is an eloquent, unsentimental reminder that a debate often conducted in moral terms feels quite different to those it affects most directly.

It was a chill day, the 6th November 2010. Chill for Allyson, at least. She hadn't been outside in two years, near enough. She was terrified of the cold, terrified of what another winter might mean for her poor, exhausted body. By then, she had no fat on her, and she couldn't exactly run around to generate warmth. Leeds Bradford airport, on top of the moor, is a windy spot and Allyson shivered in her coat, her scarf, her mittens and her blanket as I wheeled her into departures.

Allyson my old friend: my ex-wife and mother of my eldest son. We boarded a flight to Amsterdam Schiphol, two burly men lifting Allyson into her seat. With us was Allyson's sister Vivienne. We had return tickets all, just in case Ally changed her mind. From Schiphol to Zurich. From Zurich a taxi, Allyson's wheelchair strapped down and her strapped in it, comically in the centre of the back of the minibus, riding chariot and we laugh about her imperious position as the landscape of Switzerland speeds by, postcard pretty.

Pfäffikon is a pretty town, clean as a whistle and surrounded by mountains which reflect spectacularly in a deep, tranquil lake. We spent three days in Pfäffikon.

I shan't be going again. Nor will Vivienne, I shouldn't think. And Allyson...

Allyson didn't change her mind. I knew she wouldn't. She arrived back at my flat a fortnight later, a version of her. It was sooner than I had imagined. Damn efficient, the Swiss. We'll take her up to the Chevin, when the time is right. Allyson's family and I. We'll say some words while the Yorkshire wind takes her.

Sodium Pentobarbital can cause vomiting, if you swallow enough of it. So an anti-emetic is given, half an hour beforehand. You have half an hour – more if you want it – when you can phone your son, back in England, read some of the cards, remember your childhood.

A solution of Sodium Pentobarbital is the worst tasting thing you ever put in your mouth. I don't know this for certain, of course, but the grimace that Allyson pulled told you it was no milkshake. The doctor had warned her, the day before, in one of a series of careful euphemisms. *The taste is not so good. You must swallow straight down. Practise doing so. As much as a large brandy.* They give you a chocolate, afterwards. In Switzerland, they have chocolate for everything.

Later, back at the hotel, Vivienne and I are on our own. Everyone is looking at us, either that or pointedly not doing so. I don't know which is worse. We smell of Death. We smell of taboo. We are disgusting.

The following morning, in Allyson's room, we are packed and ready to go back home, stunned as cattle. A chambermaid is at the open door. We have bin liners full of redundant medicines and nappies, we have bulging suitcases and an electric wheelchair, dismantled and gaffer-taped for transportation. We are weighed down with the clutter of grief and guilt, and the chambermaid sees it all. I have seen her around, these last three days, not to speak to but they've worked around us: coming back to change the sheets when we're downstairs for cups of tea. I wave her away, signalling, *do next door first*, but she stays there. I say, in bad German, *the other room, thank you*. She stays there, sheepish but stubborn, looking at Vivienne.

Deine Schwester, she says eventually – and it's a question – your sister? I translate for Vivienne, who starts like a guilty thing as if the police have called. Yes, I say, her sister.

Ist besser für sie, says the maid, impelled to continue no matter what. In a soft tone she says, *ist besser für sie, jetzt. Ich denke so. Ist besser für sie*. Again I translate but now the tears are thick lumps in my throat and Vivienne's eyes are not her own, either.

Thank you, I say, yes, it's better. She was in a lot of pain.

My mother says the chambermaid, softly, touching her own heart, *my mother. The same*. And so it goes. The first of many who will touch her own heart, to touch ours, to show that we are not alone. In a shitty world, full of Lies and Adverts, incurable diseases and curable cruelty, the human instinct for kindness, for empathy, shines through stubborn. And there rests some kind of Hope. At least for those still living.

No Time to Die Like This: Being with the people who make you feel alive

Claire Wilson, a writer who lost her partner Alan to cancer, shares their experience of the pressure of other peoples' demands on their time during Alan's final weeks, and how they learned to fill that time with truth.

Who's at your side when you die? The people who make you love, laugh, live, who respect the poignancy of your last days? Or the people who shout loudest, hoping that out of a sense of duty you'll ease their anxiety and guilt? Dying in 'peace' is not a given.

I spent eight years of my life with Alan. Cancer butted in on the last three years. There was a lot of bad stuff... a lot. And there was a lot of beautifully good stuff; memories that dissolve the pettiness of daily life, reminding you to walk barefoot on wet grass. Alan repeatedly defied textbook timescales on recovery periods and certainly when it came to life expectancy. But in the end we knew – accepted – that Alan's time was coming to an end. There are benefits to knowing when you'll die. If you've got something to say, you are likely to say it when you believe it's 'now or never'. Alan used this clarity to tell people how he felt, to make sure he left belongings and words for his daughters that would resonate throughout their lifetimes, to ensure that practical and legal arrangements were taken care of, to laugh again with those he loved.

There was a downside to this 'window of open communication'. In through it clambered people realising their guilts, fear, anxieties, greed... shoving and pushing their way harder than any of those Alan had actually opened the window for. In the certainty of imminent death one might expect the courage to face with contempt such disingenuous requests for forgiveness, or to ignore a love once betrayed. Not so. Death makes you question, soften, forgive. Blood is a powerful contract, as is the emotion of rekindled good old times with people who were 'sort of' there, at some point. Even with each sharpened moment spilling through our grappling hands we were conscious of the needs, the demands, of others. Even now, I am saddened that for a time we let all this noise interrupt our peace. Here's an extract from the diary I kept during Alan's last months:

> It's not the time at home we talked about, prayed for. Our walks together, our time in the garden, get sabotaged by other stuff, other people. Our return home is as tough a slog as life in the hospital or hospice. I watch you dying, almost out of touch behind a barrier of routine and other people.
>
> 6.40am I'm up to get a handover from the overnight nurse. I give you breakthrough diamorphine, have shower, get dressed, make

you breakfast in bed. Help you up and shower and get settled, change the bed, the nurse arrives at 10.45/11am, doctor follows most days at 12/1pm. I do the necessary housework, then make you lunch. I try to answer some of the texts. We have visitors, I make coffees, chat when you tire, make hints for them to leave. I do meds at 1pm then 5pm, I make tea, answer more texts and phone calls, take the call from the out-of-hours nurses. We do some paperwork – not daily stuff, but the important stuff about dying that you want taken care of. All the while the home phone squawks... the mobile chirps... all the questions, all the questions, all the questions. It's not support, it's assault.

At 8pm we go upstairs. I help you get changed for bed, give you more breakthrough, the 9pm meds and we lie next to each other resting and waiting for the overnight nurse arriving at 10pm, dreading being apart. I do a handover and go to the spare room. For a while I lie and listen to the sound of a stranger in our home, then I down two sleeping pills, sleep little, listen for noises from you and get up at 6.40am and do it all again. And all the while the deafening noise of everyone else.

Our close family and friends of course respected our space. But not until we were at breaking point and our doctors intervened did we put a firm foot down on the people who were invading a private time with little regard for Alan's welfare. They didn't understand the critical importance of the medical routine we maintained, or even seem to care that the faster Alan tired, the less time he had.

We were a private couple suddenly bombarded by unruly noise. It took a while to learn how to manage the wanted and unwanted attention. I felt like I was failing in some way, but our MacMillan and Marie Curie nurses reassured me we were not alone. They'd known patients who'd put signs on their doors asking visitors to stay away and others who screamed at everyone to get out of their house or hospice room.

Given all the horrors we faced, it seems ridiculous to say that dealing with everyone else was one of the worst bits of the cancer rollercoaster as we prepared for Alan's death. It was; we nearly left home to escape it. Fortunately we found small ways to help manage the 'attention'. Here is our list of 'practical defences':

Regular group updates
- Of course, keep family and friends updated after operations and treatments, or daily as the situation deteriorates. But responding individually is overwhelming. Explain that you'll update at the end of every week/day via a group text/email/facebook. Gradually people will accept this and stop 'panic texting/calling'.
- Too tired to talk after twelve hours at the hospital? Be honest. Don't sacrifice vital rest and meals to repeat what you've already communicated.

Visiting at the hospital and at home
- Ask people to check before visiting to avoid a large group, both for your own sake and to meet hospital rules.
- The patient's energy levels and comfort are the priorities, so plan essential needs first: medicines, meals, doctor/nurse visits, personal care, rest periods. Remember that simple things like washing and dressing or moving rooms take much longer. Plan time to do it safely and comfortably.
- If you're the primary carer, what does the person you love want to do... *really* want to do? Whatever it is, make sure they have the time to do it.
- Then, only then, commit to visitors, and when you do, ask people to be aware of signs that the 'patient' is tiring. Agree a 'secret signal' with your loved one so you know when it's time to encourage guests to leave.
- Limit personal visits to times that suit you both, and keep some days free. Cancel if either one of you is unwell or too tired.

- Talk to your nurses. They see these problems every day and will help you 'manage' the attention.
- Do what's right for the person who is dying. If someone gets upset because you can't let them visit, explain the situation calmly once, then leave it. There's no time – or energy – for emotional politics.
- Often some time in the fresh air, with the trees and wildlife is truth enough.

"I'm either alive or dead, there's no in between. I know who has been there for me in life; I know who will respect my memory when I die." In the end Alan cherished the company of the people who brought truth to his time and helped him – as much as he could – to live life as if the end was nowhere in sight.

Bereavement in the Lesbian, Gay and Bisexual Community

John Parson worked with Cruse Bereavement Care as Service and Development Manager until his retirement two years ago, and is now a volunteer with the organisation.

Homosexuality and bisexuality are perhaps more tolerated in our society today than they ever have been before. But it's also undeniably true that some people still feel uncomfortable when confronted with these types of relationship and so, even in twenty-first century Britain, many gays and lesbians keep their relationships separate from family, friends or work colleagues. This is despite the fact that such a relationship could very well be the most intimate and significant in their lives. Even for those who are not 'out', most people know, though little is ever said.

But when someone dies, very little can be more hurtful to those who are grieving than for their relationship with the deceased to go unacknowledged or undervalued. In the immediate days after the death, the grieving partner might be left out of the funeral arrangements as family and friends sometimes fail to acknowledge the central role that the partner played in his or her life. Even the simple act of expressing condolences may be missing. To add further to the pain, a partner can be left with enormous financial difficulties or with their home at risk. The advent of civil partnerships has thankfully reduced such risks, but legal challenges or other disputes can add to the burden.

Grieving is a difficult process for anyone, but there can be further complicating factors for the many gays, lesbians and bi-sexuals who move away from where they grew up, often to cities. As a result, there can easily be differences of opinion about where funerals take place, unless the person who has died has made his or her wishes explicit. And even if the funeral instructions are clear and unambiguous, the service will ring hollow if it is tinged with implicit disapproval of the relationship. The funeral may even inadvertently initiate an 'outing' process because of the way it brings together disparate people who knew the deceased.

Gay men, lesbians and bisexuals often develop their own strong social networks, especially if they are not 'out', and so a death can be like the loss of a family member. Gay men, in particular, may have suffered multiple HIV-related bereavements. At its worst in the late 1980s and '90s, you could even say there was a 'culture of mourning' amongst the gay community. It decimated social net-works and increased the risk of isolation and loneliness, especially as there was often stigmatisation of HIV-related illness and death.

Large numbers of gay men and women have a significant and varied 'history of loss' in their lives. Suicide rates amongst young gay men are higher than that for the rest of that age group and, in general terms, it seems that life expectancy within the gay community is lower than in the population as a whole. Since gay men and lesbians are less likely to have children or an extended family, it opens up a greater possibility of isolation in old age.

However, every person and relationship is unique. It is so im-portant to respect the value that a bereaved person places on the relationship with someone who has died. That relationship may have been private and inexplicit or beyond the comprehension of others. To simply accept that it was and is of great consequence and value may be the first stage of providing comfort to someone who is grieving.

What Is Death?

Professor of Divinity Henry Scott Holland first delivered these words in a 1910 sermon following the death of Edward VII. The poem is also known by the title 'Death is Nothing at All'; we have chosen the title reflecting the confusion and turmoil involved in coming to terms with a loss.

Death is nothing at all.
I have only slipped away into the next room.
I am I and you are you.
Whatever we were to each other,
that we are still.

Call me by my old familiar name.
Speak to me in the easy way
you always used.
Put no difference in your tone.
Wear no forced air of solemnity or sorrow.

Laugh as we always laughed
at the little jokes we enjoyed together.
Play, smile, think of me, pray for me.
Let my name be ever the household word
that it always was.
Let it be spoken without effort,
without the trace of a shadow on it.

Life means all that it ever meant.
It is the same that it ever was.

There is absolutely unbroken continuity.
Why should I be out of mind
because I am out of sight?

I am waiting for you,
for an interval,
somewhere very near,
just around the corner.

All is well.

Death Is not The End
Peter Tatchell campaigns for civil liberties, justice, freedom and human rights. He wrote this poem in 1985.

Death is not The End,
But the beginning
Of a metamorphosis.

For matter is never destroyed,
Only rearranged –
Often more perfectly.

Witness how,
In the moment of the caterpillar's death,
The beauty of the butterfly in born,
And, released from the prison of the cocoon,
It flies free.

Mourning Becomes Electoral (and Social): Our Return to Open Grieving?

After the death-denial taboo of the twentieth century, are we coming full circle in a more open approach to grieving? Michael Kerrigan reflects.

Princess Diana's death in 1997 and the outpouring of public grief that followed have been seen as representing a turning point in British social and cultural life. Precisely what was turning to what, though, is a matter of disagreement, dividing commentators at the time and to this day. Tearful tributes in the print and broadcast media, condolence books in supermarket foyers, acres of floral bouquets outside Kensington Palace: it was an extraordinary time, no one would deny that – but what did it actually *say* about modern Britain? Was it welcome evidence, as some suggested, that the land of the stiff upper lip was at long last getting in touch with its emotions? Or was it, as others argued, just the final jettisoning of self-discipline and decorum by a society now fully in the grip of a mawkish and sensationalist celebrity culture?

Almost as noisy as the weeping and the wailing was the backlash from those who, not having known the late Princess personally, saw no compelling reason why they should mourn her. Many felt there was something almost bullying in the expectation – even the insistence – that they should. The higher-minded media rang with denunciations of the 'grief police' who were allegedly everywhere, from the columns of Fleet Street to the factory floor, ganging up on those who had the temerity to remain unmoved. Some saw something positively sinister in the spectacular show of grief – and it *was* a show, a collective performance. People were crying to conform; they weren't sincere. And even if they were, sceptics suggested, the most that could be said for this was that this very public death had enabled them to vent deeply suppressed and perhaps even subconscious feelings of loss and desolation.

No matter, they found a fluent spokesman in Prime Minister Tony Blair, whose tribute to the 'People's Princess' was generally agreed to have picked up the prevailing mood. The Labour leader had been swept to power by a landslide just a few months before and was still riding so high in the polls that it seems superfluous to speak of any sort of Diana-dividend. What can be said, however, is that his main political opponent, Conservative Party leader William Hague, was generally deemed to have misread the situation and suffered a setback in the opinion polls. This was in spite of the fact that his statement on Diana's death had been by previous standards irreproachable: brief, but solemn and dignified.

Buckingham Palace is believed to have resisted attempts by Blair's Downing Street staff to secure a major role for the Prime Minister in the ceremonial surrounding the funeral of the Queen Mother five years later, in 2002. The public mourning now had to find its own level and make its way without the guidance of its political leaders. Not only the New Labour hierarchy but the political elite more generally were badly affronted, the conservative columnist Peter Oborne was subsequently to argue, by this 'reminder of the existence of a Britain whose loyalties and allegiances went far deeper than party, but had everything to do with Queen and country, village, school, town and family'.

Of course, a death doesn't have to be of constitutional significance to be of consequence for the country – or the world: recent years have seen the rise of what might be called 'social grieving'. As many as 2.5 billion viewers worldwide watched Michael Jackson's memorial service in July, 2009, it has been claimed: even allowing for exaggeration, that's quite a crowd. Time will tell whether the fame of Apple founder Steve Jobs goes the way of the floppy disk and the daisy-wheel printer, but he was acclaimed as a maker of the twenty-first century when he died in October 2011. Britain, meanwhile, has mobilised in mourning for everyone from haulage entrepreneur Eddie Stobart (March 2011) to singer Amy Winehouse (July 2011), and from former footballer and Wales manager Gary Speed (November 2011) to Raoul Moat-victim PC David Rathband (March 2012).

There's an established etiquette, it seems: the hushed reports; the footage of flower-wielding and candle-lighting crowds; the setting up of online tribute boards so everyone can offer their RIP. But if the media and the punters swing straight into action, the backlash is quick in coming too – the cynical sniping, the disdainful accusations of excess. Indeed, the whole cycle – from shock to indifference – has accelerated, argued American journalist Megan Garber after observing the fuss that followed Whitney Houston's death in February 2012. Within an hour, she was trending worldwide on Twitter; almost immediately, though, the interest was measurably waning; within a couple of days, it had come to seem 'old news', revived only briefly by a star-studded turnout for the funeral itself. It's striking that we seem to feel so much real emotion for someone we've most of us never come close to meeting, Garber suggested, but the contrast with more traditional forms of mourning couldn't be more stark. 'Instead of four years or seven days,' she says, 'we're giving ourselves a moment, a burst to commiserate and commemorate before we shed our widow's weeds and move on.'

How we grieve for loved ones and friends is, of course, nothing like the way we respond to the death of a public figure. Yet our views on death and dying and the ways we mourn and remember those we have lost are changing, too. Now more than ever, we are coming to recognise the importance of talking more openly about death, addressing our fears and dealing with our affairs. Through this increased openness, it is hoped that more and more of us will experience greater peace of mind in later life, and a 'good death'.

✳ RECOMMENDED ✳ RESOURCES

In addition to those that appear at appropriate points in the book, here is a selection of resources whose treatment of various aspects of death and dying you may find useful, interesting or inspirational. Note that it is not intended to be comprehensive or exhaustive, but instead to provide pointers to locating further information and help.

- For a general historical overview of how the dead have been buried and commemorated over the centuries, author Michael Kerrigan's book, *The History of Death: Burial Customs and Funeral Rites, from the Ancient World to Modern Times* (Lyons Press, 2007), is an illuminating read.

- **The Dying Matters Coalition** was established in 2009 by the **National Council for Palliative Care** (www.ncpc.org.uk) to raise awareness of dying, death and bereavement. Its website offers a wealth of advice, resources and specialist links. Visit www.dyingmatters.org for more information.

- The **If I Should Die** website was set up in 2001 to provide as much independent (and non-denominational) practical information and support as possible. Visit www.ifishoulddie.co.uk for guidance on preparing for death, dealing with it and coping in its aftermath.

- The **Directgov** website, the UK government's digital service for people in England and Wales, has a section on death and bereavement that provides information on wills and probate; on what do to after a death; and on benefits, properties and money: www.direct.gov.uk/en/Governmentcitizensandrights/ Death/index.htm. Other death-related issues are addressed, too. If you live in Northern Ireland, NI Direct gives similar advice in its death and bereavement section: www.nidirect.gov. uk/index/information-and-services/government-citizens-and-rights/death-and-bereavement.htm.

- The **Centre for Death and Society** (CDAS), based at the University of Bath, is the UK's only centre devoted to the study and research of social aspects of death, dying and bereavement. Visit www.bath.ac.uk/cdas for more information.

- For a comprehensive treatment of many of the cultural and practical issues discussed in this book, Suleman Nagdi's book *Discovering through Death: Beliefs and Practices* (Muslim Burial Council of Leicestershire, 2011) is a useful reference. See pages 224–26 for the author's guidance on Muslim funerals.

1.   Last Orders: What Instructions Do You Want to Leave Behind?

- **Age UK** produces a 'LifeBook' ('a free booklet where you write important and useful information about your life, from who insures your car to where you put the TV licence'), which you can order by visiting the organisation's website, www.ageuk.org.uk/home-and-care/home-safety-and-security/lifebook, or ringing 0845 685 1061.

- If you need advice relating to trusts, estates and related issues, the website of the **Society of Trust and Estate Practitioners** (STEP) is worth a visit: www.step.org.

- If you need help finding a solicitor, the searchable database on the **Law Society**'s website may be useful: www.law-society.org.uk/choosingandusing/findasolicitor.law. **The Law Society of Scotland** is found at www.lawscot.org.uk.

- **Directgov** has a page that gives basic advice on making a will on its website: www.direct.gov.uk/en/Govern-mentcitizensandrights/Death/Preparation/DG_10029800.

- Advice on making a will is given by the **Citizens Advice Bureau**: www.adviceguide.org.uk/index/family_parent/family/wills.htm.

- **Age UK** provides basic information on making a will, and you can also download helpful factsheets from its website (www.ageuk.org.uk/money-matters/legal-issues/making-a-will). **Age UK Legal Services** can provide a will-writing pack and advise you on how to write, update and change your will (www.ageuk.org.uk/buy/legal-services/will-writing), but note that only the initial consultation may be free of charge.

- A number of useful death-related factsheets can be down-loaded from the **Age Concern Scotland** website (www.agescotland.org.uk/helping_you/factsheets), including one on making your will.

- **The Will Expert** website (www.thewillexpert.co.uk) offers guidance on aspects of will-writing, intestacy and inherit-ance in the UK (including Scotland).

- Visit the **Age UK** website for advice on dealing with a de-ceased person's estate: www.ageuk.org.uk/money-matters/legal-issues/dealing-with-an-estate.

- **Directgov** provides information on probate, www.direct.gov.uk/en/Governmentcitizensandrights/Death/Preparation/DG_10029799, and, if you are an executor, on how to apply for probate: www.direct.gov.uk/en/Governmentcitizensandrights/Death/Preparation/DG_10029716. It also gives guidance on inheritance tax (www.direct.gov.uk/en/MoneyTaxAndBenefits/Taxes/BeginnersGuideToTax/InheritanceTaxEstatesAndTrusts/index.htm), an area on which the **HM Revenue & Custom**'s website goes into more detail: www.hmrc.gov.uk/agents/forms-iht.htm.

- For more information about ownerless property that passes to the Crown, and for a list of unclaimed *bona vacantia* estates, see www.bonavacantia.gov.uk.

2. Shuffling Off This Mortal Coil: How Do You Want to Go?

- **Saga** provides information and discussion forums on all sorts of issues affecting older people. See www.saga.co.uk.

- Appointing a trusted someone to act as your 'attorney' to make decisions on your behalf should you no longer be capable of doing so yourself is worth considering. Learn more about making and registering a lasting power of attorney (LPA) by visiting the **Directgov** website: www.direct.gov.uk/en/Governmentcitizensandrights/Mentalcapacityandthelaw/Makingarrangementsincaseyoulosementalcapacity/DG_186373. **Age UK** also gives advice on powers of attorney: www.ageuk.org.uk/money-matters/legal-issues/powers-of-attorney.

- If you want to learn more about your options should you think that you'll want to refuse further medical treatment at some point, visit the **Directgov** website: www.direct.gov. uk/en/Governmentcitizensandrights/Death/Preparation/ DG_10029802.

- The issues surrounding living wills (also known as advance decisions and advance statements) are outlined on **Age UK**'s website: www.ageuk.org.uk/money-matters/legal-issues/living-wills.

- **Compassion in Dying** is a national charity that supports people at the end of their lives to have what they consider to be a good death; its website provides further information: www.compassionindying.org.uk. A national campaign and membership organisation, **Dignity in Dying** (Compassion in Dying's partner) seeks greater choice and control to alleviate suffering at the end of life. Learn more by visiting its website: www.dignityindying.org.uk.

- For information on UK hospice care and how to find a hospice, visit the hospice information service page on the **Help the Hospices** website: www.helpthehospices.org.uk/ hospiceinformation.

- The **Age UK** website lists the immediate tasks that should be performed after someone's death: www.ageuk.org.uk/money -matters/legal-issues/what-to-do-when-someone-dies.

- Visit the **Directgov** website for information on how to register a death in England and Wales, and for links relating to registering a death in Scotland and Northern Ireland: www. direct.gov.uk/bereavement_radio.dsb?pro=BDT. Directgov also provides additional guidance on what should be done after someone's death: www.direct.gov.uk/en/Govern-mentcitizensandrights/Death/WhatToDoAfterADeath/index.htm.

- More information about 'Tell Us Once', the service that (hopefully) makes it easier to inform the government about a death, can be found at www.direct.gov.uk/en/Nl1/Newsroom/DG_188740

- The **Citizens Advice Bureau** presents a comprehensive guide to what to do after someone's death on its website (www.adviceguide.org.uk/index/family_parent/family/what_to_do_after_a_death.htm), as do the **Bereavement Advice Centre** (www.bereavementadvice.org) and **Carers UK** (www.carersuk.org/Information/Whencaringends/Whenapersondies).

3. Pomp and Circumstance: What Kind of Send-Off Do You Want?

- If you are looking for a funeral director, both the **National Association of Funeral Directors** (www.nafd.org.uk) and the **National Society of Allied and Independent Funeral Directors** (www.saif.org.uk) offer a member search facility on their websites.

- For information on humanist services and finding a humanist celebrant, visit the **British Humanist Association**'s website: www.humanism.org.uk, or www.humanism-scotland.org.uk.

- The **Institute of Civil Funerals** (IOCF) was set up in 2002 to oversee the standards and quality of civil funerals in the UK. The website includes a directory of registered civil funeral celebrants, as well as other useful information: www.iocf.org.uk.

- The **Good Funeral Guide**, Charles Cowling's website (www.goodfuneralguide.co.uk) – and book – is an informative independent guide to the funeral industry, with an interesting blog: www.goodfuneralguide.co.uk/blog.

- Visit **Directgov** if you are on a low income and need to pay for a funeral as you may be able to get financial help from the Social Fund: www.direct.gov.uk/en/MoneyTaxAnd-Benefits/BenefitsTaxCreditsAndOtherSupport/Bereaved/DG_10018660

- **The Compassionate Friends** (TCF) is an organisation that supports bereaved parents and their families after a child's death; its website gives more details: www.tcf.org.uk. The **Child Death Helpline** (freephone 0800 282 986) aims to help anyone who has been affected by a child's death; learn more on its website, which also provides specialist links relating to children's deaths: www.childdeathhelpline. org.uk. **The Stillbirth and Neonatal Death Society** (SANDS) supports anyone affected by the death of a baby; details of national and regional offices are found at www. uk-sands.org.

- Certain organisations and websites are concerned trying to help children cope with a loved one's death, notably: **Winston's Wish** (www.winstonswish.org.uk), **Childline** (www.childline.org.uk/Explore/Life/Pages/WhenSome-oneDies.aspx) and **RD4U** (www.rd4u.org.uk).

4. Your Last Resting Place: Where Do You Want to End Up?

- For advice on organ donation, visit the **NHS Organ Donor Register** website (you can also join it online here): www.organdonation.nhs.uk.

- If you have a potentially life-threatening medical condition or allergy and aren't already aware of **MedicAlert** and its associated MedicAlert emblems and emergency telephone service, particularly in relation to organ donation, you may find visiting its website informative: www.medicalert.org.uk.

- If you are considering leaving your body to medical science and would like to learn more, visit the **Human Tissue Authority** (HTA) website: www.hta.gov.uk/donations/howtodonateyourbodytomedicalscience.cfm.

- Authors Michael Kerrigan and contributor Ronnie Scott have both written books on **burial places**: Michael is the author of *Who Lies Where: A Guide to Famous Graves (A Guardian Book)* (Fourth Estate, 1995), while Ronnie has published *Death by Design: The True Story of the Glasgow Necropolis* (Black and White Publishing, 2005). Catherine Arnold's *Necropolis: London and its Dead* (London Pocket Books, 2007) provides an interesting history of London's great cemeteries (and much more). Ken West's book *A Guide to Natural Burial* (Sweet & Maxwell, 2010) is an excellent resource and has been widely influential since its publication.

- Visit the website of the **Natural Death Centre** for information on family-organised and environmentally friendly funerals: www.naturaldeath.org.uk.

- For practical information on burial at sea, visit the **Marine Management Organisation** website: www.marinemanagement.org.uk/works/controls/burial.htm.

- The **Scattering Ashes** website is a source of simple advice and ideas on what do with a loved one's cremation ashes: www.scattering-ashes.co.uk.

- More information about the Living Churchyards Project can be found at the **Alliance of Religions and Conservation** (ARC) website: www.arcworld.org/projects.asp?projectID=271

5. *In Memoriam:* How Do You Want to be Remembered?

- The **Oral History Society**'s website gives advice on how to interview someone in order to record their memories or life story: www.oralhistory.org.uk/advice/index.php.

- The **StoryVault** website encourages its users to preserve people's memories by interviewing friends or family members on video and then uploading the interviews to www.storyvault.com.

- The website of the **National Association of Memorial Masons** gives advice on memorials and on finding a memorial mason: www.namm.org.uk.

- Douglas Keiter's *Stories in Stone: A Field Guide to Cemetery Symbolism and Iconography* (Gibbs Smith, Publisher, 2004) provides an interesting illustrated overview of the symbols that have traditionally been used to decorate tombstones.

6.   A Happy Ending?

- For advice on what to do when a friend or relative dies abroad, visit the **Foreign & Commonwealth Office**'s website: www.fco.gov.uk/en/travel-and-living-abroad/when-things-go-wrong/death-abroad.

- If you were married or in a civil partnership when your partner died, you may be entitled to bereavement benefits. **The Citizens Advice Bureau** outlines these on its website: www.adviceguide.org.uk/index/your_money/benefits/benefits_and_bereavement.htm.

- For emotional support following a bereavement, you may find it helpful to visit the **Cruse Bereavement Care** website, www.crusebereavementcare.org.uk (or www.cruse-escotland.org.uk) and the **Facing Bereavement** website: www.facingbereavement.co.uk.

- The **National Association of Widows** is run by the widowed for widowed men and women of all ages; for further details, visit its website: www.nawidows.org.uk.

- If you are a young person who has been widowed, you may be interested in the support offered by the **WAY Foundation**: www.wayfoundation.org.uk.

- If you are struggling to come to terms with a loved one's suicide, you may find it beneficial to visit the **Survivors of Bereavement by Suicide** website: www.uk-sobs.org.uk or the **Choose Life** website: www.chooselife.net. **The Samaritans**' website also focuses on bereavement by suicide: www.samaritans.org/your_emotional_health/about_suicide/bereaved_by_suicide.aspx.

- The **Directgov** website gives advice on what to do when someone has died intestate, or without making a will: www.direct.gov.uk/en/Governmentcitizensandrights/Death/Preparation/DG_10029802.

- Receiving mail addressed to a loved one who has died can be upsetting. You can take steps to stop this by registering with the **Bereavement Register**: www.the-bereavement-register.org.uk.

INDEX

Academy of Medical Royal Colleges 84

accidental deaths 13, 60, 80, 87, 101, 103, 169, 196, 214

advance decisions 76–77, 227, 248

Aeschylus 16, 191, 194

Afghanistan 102

Africa 14, 96, 118, 183, 224, 231

afterlife, the 13, 16, 17, 25, 92, 97, 98, 99, 143, 149, 152, 161, 163, 194, 216

Age UK 37 (*see also* Recommended Resources)

Alexander the Great 204

Alliance of Religions and Conservation 139, 252

ancestor worship 118, 173, 178–79

anniversaries 185, 211

armed forces 18, 38, 60, 102, 109, 132, 135, 148, 175

ashes 26, 92, 128, 132, 133, 148, 150, 151, 154–58, 160, 164, 172, 174, 188, 252: impact on the environment 155–56, 157, 158

Association of Natural Burial Grounds 146

assisted dying 68, 69, 82–83, 231–33: attitudes to assisted dying 70–72, 73–75;

atheist and agnostic attitudes to death 10, 71, 100, 104, 118, 151, 161, 210–14

baby boomers 36, 145

banking, banks 24, 28, 29, 30, 41, 43, 44, 45, 88, 122: banking crashes 44, 45

BBC, the 83, 94, 105, 122

bequests 34, 43, 47, 48: charities, bequests to 42, 47–48, 168, 175, 179–181, 204; unusual bequests 54, 56–57 *see also* inheritances, memorials, wills.

bereavement 7, 11, 27, 48, 78, 93, 119, 123, 127, 168, 181, 184, 185, 186, 187, 188, 189, 190, 191, 195, 196, 197, 198–200, 201, 202, 222, 237–39, 253

births 11, 12, 41, 71, 117, 126, 127, 128, 189, 214

Blair, Tony 136, 242

bodies 67, 84, 85, 88, 103, 114, 143, 149, 152, 153, 195, 204: decomposition 12, 101, 140; 148, 149, 153, 160–61; disposal of 28, 114, 132–33, 135, 140, 146, 147, 148, 153, 154, 164; donating to medical science 28, 101, 132, 133–34; 'green' body-disposal 158–60, 161; preparation before burial 99–102, 116, 117, 118, 119, 120–21, 126, 226; preservation 161–63, 167; repatriation 197

bona vacantia 57, 247
Bowlby, John 190
Brazil 12
British Humanist Association 213, 249
British Museum, the 97
Buddhism 95, 106, 117, 152, 221
burials 12, 26, 44, 50, 88, 95, 98, 99,
    100, 102, 103, 116, 118, 132, 135–48,
    151, 152, 153, 156, 158, 160, 204; at
    sea 148; certificates 88, 120; garden
    burials 146–47, 156, 244, 251;
    Tibetan Sky Burial, the 152; with
    possessions 97–99, 117; woodland
    burials 96, 124, 125, 145–46
Canada 96
cancer 68, 75, 206, 207, 233–37
Carbon Trust, the 158, 159
Cartland, Dame Barbara 146
cemeteries 12, 26, 56, 96, 102, 105,
    132, 135, 137, 139–42, 143–45, 150,
    154, 164; 174, 175, 176, 178
Centre for Death and Society 245
ceremonies 92, 93, 95, 99, 105, 106,
    110, 113, 114, 116, 117, 118, 143,
    148, 151, 162, 173, 178–79
children 18, 25, 27, 32, 35, 37, 39,
    40, 51, 63, 94, 97, 121, 143, 151,
    177, 180, 189, 250: death of a child
    125–28, 214, 216–20, 250; guardians
    53–54 *see also* inheritances, wills
China 118, 129, 167, 221
Christianity 13, 14, 73, 116, 148, 149,
    152, 178, 179, 191: Catholicism 71,
    103–4, 116, 118, 149–50; chap-
    lains 214–16; Presbyterianism 103;
    Protestantism 103–4, 116, 118 *see also*
    funerals, religious attitudes to death
churchyards 96, 98, 132, 135, 136–39,
    140, 141, 149, 164, 170, 174, 179:
    Living Churchyards Project 138–39,
    252
civil partners 28, 33, 35, 40, 42, 43, 47,

51, 53, 92, 94, 128, 237–38, 253
class 12, 33, 42, 44, 45, 137, 140, 141,
    142, 147, 187, 199
cloning 162
clutter 48–49
CNN 183, 184
coffins 95–97, 98, 105, 106, 107, 116,
    117, 120, 124, 125, 136, 147, 148,
    149, 150, 163, 204
Commission on Assisted Dying 74, 83
'common-law' partners 35, 51, 52–53,
    128
communication 10, 11, 30, 49, 65, 66,
    83–84, 109, 138, 177–78, 183, 208,
    215–16, 218, 221, 234, 236–37: im-
    portance of talking 18, 53, 56, 77, 82,
    90, 124, 163, 164, 172, 178, 203, 207,
    243; communicating wishes 25, 26,
    27–29, 35, 53, 55, 68, 70, 76, 89, 90,
    94, 95, 98, 106, 108, 111, 112, 121,
    128, 129, 134, 162–63 *see also* family/
    families, funerals, preparing for death
computers 18, 27, 29–32, 183, 202
condolence messages 113, 168,
    184–85, , 226, 238
confirmation of wills *see* wills: probate
confusion 19, 24, 183, 189, 190, 194,
    198–200, 201, 202, 203, 205
Conservative Party, the 205–6
Cooperative Funeralcare 93, 94, 108
coroners 87–88, 89
creditors 46, 47, 180
cremation 88, 95, 96, 100, 102, 116,
    117, 137, 148–53, 154, 158–59, 174,
    213: certificates 120; columbaria 150;
    cost 124–25; crematoria 98, 106, 107,
    110, 112, 125, 159; funeral pyres 119,
    151, 192
Cruse Bereavement Care 237, 253
cryomation 159
cryonics 161–62
Czech Republic, the 176

Day of the Dead 178–79
death certificates 87, 88, 120
death notices 181–82, 185
debts 26, 36–37, 46–47
declaring death 84–85
denial 10, 19, 24–25, 35, 55, 56, 120, 124, 127, 161, 187, 189, 196 , 212, 241
Diana, Princess of Wales 93, 241–42
Dickens, Charles 14–15, 33
dignity in dying 7, 60, 70, 72, 79, 145, 208, 220
Dignitas 73–75, 83, 231–33
disease *see* illness
'Do Not Resuscitate' orders 77, 80
dying 68–83, 206–8, 214–16, 240:
    death abroad 197, 253; making choices 69–70, 76–78, 79; sudden death 185, 194, 196–97, 214ß *see also* advance decisions, assisted dying, ethics of mortality, law
Edmiston, Jean 222
Egypt, ancient 50, 92, 97, 98–99, 167, 204
elderly, the 24, 60–61, 62–82, 109, 222:
    as a burden 65–66; attitudes to death 69; attitudes to the elderly 62, 63, 64; contributing to society 66; enjoying retirement 66–67; financial difficulties 67–68 *see also* retirement
Eliot, TS 194, 195
embalming 99–102, 116, 125, 133, 147, 162, 167
Environment Agency, the 155
epitaphs 18, 168, 169–70, 174: famous epitaphs 21–22, 171–72
estate planning 32–43, 122, 245:
    increasing complexity of 44–46; trust funds 43;
ethics of mortality 61, 69, 70–75, 78, 81–83, 84, 204, 216–20, 227–33
Evelyn, John 140
executors 26, 27, 29, 30, 31, 32, 38–39,

41, 42, 46, 50, 94, 128, 134, 164, 180 *see also* wills
euphemisms 19–20
euthanasia *see* assisted dying
Facebook 18, 29, 30, 31, 176, 177, 192, 202
family/families 13, 17, 32–33, 36, 47, 48, 51, 53, 54–56, 57, 61, 63, 78, 89, 90, 92, 102, 103, 106, 110, 118, 119, 120, 121, 138, 147, 164, 168, 178, 180, 181, 191, 199, 201–2, 203–4, 208, 211, 215: 'blended families' (step-families) 33, 39; caring for elderly relatives 62, 63, 65–66; changing shape of 63–65; history 49–50, 252; tensions 48, 54–56, 128–29, 189 *see also* communication, children, civil partners, 'common-law' partners, spouses
fear 7, 10, 13, 16, 19, 20, 21, 24, 35, 56, 60, 70, 71, 72, 149, 153, 150, 169, 194
financial planning & documentation 24, 26, 28, 29, 32, 44–46, 47, 56, 77, 202, 203: equity loans 36–37; online banking and finances 29, 30, 45; trust funds 43
Four Weddings and a Funeral 110
France 12, 129, 174, 175–76
funeral directors 94, 106, 109, 119, 120, 121, 122, 123, 124, 125, 128, 129, 144, 249
funerals 26, 28, 92–129, 132, 138, 143, 162, 238, 243: announcements 108–9, 187; as part of the grieving process 92, 104, 119, 120, 121, 127; clothing 102, 109, 116, 117, 118, 187, 226; costs 96, 121, 122–25, 147; environmentally friendly funerals 96, 101, 102, 146, 147–48, 160, 161, 251; eulogies 110, 113, 114–16; flowers 109, 116, 117; home funerals 119–20, 121, 122, 126, 128, 251; music 107–8,

110, 113, 114, 118, 212, 214; New Orleans jazz funerals 118; non-religious funerals 106, 110–12, 113, 210–14; order of service, the 112–14, 210–14; planning 93–95, 106, 108, 111, 112, 120, 197; prepaid funeral plans 26, 93–95; readings 110–11, 113, 212–13, 214; reception 114, 118–19; recording a funeral 112; religious funeral practices 93, 103, 110, 113, 116–17, 119, 224–26; transport 105–6, 114, 125

Garber, Megan 243

gay and lesbian bereavement 237–39

Germany 133

Ghana 96

Gibson, Clare 99, 188

Grainger, Tamsin 220

graves 97, 98–99, 116, 117, 118, 124, 125, 137–38, 140, 143, 145, 146, 147, 172, 251

gravestones 168, 169, 170, 172, 173–74, 179, 252

Gray, Thomas 136, 137

Greece, ancient 11–12, 16, 97

grief 88, 114, 125, 126, 166, 185, 187, 190, 191, 192, 196–97, 198–200, 202, 208, 211, 216, 218, 225, 237–39, 241–43 see also mourning

Halloween 179

health 12–13, 16, 60, 135, 142, 153, 161, 207, 220–22, 227–37

heirlooms 49

Henley, William Ernest 71

Hillary, Sir Edmund 155

Hinduism 117, 119, 152, 155

HIV/Aids 238

HM Revenue & Customs 42–43, 247

HM Treasury 57

Holland, Henry Scott 239

hospices 63, 69, 78, 79–80, 90, 175, 223, 248

Houston, Whitney 243

humanism 106, 110, 113, 155, 210, 213, 249

Human Tissue Authority 134, 251

illness 12, 13, 60, 63, 68, 75, 82, 87, 140, 189, 207, 214, 231–37; terminal illness 68, 79, 90, 189

India 92, 152, 153, 167, 191–92

Industrial Revolution 140

inheritances 32, 33, 34, 36–37, 40, 41, 43, 47, 49, 51, 52, 203

inquests 88, 89

Iraq 175

Ireland 103

Islam 99, 117, 139, 148, 152, 224–26

Isle of Wight 96

Jackson, Michael 242

Jainism 152

Japan 95, 106, 133

Jehovah's witnesses 73

Jobs, Steve 242

Judaism 13, 21, 99, 103, 116, 148, 149, 152

Kerrigan, Michael 8, 241, 244, 251

keys 27, 28

Kostic, Branislav 205–206

Kübler-Ross, Elisabeth 189–90

Lancet, the 86

Larner, Chris 231

Lasting Power of Attorney 76, 77–78, 227, 247

law 35, 38, 50–53, 54, 57, 73, 74, 76–78, 83, 84, 88–89, 94, 120, 128, 146, 151, 159, 179, 203, 204–5, 206: Law Society, the 35, 246; legal aid 40; overseas law 12, 87, 94, 129, 157, 197; Scottish law 37–38, 41, 76, 88, 246

Lee, Jae Rhim 160–161

Lenin, Vladimir Ilyich 162, 183

life expectancy 14, 15–16, 63: increase in 60, 61

life insurance 24, 26, 28, 46

'life stories' 17, 18, 19, 189, 194, 195, 196, 198–99, 200, 201–3, 213, 222–24, 252

life support 61, 72, 80, 81

Liverpool 155, 157

Liverpool Care Pathway 78

London 14, 34, 56, 93, 105, 107, 122, 139, 142, 143, 144, 154, 183, 251: Brookwood Cemetery 143–44, 145; Golders Green 151; Highgate Cemetery 141, 142, 146; Islington 140; Kensal Green Cemetery 105, 141, 142; Kensington & Chelsea 16; Kensington Palace 92, 241; St Christopher's Hospice 79; St Martin-in-the-Fields 140; St Thomas' Hospital 12; Waterloo 144; Westminster 12; Westminster Abbey 93, 167

Macmillan, Harold 62

Major, John 135, 136

mausoleums 92, 167, 204

McGregor, Stewart 214

McHaffie, Hazel 216

McQueen, Alexander 154

meaning of life 15, 194, 195, 200, 201, 202, 212, 221

medical care and treatment 10, 27, 60, 61, 68, 70, 72, 73, 76, 78, 79–80, 81, 83–84, 86, 206, 216–20, 221, 227–37; ascertaining death 85

memorials 167–68, 170, 172–78, 179–81, 182, 204, 252: electronic memorials 31, 176–78, 243; ossuaries 175–76

Mexico 178–79

Milligan, Spike 170

Mitchell, Prof. Richard 16

Monty Python 115

mourning 20–21, 92, 109, 113, 116, 117, 121, 125, 126, 142, 166, 172, 185–92, 199, 207, 211–12, 213, 242: clothing 186, 187, 188, 191; gender differences in 191–92; mourning period 185, 186, 187 see also grief

mummification 98, 99, 162–63

Muslims see Islam

Muslim Burial Council of Leicestershire 224, 225, 245

National Council for Palliative Care 244

National Health Service, the 62, 63, 78, 134, 215, 251

Nagdi, Suleman 224, 245

near-death experiences 86

Northern Ireland 41, 76

Norway 12

Nottingham 96

obituaries 168, 182, 183–84

old age, see elderly, the

organ donation 27, 134–35, 251

Orwell, George 135, 136

pain management 21, 24, 32, 60, 70, 73, 78, 79, 80, 196

palliative care 78, 79, 236

paperwork 87–88, 120, 163, 164: important documents 28, 30, 31, 41; organising your papers 7, 24, 25–26, 27, 46; passwords 24, 28, 29, 30, 31 see also death certificates, financial planning & documentation, wills

Parson, John 237

pensions 36, 45, 62, 63, 64, 65, 67, 88

personal documents (address books, diaries, journals, letters) 27, 31, 32, 49, 97, 202

pets 29, 54, 57, 160, 163

photographs 29, 31, 96, 97, 111, 126, 172, 177, 182

plastination 133

Pope, Alexander 168–69

post-mortem examinations 61, 88–89

Pratchett, Sir Terry 82–83

preparing for death 7, 10, 11, 12, 13, 19, 20–21, 24–32, 34, 35, 46, 55, 61, 68–70, 73, 75–78, 89–90, 163, 164, 167–68, 170, 172, 178, 180, 181, 206–8, 244

Price, Dr William 150–51

primogeniture 33

privacy 18, 30, 41, 88, 90, 112, 126, 177

probate *see* wills

Probate Service, the 41

property 34, 35, 37, 38, 40–41, 42, 44, 47, 53, 57, 69, 77

psychology 10, 78, 104, 122, 166, 187, 189–90, 194, 196, 198–200, 201, 202, 203–4, 206–8, 221

Queen Mother, the 184, 242

Queen Victoria 188

religious attitudes to death 10, 11, 13, 25, 32, 71, 73, 81, 103–4, 116, 117, 128, 135, 147, 148, 149–50, 152, 153, 215, 224–26 see also funerals

remembrance 18, 47, 48, 50, 103, 107, 111–12, 113, 114, 132, 150, 155, 166–67, 179, 182, 184, 185, 188, 190, 211, 213, 219, 224, 239–40, 252

resomation 159

retirement 62, 66–67, 144 *see also* elderly, the

risk 16–17, 37, 60, 76

Romans, ancient 97, 142, 143, 150

Rossetti, Christina 111, 112

Russell, Bertrand 151, 153

Russell, Dr James 210

Saga 61, 247

Serbia 176

Scotland 54, 102, 103, 107, 118, 136, 154, 169: Dundee 102; Edinburgh 210, 214, 217, 220; Glasgow 14, 15, 141, 159, 251

Scott, Ronnie 8, 251

Second World War 223

secrecy 50, 201–4: secret documents 30, 31, 49

Shakespeare, William 48, 132, 166, 171

shiatsu 220–22

Shipman, Dr Harold 89

Sikhism 117, 119, 152

social networking 18, 29, 30, 31, 109, 176, 192, 243

solicitors 28, 38, 39–40, 41, 43, 76, 180, 203, 205, 246

Spain 12

Speed, Gary 243

spouses 20, 35, 40, 42, 43, 47, 51, 53, 94, 128, 129, 156

Stevenson, Robert Louis 54

storytelling 222–24, 252

suicide 74, 83, 97, 154, 183, 195–96, 214, 238, 253 *see also* assisted dying

support for those close to death 10–11, 61, 70, 78, 79, 90, 208, 214–16, 220–22, 225, 233–37

Switzerland 74, 231–33

taboo 11, 19, 79, 149, 232, 241

Tatchell, Peter 240

taxes 11, 46, 65, 180: inheritance tax/relief 42, 43, 48

Thatcher government, the 44

Twitter 29, 188

USA 87, 94, 100, 103, 118, 119, 120, 122, 146, 159, 162, 183, 184: Americans 21, 22, 56, 57, 86, 87, 152, 157, 207

Victorians, the 33, 35, 105, 140, 142, 144, 186–87, 188, 191, 199

video messages 18, 29, 31, 43, 111

Vikings 92

wakes 100, 101, 103–4, 113

Wales 136, 137, 151

weddings 129

West, Ken 145, 146

wills 24, 25–27, 29, 34–39, 48, 50–53, 57, 94, 134, 180, 203: *bona vacantia* 57; challenging wills 204–206; changing and updating wills 38, 41; digital wills 43; intestacy 35, 50–53, 55, 57, 204; legal requirements for validity 40–41; living wills 75–78; making a will 25, 34, 35–36, 37–39, 53; pets 54; 'privileged wills' 38; probate 38, 41–42, 88; 'revenge wills' 56–57 *see also* executors

Wilson, Claire 233–37

YouTube 31–32, 43, 176

Zoroastrianism 152

Acknowledgements

The publisher, author and editors are indebted to many people who have provided help during the preparation of this book, including those listed below:

Contributors:
Ronnie Scott, Dr James Russell, Stewart McGregor, Hazel McHaffie, Tamsin Grainger, Jean Edmiston, Chris Larner, Clare Gibson, Suleman Nagdi MBE, Richard Mitchell, Jennie Renton, Craig Hillsley, John Parson, Claire Wilson.

Readers and consultants:
We are indebted to Reverend Dr. Peter Jupp for invaluable advice and detailed comments on an early draft of the book.

We are also grateful to Emma Williams, solicitor (and great-granddaughter of Sir William J. Williams, author of the definitive practitioner textbook on writing wills), for comments and clarifications on legal points in chapters One and Two.

Thanks also to Lucian J. Hudson, for comments on an early draft, and Sara Myers and Debbie White for additional research.

In addition, we would like to thank those whose comments and contributions have been made anonymously because of the sensitive nature of their circumstances.

Whilst many people have helped by generously providing their time and expertise, responsibility for any errors remains with the editors.

Thanks are also due to Lesley Barnes for the cover illustration and Marta Wawro for text design.